Australia's Creative Native CUISINE

For my amazing family, wife Kaye for all the love and support, my dearest twin daughters, Kristen and Cailin, whose help on shopping and prep for recipe testing and photography was invaluable, and for Dale's love and encouragement from the other side of the world.

— Andrew Fielke

For my loving and supportive family, Andrew A., Holly and Bridgette.

— Luisa Alice Adam

Brolly Books,
(an imprint of Borghesi & Adam Publishers Pty Ltd)
Suite 330/45 Glenferrie Road Malvern, Vic., 3144 Australia.
www.brollybooks.com | email: emma@brollybooks.com

First published in Australia by Brolly Books, 2020.
Reprinted with index 2020.

Author: Andrew Fielke: Introduction, 'Getting the best from your BBQ or char-grill', 'Cooking with paperbark', 'Wattleseed' chapter, and all recipes.
Co-author: Luisa Adam: 'Chef's notes', ingredients summary tables, ingredients chapters (excluding recipes), Index.
This Work is a collaboration between the Author and Co-Author, who have each asserted their Moral Rights in the Work.

Photographer: Tony Lewis (except as otherwise stated below)
Designer (text and cover): Emma Borghesi
Indexer: Luisa Adam

ISBNs: 978-0-6486918-2-2 hb | 978-0-9873895-7-2

NATIONAL LIBRARY OF AUSTRALIA
A catalogue record for this book is available from the National Library of Australia

Australia's Creative Native CUISINE

— Andrew Fielke —

Published by Brolly Books
Melbourne | Australia

Acknowledgements

The Authors and the Publisher respect and acknowledge the traditional owners, past, present and future, of the land on which we live and work, as the first people and custodians of this country and its foods.

Our First Nation peoples have an intimate knowledge and understanding of the amazing ingredients that formed part of their diet and culture for many thousands of years. Their knowledge and connection to the land and its bounty are awe-inspiring and we are indeed lucky to tap into this knowledge and the foods. The right way forward for the development of an Australian native food industry is with the involvement, expertise, and consultation of Indigenous Australians.

Additionally, the Authors consulted several sources in the writing of this book but are particularly indebted to the expertise of Frances Bodkin (*Encyclopaedia Botanica: the essential reference guide to native and exotic plants in Australia*); John Newton (*The Oldest Foods on Earth* and *Cooking with the Oldest Foods on Earth*); Tim Low (*Wild Food Plants of Australia*); Australian Native Food and Botanicals (www.anfab.org.au); Australian Native Plants Association of Australia (www.anpsa.org.au); and Australian Bush Foods (www.ausbushfoods.com), among many others.

Authors' and publisher's note

This book does not advocate the sourcing of native ingredients from the wild because of the risk of damage to the environment and/or plant identification errors. The best sources for native ingredients are the home garden, native plant nurseries, reputable retail outlets, as well as reputable online suppliers. See page 272 for more information. The Authors and the Publisher have taken all care in the creation of this Work but accept no responsibility whatsoever for any unwitting error.

front cover painting:
detail from 'Westbound' (left) by Gus Leunig,
Acrylic on canvas, 51 x 51cm,
reproduced by kind permission of Gus Leunig and Libby Edwards Galleries,
163A Williams Road, South Yarra Vic. 3141,
tel: +61 (3) 9826 1043 | email: melb@libbyedwardsgalleries.com
www.libbyedwardsgalleries.com. ©Gus Leunig, 2019

Questions or comments?

- Email Andrew Fielke and his team at info@creativenativefoods.com.au
- Email Brolly Books at andrew@brollybooks.com
- Email Luisa Adam, care of the publisher, Brolly Books, andrew@brollybooks.com

Information and events

Andrew and his team regularly post new product information, specials, what's in season, and details about where Andrew will be cooking up a storm with demonstrations or events. To find out more, visit:

facebook.com/creativenativefoods/ instagram.com/creativenativefoods/ creativenativefoods.com.au

PREFACE

For over 35 years, chef, producer and educator Andrew Fielke has had one focus: to spread the word about Australia's remarkable and, for many years, under-appreciated native foods. He opened his first native food restaurant, Red Ochre Grill, in 1992 and has dedicated his work to researching and developing native foods and introducing them to the mainstream food supply chain. He is deeply respectful of Indigenous knowledge of Australian native foods and traditional practices and works closely with Indigenous associates to educate the wider Australian population of their benefits.

His persistence has paid off. Increasingly chefs and home cooks around the country are now exploring, experimenting with, and using these foods in their kitchens as a result of his work.

The recipes in this book are the culmination of Andrew's hard work and vision and bring together his practical knowledge and understanding of Australian native foods to offer all who want to know the fundamentals of preparing, cooking, and storing these healthy and flavoursome foods.

— JOHN NEWTON, 2020

CONTENTS

The stunning Australian boab tree (Adansonia gregorii), of the Kimberley. As at the time of writing, I am just beginning to introduce the young boab plants into Creative Native Food distribution. They are wholly edible and delicious: the leaves for salads and stir-fries, the tuber baked like a yam, or thinly sliced in salads or fried into crisps, and so on. Even the huge nut yields a white sherbet-like powdery pith — we continue to learn!

INTRODUCTION

MY EARLIEST MEMORY OF COOKING is of making crumpets over a little camp-stove toaster with my long-time best mate, Tony Sharley, in the back of his family-home block in Renmark (South Australia). We must have been 10 or so. (He still jokes now about how he helped forge my career path in the culinary field!)

They were wonderful carefree days with endless summers of camping, hunting, setting rabbit traps, cutting apricots, fishing, skiing and swimming in that marvellous Murray River. But things took another turn towards food during my early high-school years in the Riverland. I distinctly remember my mum's cheesecakes; they were awesome in the eyes of a hungry teenager, etched in my memory. One day, I raced home from school on my bike at the highest speed possible knowing there was only one slice of Mum's cheesecake left, and that I had four brothers and a sister to beat to claim that prize. Imagine my disappointment when I got home and there was nothing left but crumbs. I implored my dear mum to teach me how to make cheesecakes – immediately!

I guess that was what got me into the kitchen a lot earlier than many. Then, in my third year at high school, there was an elective subject choice, and strangely enough, for a male at the time, I chose Home Economics. But, in honesty, it wasn't because I wanted to cook or play with food; it was the thought of getting in amongst all the girls that influenced my selection. Not surprisingly, really, I did well with cooking against the girls, but was lousy with them in the other sense. Yet, from that point on I thought, this is where I'm heading, I can do this . . . I want to be a chef and travel the world!

I have always been driven to succeed and to innovate, and I was truly blessed as a young apprentice to have great mentors who helped me achieve some amazing accolades and awards. This certainly opened doors, enabling me to get work in Europe straight after my apprenticeship finished in 1980. It was those years working in Switzerland, in London's famous Savoy Hotel, and in Austria, not to mention the incredible camper-van travel around Europe (in between work stints) that really opened my eyes on how to appreciate food. I realised it was such a part of the life-style and culture in countries like France and Italy. These people live and breathe food and wine, I thought. It's a really important part of their day, and I wondered why it was so different in Australia. I couldn't see anything substantial beyond an Australian cuisine of meat pies, barbecues, roast lamb and three over-cooked veggies and the occasional pavlova.

It wasn't until I came back to Australia brimming with a wealth of new knowledge based on very classic European techniques and philosophy that I found myself taking a job as executive chef in a stunning country estate, Mount Lofty House in the Adelaide Hills, which was recently resurrected from devastating bushfires. It's there I first had the kangaroo meat offered by our butcher – what a revelation! I was amazed how good it was. Why had we never cooked it at home when I was young? At the same time, I read an article on Brian Powell, who was the first person to commercialise the famous quandong, or desert peach, in Quorn in the mid-north of South Australia. I connected with him and he sent me some samples, and I was 'blown away' by the flavour. It was such a light-bulb moment in my career, to try the fruit of the quandong for the first time at age 25, yet I clearly remembered playing marbles in the sand with quandong seeds, the beautiful, round, dimpled stone of this desert fruit, when growing up in Renmark. I couldn't understand why we never ate quandongs, never used them in our pies and jams or on our toast, and why we had ignored this fabulous food resource right on our doorstep. I was convinced we were missing something really important here. And so, I experimented, and my first-ever combination of two native ingredients, kangaroo and quandong (back in 1985) was a great pairing and later became my signature dish at the Red Ochre Grill. It is of course included as a recipe in this book. From that point on, my career switched to a 100% focus on the Indigenous foods of our country .

My next big break was to connect with Vic Cherikoff that same year, who had started Bush Tucker Supply. He sent me a box of 20 or so samples of the most weird and wonderful ingredients, things I never dreamed existed. It was so exciting – a whole new cornucopia of flavours to explore. Chefs get so excited with one new ingredient to play with, and here I had dozens! I also drew inspiration from an old friend, Jean-Paul Bruneteau, an Australian-French chef who opened the first specialist native food restaurant in Hornsby in Sydney, also in the 1980s. This was ground-breaking stuff. From there, I became obsessed with learning how to use these ingredients and building my repertoire of dishes and supplier contacts. Eventually this led to opening the first Red Ochre Grill restaurant in 1992 in Gouger Street, Adelaide, where we very quickly had incredible success. I was staggered with the international media exposure we achieved, because the menu was so unique. Tourists to Australia had a special interest in trying a unique Australian cuisine – that's what you do when you travel, try the true local cuisine. The South Australia and the Australian tourism commissions kindly fed us a constant stream of journalists, media and TV crews, whose generous reviews included:

> What sets the Red Ochre apart, and what attracts the flocks of people who have been filling up the restaurant every day since it opened, is its menu.
>
> – *Marie Claire*, Singapore

> A sophisticated restaurant style which uses flavours the original Australians were aware of centuries ago.
>
> – *The Sunday Times*, London

Such was the success of the restaurant, I decided to expand firstly into Cairns and then later Alice Springs. Those three restaurants still trade today in similar ways, although for most of the past twenty years my role has been to supply them with native ingredients. It was not all 'roses and chocolates', though. I did have tough times with similar restaurants in Brisbane and Melbourne. In the end, after missing out way too much of the early growing years of my three children, and being physically and mentally exhausted, I left the restaurant game and kitchen full-time in 2001 and started Creative Native Food Service, my supply and procurement business. I could see quite clearly there was a largely untapped potential for a new industry for Australia, but with lots of work needing to be done on the supply side. To build an industry, there need to be consistent and affordable harvests. I also wanted to spend more time engaging with and learning from Indigenous Australians, something that was not possible during the restaurant years, working 12–14 hours a day, six days a week, for years on end.

Over all the years since 1985, my network of passionate 'native foodies', growers and suppliers, had grown, and this led to my involvement in forming firstly a national native foods committee, then later a 'peak industry body' to help advocate for the growing industry sector. ANFIL, or Australian Native Food Industries Limited, was incorporated in 2006, and I was privileged to be the inaugural chair. I served on the board for ten years. I have also been blessed, in my post-restaurant years, to be taken all over the world many times as a guest chef, cooking for Australian events and promotions, as well as presenting a food-and-wine TV series on ABC's Asia Pacific program *Nexus*.

As is often the way with us Australians, we often don't appreciate what we have in our own backyards and look to Europe and other parts of the world for inspiration. Yet, then the world looked to us, when the world-renowned René Redzepi of Noma in Copenhagen opened his pop-up restaurant in Sydney in 2016. This shone an international spotlight on native foods. I was privileged to host René on a foraging trip with the Adnyamathanha people in the northern Flinders Ranges during this time. And, since then, we have seen an unprecedented take-up of native ingredients by the very best chefs and restaurants in Australia. It's amazing what chefs like Ben Shewry, Dan Hunter, Kylie Kwong, Jock Zonfrillo, Peter Gilmore and many others are doing with native ingredients today – absolutely fantastic!

Now is an exciting time in the history of Australian cuisine, and given its strong cultural connection, and nutritional and sustainable aspects, as well as superb flavours, it is set to go from strength to strength. It is my hope that this book will help people to introduce more of these foods into their family homes and to make them a part of their regular family fare. This will in turn support a local industry that is at one with the environment and also the people, Indigenous and non-Indigenous, through all stages from growing through to consumption.

Alongside working on this book, I am very proud of another current project, the 'Native Foods Education Kit', which seeks to educate a new generation on the use of these foods. It would be so great to see every young Australian student in Middle School Home Economics classes learning about Australia's true native food and Indigenous culture, and cooking with these ingredients. What a different cuisine Australia may have had now if our explorers and pioneers had been more open to the native flora and fauna of the bushland and had an embracing attitude to Indigenous culture. Importantly, we can now all play an important role in educating ourselves and the youngest Australians about the true food and cultural history of Australia, fascinating facts and information that were never taught when I was at school many years ago. I love this quote:

> Food is a central activity of mankind and one of the single most significant trademarks of a culture.
>
> – Mark Kurlansky, *Choice Cuts*, 2002

It's often said 'You are what you eat', so I challenge all Australians from all ethnic backgrounds to help the evolution of a true Australian cuisine that comes from the heart and the home and that includes Indigenous foods and culture . . . I hope you enjoy this book and all the wonderful native foods Australia has to offer.

Andrew Fielke

CHEF'S NOTES

All my recipes follow usual conventions, but below are a few notes I hope you will find helpful. I also always suggest that you read each recipe in full before starting, so you can familiarise yourself with the ingredients, method, equipment, and time required.

Native and wild ingredients

I recommend that you always source your ingredients from quality food stores or from reputable on-line suppliers – like Creative Native of course 🙂. Where practical, you can also purchase seeds or seedlings from native plant nurseries – so many nurseries now include native plants in their stock – and grow your own herbs, fruits, vegetables and other plants in your garden.

Generally, I discourage foraging in the wild because it can be damaging to the environment, and also because there is always some risk of incorrectly identifying native plants, even though Australia's native foods have been eaten for thousands of years and sustained generations of Indigenous people.

There is also the advantage that native ingredients grown in your own garden or purchased from native food suppliers will have the benefits of good growing conditions. Some of the leafy herbs and vegetables can become a bit dry and bitter when growing in a naturally arid or stressed environment, but enjoy the benefits of lush, well-watered conditions when grown in a controlled environment; this produces softer and more pleasantly flavoured leaves. But the opposite can also be true, especially for the salty beach succulents like sea blight, samphire and karkalla, where the real flavour comes from the saline environment in which they thrive.

The recipes in this book also provide loads of substitute ingredients, so you have plenty of options to choose from if ever a suggested ingredient is unavailable.

A few other special ingredients

The best ingredients lead to the best results, so always choose quality ingredients. See the notes on some important ones on the following pages, as well as some other general notes on common ingredients.

OLIVE OIL	When a recipe calls for olive oil, I always use best quality Australian extra virgin olive oil (EVOO) for the flavour and texture it delivers. If you don't have EVOO, standard olive oil will work almost as well, and it is fine for frying, but don't substitute other oils when olive oil is needed.
UNSALTED BUTTER	I always prefer unsalted butter because I can then determine the level of seasoning according to taste; it's also what is required in sweet preparations, of course. But, if you like using salted butter, that is your choice – although I am not a fan of using margarine in cooking if it can be avoided
COOKING OILS	Olive oil is not suitable for frying some ingredients as its taste can be too intense, and it has a Mediterranean flavour bias. In these recipes if a vegetable oil is needed, I prefer peanut oil or a neutral oil like sunflower or canola. Take care to avoid blended oils that hide palm oil, as it's clear this supports poor environmental practices. Our native macadamia oil is also a great option.
NEUTRAL COOKING SPRAY	This does the same job as what was once commonly known as 'greasing', but is quicker, cleaner, and easier, and if it is neutral (flavourless) it won't add any unwanted flavours to whatever it is that you are cooking.
NUTS	It's worth mentioning that most purchased nuts, even if they are said to be 'raw', have undergone some kind of processing. I recommend buying unroasted, unsalted varieties (you can always roast and salt them at home, and they're far more delicious when fresh and lightly dry-roasted anyway!). A big 'no no' for me is pan-roasting over a flame or toasting nuts under a griller or salamander. I'm amazed at how many professional chefs and even celebrity TV cooks recommend tossing nuts in a frypan or under a griller – it's a really poor option. There is only one way in my book, and that is to slowly and gently roast them in a cool oven, about 160°C (320°F), and to use a timer to get it spot on (the recipes in this book give guidelines on the time required – but you should still keep an eye on them as they cook). This way, you can achieve a most beautiful, even, light golden brown throughout the entire nut, including the centre. On the other hand, if you toast in a frypan or under a griller, you're really only toasting the outside surface and the risk of burning or overdoing it is extremely high, especially if you are just slightly distracted or stop shaking the pan, even momentarily. It's risky, and the results are never as good. I have seen many loads of flaked almonds go in the bin during my career because chefs have tried to rush the process using a salamander, then look away momentarily, only to be left with a burnt mess.

CORN-FLOUR *or* CORN STARCH — This can be a source of confusion. The recipes in this book use pure cornflour, being made from corn (maize), and which is also known in some countries as corn starch. Make sure you use pure cornflour if gluten-free is important to you.

YEAST — 'Instant' and 'dried' yeast are really one and the same. For the home cook (and this includes me for the last 20 years since I left the restaurant game), I recommend using the 7-gram (about ¼ oz) sachets of dried yeast. I use them all the time for reliable results and convenience.

CORIANDER (CILANTRO) — The leaves and stems of coriander (cilantro) provide fresh, herbal notes to many dishes, but the roots should not be overlooked. They provide great flavours that are deeper and more intense than that of the leaves and stems, and they are largely responsible for the distinctive flavour of many Thai curries and pastes. The ground seeds of this plant are also used widely around the world as a spice.

THAI LIME — This is the same lime as commonly known as the 'kaffir' lime but the alternative name 'thai lime' is used here because the term 'kaffir' is considered offensive in several contexts.

FROZEN *or* FRESH? — It is always best to use fresh, not frozen, ingredients whenever they are available. If frozen ingredients are being used, unless the recipe suggests otherwise I suggest thawing them over 12–24 hours in a refrigerator before use, and draining off any excess liquid.

If substituting large amounts of frozen for fresh ingredients, you may need to adjust the liquid level in your recipe to compensate. In this book, general guidelines are given on these details, but some experimentation may be needed. Don't shy away from that — it's part of the fun.

Storing foods

Most foods should be kept in the fridge, covered or in air-tight containers, and consumed within 2–3 days of making. The exceptions are condiments, which can be kept in air-tight jars in the fridge for longer periods, and frozen items. Some bottled sauces will keep in the fridge for some time until opened, but generally they should then be consumed in a few days (although sauces with high acid and sugar content are quite stable and tend to keep for longer). With all foods, follow usual hygiene and storage instructions and watch for signs of spoilage, which can include strange or unpleasant odours, discolouration, changes in texture, and mould growth. It's always best to play it safe, so if in doubt, throw it out!

Measuring and weighing ingredients

Wherever possible, I recommend that ingredients (even liquids) be weighed rather than measured out in cups and spoons as weighing leads to far more accurate and predictable results. I understand, though, that individual cooking methods are well entrenched and often handed down from generation to generation, so if you prefer to use cups and spoons, please do so! But, if any doubt, use the weighed amount.

Personally, I think a tablespoon, half a cup, or a teaspoon of, say, butter can be such a variable thing as people are different, and see things differently visually. Is it heaped? Rounded? Flat? Packed firmly? It can change every time and be different by a large amount from person to person, especially if you need 4 tablespoons and they all vary! For some recipes, of course, the variances don't matter a lot, but it's critical to have the correct amounts when making pastries and baked goods, and where strong spices are used, of course. If it is weighed, you will have 100% accuracy every time. Electronic scales are so cheap and available today, and the amount of washing up avoided by adding ingredients into the one container or straight into the pot on the scales, then taring (zeroing) off before adding the next, is surprising. And everyone I know loves to save on washing up, by using less containers. So, if you don't have electronic scales, please get a set!

Additionally, if you are going to scale up a recipe to serve more people, it is much better to use weighed rather than measured ingredients as the correct proportions will be maintained. If that is not an option and you are cooking for lots of people, cook up batches, rather than one large recipe. (That is not to say that scaling up recipes does not require some adjustments: sometimes it does.)

In this book, for the most part teaspoons are used for very small amounts only, but weight for large amounts. Cups are used only when the weighed amount converts neatly to standard cup or part-cup measure. I don't differentiate between US and English/Australian cup measures, as for the recipes in this book the difference between those two volumes (about 10ml or ⅓ fl oz) is not significant.

In a very small number of recipes, I have urged for the ingredients to be weighed because the precise proportions are so important. An electronic scale with both metric and imperial units is best for this.

Finally, this book uses both metric and imperial measurements. The conversion to imperial is, where necessary, rounded up or down to the nearest practical measure. These slight adjustments will not impact on the result.

strawberry gum

Some special, basic equipment

There are a few things every home or professional chef should have handy at all times in the kitchen. Assuming you have all the basics – pots and pans, knives, spoons, chopping boards, mixing bowls, sieves, and so on – here are some other basic items that I couldn't do without:

SILICONE BAKING PAPER	This is parchment-style baking paper but with silicone in its composition. It is superior to parchment baking paper or waxed baking paper because of its non-stick capabilities. It is invaluable for lining trays, tins, ramekins and other cooking items. Just a light spray of oil or grease (with butter) on the downward-facing side is all that is needed to hold it in position – and sometimes even that is not needed, if the weight of the ingredients being placed on top is sufficient to hold it in place.
FOIL	Aluminium (aluminum) foil is used in many ways. Always have the good, heavy-duty strong foil on hand, not the flimsy type that tears too easily.
KITCHEN FILM	Alway use good, kitchen-quality kitchen film, also known as cling film. Micro-wave-safe types are best. In recent times, though, reusable silicone-based plastic covers have become more available, and if this means we can avoid single-use plastic, let's all get on board.
MASON JARS	Mason jars, or pickling jars, are useful for storing all kinds of things. They should be sterilized, in boiling water or by other usual sterilization means, before use.
MORTAR-AND-PESTLE	A mortar-and-pestle is invaluable for extracting the most flavour out of seeds and spices and for grinding and blending ingredients to the desired texture, from coarse to smooth and everything in between.
SCALES	Electronic scales, with metric and imperial units, are the best way for ensuring accurate amounts of various ingredients – and are cheap, quick and easy to use.
THERMO-METER	Cooking thermometers always come in handy, even if many larger pieces of equipment have in-built thermometers.

Some bigger equipment

STOVE The recipes in this book assume a fan-forced oven is being used for any baked goods. If you don't have a fan-forced oven, you may need to increase the temperature a little or cook the food for a little longer. There is, regardless, always variations in temperatures and cooking times, so it pays to get to know your own oven and its idiosyncrasies, and use the times and temperatures in this book as a guide.

MIXERS When it comes to electric mixers, I always favour the strong bench- or stand-type, rather than a hand-held mixer, as they are just more powerful, especially when it comes to blending heavy thick mixes such as doughs. You can get by with a hand-held mixer for whipping cream or beating eggs, but if you are serious about cooking, do try to invest in a bigger, stronger, mixer.

BLENDERS These come in all shapes and sizes. At one end of the spectrum are the more expensive food processors which are capable of chopping and blending everything: these are a super option if they are within your budget and you have the shelf or storage space. They will always give great results. Other options include jug blenders and bullet-type blenders, often used for making smoothies and fruit drinks. They vary greatly in power, but provided you are using a powerful one they are a quick and convenient way of chopping and blending lots of ingredients. The most powerful ones have the ability to crush ice: that's really what you need. Then there are the stick blenders: these are limited in what they can chop and blend, but are great for quickly and easily puréeing softer or cooked ingredients.

THERMOMIX® Of all the blender options, this is the most versatile. It is very powerful and delivers wonderful results. As the name implies, it has the added bonus of combining heat functions with various blending functions, and it also includes scales and other useful features. It will deliver the smoothest and most well-blended concoctions. I'm a big fan, and they are well worth the investment and will last for many years if looked after properly.

SOUS VIDE UNITS 'Sous vide' means 'under vacuum', and here it refers to a method of cooking akin to using a water bath or a low-steam environment, but at precisely controlled temperatures and at a very slow cooking pace. Although the best option is to vacuum-pack items before lowering them into the 'bath', you can also cook 'sous vide' by placing the ingredients in plastic snap-lock bags and then use pegs or bulldog clips to attach the bag to the side of the pot. This way, the ingredients inside the bag can be submerged in the water, but the top of the bag will be above the water level, so water can't leak in.

This cooking method produces incredibly tender results and maximizes retention of nutrients. The precise temperature control also gives the most perfect, even results for under-cooked meats and fish etc. (where 'rare' or 'medium' is desired). I have an Anova® sous vide unit at home, which is brilliant and not too expensive. It even includes a phone app which is a cool way to load your settings and also access some great recipes on line. I highly recommend it – every home chef should have one!

VACUUM SEALERS Small home-style units that use the channel-style vacuum bags are great for home cooks, and I use them regularly, especially when batch-cooking. They provide the best way to portion up, say, a nice curry or spice paste or soups or pestos for freezing down for later use, or packing foods efficiently for a camping trip. I also love to buy a really good cut of meat such as kangaroo loin fillet or a prime beef scotch fillet, then vacuum down portions with marinades such as native pepperleaf and truffle oil – even a few days under vacuum will impregnate the meat so much more effectively than a standard marinade. And, of course, you can extend the life of fresh foods a good deal longer with vacuum-packing. I have had an Orved® home unit for years and highly recommend it.

BAIN MARIE Literally meaning 'Mary's bath', this is also a water bath, but it is generally used to gently warm or melt foods that might burn or spit with more intense heat and also to cook delicate foods such as custards. The most common type is that where ramekins containing the ingredients are placed in a deep baking tray. Hot water is then poured into the tray, so it goes some way up the sides of the ramekins. Everything is then placed in the oven so that the ingredients gently cook in their hot bath – without getting wet.

DOUBLE-BOILERS These are also used to gently melt and sometimes emulsify and cook delicate ingredients and recipes such as hollandaise sauce. They are sometimes also referred to as 'bain maries' but technically they are not a water bath: rather, they use steam to warm the ingredients. They comprise two parts: a larger, lower pot containing boiling water and then, a second, suitably sized, heat-proof bowl that sits over the top. It should be just large enough to sit snugly in the top of the pot without falling in. Ceramic or glass works best, but stainless-steel bowls can also be used. Double boilers can be purchased from various stores, but if making your own take care to select properly sized pots and bowls. Most importantly, the base of the bowl must not come in contact with the hot water in the pot below. You only need to have 2.5–5 cm (1–2 in.) of boiling water in the bottom of the pot, while making sure there is enough so it won't boil dry. There should be quite a lot of space (ideally 10 cm or about 4 in.) between the water level in the pot and the base of the bowl above it.

BARBECUES For use at home, gas barbecues are generally the most practical. Their proper maintenance is a key factor in ensuring great cooking results. See some notes for keeping them in as-new condition on the facing page.

WOOD OVENS These wonderful out-door ovens need to be properly installed and require lots of time to heat up – but what they deliver in flavour and speed by virtue of their super-high temperatures is unmatched by other cooking methods. See also page 267 (Pizza Dough recipe) which includes some general notes on how to prepare your wood oven.

With all these pieces of equipment, keep the manufacturer's manual in a safe place and always consult it regarding correct use and maintenance.

GETTING THE BEST *from* YOUR BBQ *or* CHAR-GRILL

Far too many Australian backyard barbecues or char-grills are often left in quite a messy state, and even rusty in some cases. Here are my recommendations to get the best possible results, especially on the grill bars, where a lot of people have trouble with foods such as fish sticking.

After using your barbecue / char-grill

- For the bars, always use a wire brush to thoroughly scrub them down so they are free of crusted food deposits.
- Oil generously with an oily cloth rag or paper towel that has been dipped in cooking oil (plain old vegetable oil is fine).
- For the hotplate, scrape it down with a strong (heavy-duty) barbecue scraper, then oil the surface in the same way as above.
- Cover the barbecue and keep it out of the rain (rust is a real enemy).

To prepare your barbecue / char-grill before cooking

- Pre-heat for at least 10–15 minutes with the cover down; this really helps to equalize the heat evenly across the cooking surfaces.
- 5 minutes before cooking, open the lid and thoroughly scrub down the bars again with a wire brush, or scrape the hotplate with the scraper.
- Oil generously again with an oily cloth rag or paper towel so the surfaces glisten.
- Make sure your food is lightly coated with cooking oil (not dripping in oil).
- Again, immediately before putting food on the grill, give the surfaces another quick wipe (of the grill bars especially) of oil, so they glisten even more, then add your food. Always be quick and careful – barbecues do bite!

What works best for your favourite barbecued foods will take some experimentation (cooking times and temperatures will vary according to the food and personal taste), but overleaf are a few general guidelines.

When cooking whole fish or fillets, or skin-on chicken

- Moisture is what makes these foods stick so, if you can, pat dry the skin with paper towels and air-dry in the fridge at least 2–3 hours before cooking. It will stick less if the surface is touch-dry.
- Coat the fish (or chicken) skin liberally with flour (gluten-free options work, too).
- Just before grilling, shake off the excess flour.
- Now, rub the floured, dry surface so it's shiny with oil.
- Again, oil the grill bars lightly before adding the food.

Wet and/or marinated foods (including meat cuts, hamburgers, skinless chicken, sausages, marinated vegetables, meat kebabs, etc.)

- Drain the foods thoroughly from the marinade, if using.
- Flour-coating (as suggested for fish and chicken, above) can help develop a nice crust on some ingredients.
- Oil the food lightly before grilling, using either a brush or clean cloth dipped in cooking oil.
- The left-over marinade can be used to baste the cooking, marinated food once it has started to develop a nice crust.

Vegetables

- For vegetables, follow the general guidelines for cooking fish and skinless chicken above. The vegetables should be surface-dry, but air-drying and flouring is not required.

COOKING *with* PAPERBARK

Cooking with paperbark is a fantastic traditional Indigenous method which can be easily adapted for home use. I have referred to it as the 'Aboriginal aluminium foil' over the years, but it is better than foil. Not only does it trap moisture and flavours within, it imparts a subtle earthy woodiness in both flavour and aroma to the food.

Where to get the paperbark

Large sheets of bark are easily stripped from the *Melaleuca quinquinvera* (broad leaf paperbark) which is the species most commonly used, but there are others. I use a sharp utility knife to cut the bark into large strips or squares. If getting bark from a tree on your property, take it only from the outer dry layer (this won't damage the tree and is completely renewable). You can also buy paperbark from certain shops or on-line, in plastic packets, but it can be quite dry, or moist, depending on the conditions when it was harvested and packed. I sometimes pour hot or boiling water over it a few hours or the day before I want to use it, to make it soft and pliable. It can then be separated easily into thinner layers. (A friend of mine, Chris, recently soaked the bark in beer before cooking a joint of meat – what a great idea! I'll be trying that one next.)

How much to use

If you're preparing foods such as vegetables or fish that take a relatively short time to cook, a thinner layer of paperbark is o.k. On the other hand, I recommend that you use much thicker layers of bark when slow-roasting meat.

I also use an extra layer of bark if I'm cooking in the hot ash or sand of a campfire or ground oven, just to help keep sand and ash from getting onto the food.

Always be careful cooking paperback-wrapped foods in a really hot oven or a roll-top barbecue at home, as the bark certainly dries out and can start burning. Some smouldering is fine as it can add a hint of smokiness to the food, but you don't want it to catch alight and burn away, and then expose the food.

What to expect . . .

Opening paperbark-cooked foods at the table in front of your guests is great fun – people love that rush of steam and wonderful aromas. But, be warned: the brittle shards of bark can make a mess of your dinner table, so I always lay down an old tablecloth first, to catch and then easily remove the debris.

Chicken cooked in paperbark with white kunzea (p. 77)

Using Wattleseed

USING WATTLESEEDS: Methods *and* Options

* For more information on and recipes for wattleseeds, see Nuts and Seeds section, starting on page 198.

Since the early to mid 1980s, most native food suppliers have focused on promoting just one type of wattleseed, or 'acacia seed': the darkly roasted and finely ground 'flour' of the 'elegant' or 'prickly' wattle, *Acacia victoriae*. This is what most people are familiar with, and it has a lovely coffee/chicory, nutty flavour but can also have bitter notes if over-done. I have used it for years, and it's great in sweet recipes such as pancakes, biscuits, muffins and, of course, Wattleseed Pavlova (p. 238).

Over the last five or six years, however, I've really come to appreciate the wide variety of other edible wattleseeds. There are so many recorded species that Aboriginal people ate, from all the diverse regions and climate zones across Australia. They all vary significantly in size, shape, colour, weight, oil, nutrient content and, of course, flavour. Light, medium or dark roasting also alters the flavours, to give endless possibilities and profiles. But, the greatest fun for me has been sprouting, malting and cooking the wattleseeds, just as I would any other grain – rice, barley, wheat, etc. – or pulses (dried beans), and rarely grinding them at all.

Today, quickly roasting (heat-treating) the wattleseeds before cooking is recommended to assist the cooking process. Yet Indigenous Australians have long appreciated whole wattleseeds as a nutritious food source and knew of the need to 'heat-treat' them. They used hot ashes and the coals of fires for this purpose.

USING WATTLESEEDS *in* WATTLESEED 'RISOTTO' *and* OTHER DISHES

Preparing wattleseed for cooking: the quick and easy method

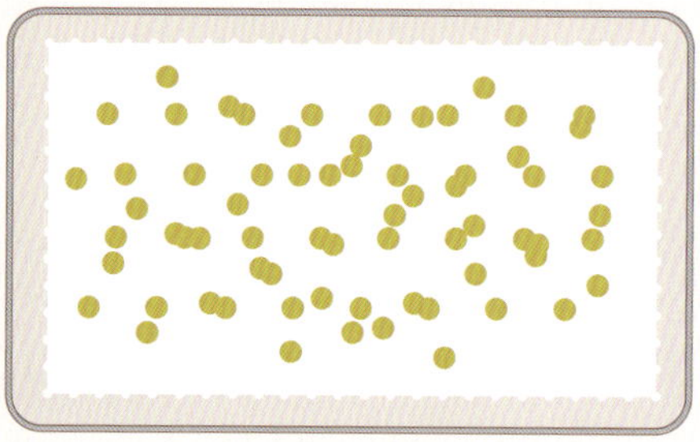

Before cooking wattleseeds, their tough outer shells need to be weakened to allow water and other cooking liquids to penetrate. The easy way is to briefly roast them in a low-moderate oven ('flash-roasting'). Just spread the seeds out in a baking tray and pop them in a 160–170°C (300–320°F) oven for a few minutes.

That's all you need to do, and then you're ready to start cooking with them as you would rice or any other grain – but keep in mind that wattleseeds are a legume, rather than a true 'grain', so contain much higher amounts of protein, along with carbohydrates and other nutrients.

You can choose to roast the seeds lightly (for a nutty, grainy, and meal-like character) or more darkly (for more roasted, bitter, coffee-like notes). Once roasted they can be cooked in just water or stock or any number of flavourings and accompaniments. Cooking times will vary, but generally 5–6 minutes for this type of roasting is sufficient. Use shorter roasting times for the smaller seeds and longer for larger seeds such as that of the desert oak (see Wattleseed and Sea Parsley Tabbouleh, p. 209). They have a much tougher shell and need more time to crack, otherwise it's very difficult to hydrate them in liquid when cooking them.

broom wattleseed

Monitor the seeds during the roasting and remove from the oven as soon as they start popping (for the lighter roast). Leave in longer (when lots are popping) for a darker roast (note: if doing a dark roast, I cover the tray with foil to stop a lot of popping seed ending up all over the oven floor!) They might start to smoke very slightly; that is o.k., but don't allow them to burn, of course. Seeds that don't pop will still soften further in the later cooking process or be ground to powder.

Activating wattleseeds for nutritional purposes – optional

In simple terms, 'activating' in this context means treating the seeds so that their nutrients are released and become 'available' to the body. This is usually done by soaking them in hot water – easy as that.

Without 'activation', many nutrients stay trapped inside the seeds, so they pass through the digestive system without being aborbed, so then we miss out on all those nutritional benefits. It's well-documented that activation releases nutritents in other seeds, so logically this would apply to wattleseeds, too. Note that activating wattleseeds must be done before any flash-roasting or slower roasting takes place.

To activate the wattleseeds, first find a suitable, small container with a lid that can be placed on top but not sealed tight (air needs to get in). Mix 1 cup of seeds to 3 cups of boiling water and leave to soak overnight and into the next morning on a bench or window sill (in good light but not direct sunlight). The ideal temperature for this is around 18–22°C (65–70°F). Small seeds such as Halls Creek wattleseed need 8–12 hours of soaking, while larger ones such as elegant wattleseed need 24 hours or more. During soaking, the seeds will start to swell and become 'activated', meaning they are coming to life. After the seeds have been soaked, drain them through a small sieve and rinse under running water. Allow them to drain thoroughly. They can now be roasted or cooked in soups, stews or used instead of rice in a risotto.

Malting the wattleseeds – optional

(My favourite way to use small wattleseeds!)

'Malting' wattleseeds is a two-step process that can take place after 'activation'. First, the seeds are left to sprout ('germinate', or start to grow) and, second, they are roasted slowly at quite a moderate temperature to allow the sugars in the seeds to caramelize and develop their distinctive sweet, nutty flavours and rich colours.

Step 1: Sprouting the wattleseeds

After the seeds have been soaked ('activated') over 8–24 hours (see 'Activating wattleseeds for nutritional purposes'), they need to be left for a further 1–5 days (depending on the size of the seed) to 'sprout'. This is when tiny roots, or sprouts, will begin to emerge from the seed. First, drain the seeds through a sieve and rinse throughly under running cold water. Next, line the base of a container with a wet Chux® or absorbent kitchen paper. The seeds can then rest in this damp bed until they begin to sprout (they need to be in a moist environment but not sitting in water). Loosely place the lid on top, not tightly, as air needs to get in (you can punch a few holes in the lid, if possible).

While waiting for the seeds to sprout, it's very important to rinse and drain them once or twice a day then return them to the moist, light environment in the covered (but not sealed tight!) container.

You can buy a seed-sprouting kit and use the special container, but I have great results regularly by just using clear plastic tubs with close-fitting (not tight) lids, such as those often bought for storing pantry items.

Step 2: Caramelizing the sprouted wattleseeds

This is where the fun really begins and when the flavours and colours start to develop!

It's not an essential step, but it is one of the best ways to enjoy wattleseeds and to introduce endless combinations of new flavours into your cooking. Once the seeds have visible tiny roots or sprouts half or as long as the seeds themselves, it's time to roast the sprouted seeds (the 'malt'). I use a slow or moderate oven (150–170°C / 300–340°F), and roast slowly (much more slowly than the 'flash-roasting' used to prepare seeds that have not been soaked beforehand). This lower heat and slower roasting time is required so to first dry the seed crisp before it starts to caramelize (this is essential).

Before roasting, first drain the sprouted wattleseeds (your 'malt') thoroughly then place them onto a baking tray lined with silicone baking paper. Spread the wattleseed thinly, not in a pile, then put them in the oven to roast. Just as brewers select a light or a dark 'caramel' malt for lighter style beers or very dark ales, you can now decide whether you want to caramelize the seeds lightly (this takes 30–40 minutes), or take them to a darker caramel malt, which will need 60 minutes or more – it's your choice.

Once roasted to your liking, allow the seeds to cool. You will then have the most wonderful light, healthy and crunchy little crisps (I call these 'Malted Wattleseed Crisps') that will add amazing texture when scattered through salads or used with other cooked dishes (e.g. Braised Red Cabbage with Wattleseed Crisps, p. 228). Try them also in seed crackers, breads, biscuits and tuiles, sweet crumbles, savoury crumbings over meats and fish – or just munch on them as is. Oh, if you are a home brewer, go for it!

Fermenting the malted seeds – optional

If you like making your own sourdough breads, fermented foods or beers, fermenting the malted wattleseeds gives another dimension in which to play. Simply carry on from 'Step 2: Caramelizing the sprouted wattleseeds', above. Just cover your light- or dark-malted wattleseeds in warm water in a small tub with a loose-fitting lid and leave in the same warm and light conditions for 2–4 days as you did in the 'activating' stage. Wait until the mixture is starting to bubble and develop sour notes that are 'on the nose'. The fermented seeds can be used in kombucha-style drinks, sourdough breads or crumpets, with pickled vegetables, and so forth. Note that you can also ferment the seeds after a light roast, without malting, if desired.

Growing salad sprouts – optional

Another option, instead of caramelizing the wattleseeds, is to grow the seeds into full sprouts. To do this, just continue on from the first malting step on the previous page ('Step 1: Sprouting the wattleseeds') and allow the sprouts to continue growing for a further 2–3 days (5–10 days in total, depending on the species and conditions). Make sure you continue the daily draining-and-rinsing routine over this period. The roots will grow quite long, to about 3–4 cm (1–1½ in.) and look very similar to alfalfa sprouts. Stored in the refrigerator after fully sprouting; they will last for 5–7 days and can be used just like alfalfa sprouts in salads, sandwiches, wraps and the like. Note that as with any sprouting, hygiene and the use of clean filtered rinsing water is important

There are so many ways to use wattleseeds that I am sure there is another book just waiting to be written!

Australia's
Wild Herbs *and* Spices

Anise myrtle — *Syzygium anisatum*

AUSTRALIA'S WILD HERBS *and* SPICES

Summary

This table is a summary of the notes on Australia's wild herbs and spices and is intended as a brief introduction to their use in home cooking. A list of suppliers and wild food stores is included on page 280. The table includes information about the commonly eaten parts ('edible parts'). It should be noted that some plants might include other edible parts but only those that are used in this book and tested in the recipes are listed here.

Common name	Botanical name	Edible part	Form	Preparation and use	Flavour	Sourcing
BUSH TOMATO						
Bush tomato (also known as 'akudjura') 	*Solanum centrale*	fruit	dried	*The crisp dried whole fruit of the bush tomato can be coarsely ground to make a concentrated spice that is added to foods during preparation and cooking. It is also eaten raw.*	*The robust earthy flavours are reminiscent of caramelized tamarillo and sun-dried tomatoes.*	*Mostly whole crisp or semi-dried fruit is sold, although sometimes the ground powder is also available through various native food stores and on-line suppliers — or you can easily make your own powder from the crisp dried fruit (see pp. 172 and 174).*
GERALDTON WAX						
Geraldton wax 	*Chamelaucium uncinatum*	leaves	fresh	*The small leaves can be puréed or shredded and used in food, both cooked and uncooked.*	*Sharp, citrus flavours.*	*The dried leaves and the ground leaves are available from various stores and on-line suppliers. For commercial convenience, dried forms are more readily available than fresh, although some suppliers might offer fresh leaves from time to time. The fresh stems with or without flowers may be purchased from various stores and on-line suppliers, subject to seasonal availability.*
			dried	*Coarse leaves are great in teas or infusions, then strained. They can also be used in the same way as fresh leaves (above).*		
			ground	*Dried and finely ground leaves are used like a spice, added to foods while cooking to impart their flavours.*		
		flowers	fresh	*Can be used as a decorative and edible garnish but are very strong on the palate.*	*Strong and astringent (I'm not a fan).*	

Common name	Botanical name	Edible part	Form	Preparation and use	Flavour	Sourcing
THE GUMS (eucalypts)						
peppermint gum strawberry gum  *peppermint gum*  *strawberry gum*	*Eucalyptus dives* *Eucalyptus olida*	leaves	fresh	*May be used to infuse flavour into foods, in a similar way to a bayleaf. They are generally discarded once spent, but may also be used as a garnish. They are sometimes chewed for flavour, but are too fibrous to be eaten.*	*Peppermint gum: peppery and minty (as the name suggests!), with eucalyptus notes.* *Strawberry gum: sweet, fruity flavour with eucalyptus notes.*	*The dried leaves and the ground leaves are available from various stores and on-line suppliers. Some suppliers might offer fresh leaves from time to time.*
			dried	*Used to infuse flavour into foods, in the same way as fresh leaves (above). Can also be used to make a hot tea-like beverage but are too fibrous to be eaten.*		
			ground	*Dried and ground gum leaves are used like a spice, added to foods while cooking to impart their unique flavours.*		
THE 'MYRTLE HERBS'						
anise myrtle cinnamon myrtle lemon myrtle  *anise myrtle*  *cinnamon myrtle*  *lemon myrtle*	*Syzygium anisatum* *Backhousia myrtifolia* *Backhousia citriodora*	leaves	fresh	*May be used to infuse flavour into foods, in a similar way to a bayleaf. They are generally discarded once spent, but may also be used as a garnish.*	*Anise myrtle: strong aniseed flavours and sweet aroma.* *Cinnamon myrtle: subtle nutmeg and cinnamon flavour and aroma.* *Lemon myrtle: strong, fresh floral and citrus flavours and aroma.*	*The dried leaves and the ground leaves are available from various stores and on-line suppliers. Some suppliers might offer fresh leaves from time to time.*
			dried	*As above.*		
			ground	*Dried and ground leaves are used like a spice, added to foods while cooking to impart their unique flavours.*		

Common name	Botanical name	Edible part	Form	Preparation and use	Flavour	Sourcing
NATIVE VOILET						
native violet 	*Viola hederacea*	petals	fresh	*Generally used freshly picked and whole.*	*Very mild; they are used more for delicate texture and decoration than for their flavour.*	*From home gardens although may occasionally be available through commercial outlets.*
OLD MAN SALTBUSH						
old man saltbush 	*Atriplex nummularia*	leaves	fresh	*Blanched, wilted, or quickly fried, can be used as a salty seasoning or, in larger quantities, as a vegetable.*	*Salty, herbaceous flavours.*	*The dried leaves and the ground leaves are available from various stores and on-line suppliers. Some suppliers might offer fresh leaves from time to time. Whole seeds may be available for purchase from various stores and suppliers but must be toasted and ground before use.*
			dried	*May be used like a herb, to add salty notes to generally cooked foods.*		
			ground	*May be used like salt, to add salty flavours to both cooked and uncooked foods.*		
		seeds	ground	*Toasted and ground, the seeds are used to add a salty crunch to cooked foods.*		
PEPPERLEAF						
pepperleaves and pepperberries  	*Tasmannia lanceolata*	leaves	fresh	*May be used to infuse flavour into foods, in a similar way to a bayleaf. They are generally discarded once spent.*	*Intense peppery flavours.*	*The dried leaves, ground leaves, and berries are available from various stores and on-line suppliers. Some suppliers might offer fresh leaves from time to time. Fresh leaves and berries may be available from correctly identified growing trees but this book does not recommend the sourcing of fresh ingredients from the wild.*
			dried	*May be used like a herb, to add peppery notes to generally cooked foods.*		
			ground	*Dried and ground leaves are used like a spice, to add peppery flavours to food generally at the end of the cooking process (to preserve their heat properties).*		
		berries	dried	*dried and ground berries are used like ground peppercorns, to add heat to food, uncooked or cooked.*		

Common name	Botanical name	Edible part	Form	Preparation and use	Flavour	Sourcing
RIVERMINT						
rivermint 	*Mentha australis*	leaves	fresh	*Leaves can be torn or shredded and used in food, both cooked and uncooked.*	*Strong peppery-mint flavours.*	*The dried leaves and the ground leaves are available from various stores and on-line suppliers. For commercial convenience, dried forms are more readily available than fresh, although some suppliers might offer fresh leaves from time to time.*
				May be used in the same way as fresh leaves (above).		
				Dried and ground leaves are used like a spice during food preparation and cooking to impart flavour.		
COASTAL ROSEMARY						
coastal rosemary 	*Olearia axillaris*	leaves and stalks	fresh	*This species is also known as 'coastal daisy'. Fresh or dried, it can be used like rosemary with generally heartier foods such as meats and cooked vegetables, although it is much milder.*	*Resembles rosemary in appearance only, not in taste! It has a mellow, almost sage-like, and herbaceous flavour, and is quite perfumed.*	*The dried leaves and the ground leaves are available from various stores and on-line suppliers. Some suppliers might offer fresh leaves from time to time.*
			dried			
ROSELLA						
rosella 	*Hibiscus heterophyllus* *Hibiscus sabdariffa*	flowers	fresh	*The petals, fresh or dried, can be added to various recipes, cooked and uncooked.*	*Tart, berry-like flavour.*	*The whole flowers of Hibiscus heterophyllus, seed in, are generally purchased fresh, subject to seasonal availability. Mostly the seeded flowers (petals) are sold frozen or dried. The related introduced species Hibiscus sabdariffa can also be used.*
			dried	*Dried flower 'chips' are mostly used as a tea.*		
SEA PARSLEY						
sea parsley 	*Apium prostratum*	leaves and stalks	fresh	*Can be used like continental parsley, as a fresh herb added to salads and cooked foods. It can also be blanched, wilted, or quickly fried, and served as a vegetable.*	*fresh, parsley- and celery-like flavour with peppery and sometimes mild bitter notes.*	*The dried leaves and the ground leaves are available from various stores and on-line suppliers. Some suppliers might offer fresh leaves from time to time.*
			dried	*May be used like a herb, to add herbaceous notes to salads and cooked foods.*		
			ground	*Dried and ground sea parsley can be used as a seasoning, to add herbaceous flavourings.*		

Common name	Botanical name	Edible part	Form	Preparation and use	Flavour	Sourcing
WHITE KUNZEA						
white kunzea 	*Kunzea ambigua*	leaves	fresh	*The whole leaves and stalks can be used like a tea or a 'bouquet garni' for infusions then strained.*	*Subtle and elusive hints of eucalyptus, honey and citrus, with a honey-like scent.*	*Limited availability as a 'dried leaf tea' through native food suppliers. As at the time of writing, it is still only on the horizon of the mainstream food chain, although this is expected to change.*
			dried	*The whole small leaf or ground powder can be added to various dishes during preparation and cooking.*		
WILD BASIL						
wild basil 	*Ocimum tenuiflorum* *Plectranthus graveolens** **Ocimum tenuiflorum, the highly aromatic 'wild basil' (also known as 'holy basil' and by various other names) originated in India but was introduced long ago to neighbouring countries and now grows throughout South East Asia and Australia. It is more readily available in stores than Plectranthus graveolens, the true 'bush basil' (although it is in fact a type of mint), which early European settlers called the 'five spice plant' on account of its herbacious notes of basil, mint, sage and other herbs.*	leaves	fresh	*Leaves can be torn or shredded and used in food, both cooked and uncooked.*	*Strong hints of basil, but also mint, sage, pepper and other herbaceous flavours.*	*The dried leaves and the ground leaves are available from various stores and on-line suppliers. Dried forms are more readily available than fresh, although some suppliers might offer fresh leaves from time to time.*
			dried	*May be used in the same way as fresh leaves (above).*	*May be used in the same way as fresh leaves (above).*	
			ground	*Dried and ground leaves are used like a spice, added to foods while cooking to impart flavour.*	*Dried and ground leaves are used like a spice, added to foods while cooking to impart flavour.*	
WILD THYME						
wild thyme 	*Prostanthera incisis*	leaves	fresh	*Leaves can be torn or shredded and used in food, both cooked and uncooked.*	*Similar to thyme and oregano.*	*The dried leaves and the ground leaves are available from various stores and on-line suppliers. Some suppliers might offer fresh leaves from time to time.*
			dried	*May be used in the same way as fresh leaves (above).*		
			ground	*Dried and ground leaves are used like a spice, added to foods while cooking to impart flavour.*		

AUSTRALIA'S WILD HERBS *and* SPICES

Australia has a number of wild herbs that are botanically close to their relatives overseas, but with their own distinctive characteristics. They often have slightly sharper, bolder flavours. As well as these herbs, there are the flavoursome and highly aromatic leaves of certain trees that are also used as flavourings, and so for culinary purposes they too are considered 'herbs'. These include the various 'myrtle herbs' – anise, cinnamon, and lemon – as well as the leaves of some eucalypts, such as strawberry gum and peppermint gum. Many of the true herbs, such as wild basil, can be grown in vegetable plots, while some of the larger trees may already be growing in the home garden (or might soon be planted) or in neighbourhood streets but, as always, care is needed in identifying any plants used for food. The Australian herbs, whether they be true herbs or the leaves of larger trees, can generally be used fresh or dried. Those that are the leaves of large trees, unlike true herbs or leaves from smaller shrubs, can be tough and indigestible in their raw state, but easily used, like a bay leaf, to infuse flavour then removed when spent. They are also used in their dried form, as flakes, or ground into powder to use as a seasoning or spice. On the other hand, the true herbs have softer, more digestible leaves and are at their most invigorating and appetisingly aromatic and colourful when used fresh. For convenience, though, many are also available dried or ground. In some cases, both the leaves and the berries may be used as a herb or spice for flavour. For example, the leaves and the berries of the Tasmanian peppertree are prized for their unique peppery flavours. It works well to combine Australian herbs with other Australian wild foods as they tend to be naturally complementary in flavour, suggesting at some deep level their connection through the earth in which they grow. Indigenous Australians have long used Australian herbs as flavourings in foods as well as for certain medicinal purposes and health care.

Bush Tomato, dried or ground

Dried bush tomato, sometimes know as 'akudjura' (one of its many Aboriginal names) is mostly sold semi- or crisp-dried (there is a huge variance in terms of moisture content), whole, or ground, and is used as a spice or flavouring (although not all varieties are edible). Fully ripe fresh bush tomatoes or the dried can be eaten whole but are quite pungent, yet 'moreish'.

Bush tomato — *Solanum centrale* — dried or ground
This pungent dried fruit varies in colour from light and sandy through to reddish dark browns. You can make a spice powder by grinding very crisp dry bush tomatoes into a coarse powder. It has strong, slightly sweet and savoury flavours reminiscent of tamarillo and sun-dried tomatoes, with some bitter notes on the finish, but is very concentrated so a little goes a long way. It can be combined with other ingredients such as pepper and sugar to make spice mixes for rubbing on meats prior to cooking, or as an ingredient in sauces, chutneys, marinades, and also in other condiments. See also 'Bush tomatoes' (see p. 174).

bush tomato, dried and as akudjura (ground)

Geraldton Wax

Geraldton wax is a flowering, evergreen shrub endemic to Western Australia. While not a true herb, the leaves of certain varieties are used as a flavouring in food, and its attractive scented flowers for floral displays.

Geraldton wax — *Chamelaucium uncinatum*
The small, pale green leaves of this plant are highly aromatic with a sharp citrus flavour. They can be used whole or pounded or shredded, fresh or dried, in place of thai lime leaves or other citrus flavourings to add a uniquely Australian zing to curries, sauces and soups, as well as jams, salads and condiments. The waxy pink, red and cream flowers are also edible, but very strong. They work best as a garnish.

Geraldton wax

'I love to use this herb infused into olive oil.'

The Gums

Gums (eucalypts) are of the myrtle family, Myrtaceae. They have highly aromatic leaves that emit the scent of eucalyptus (produced by the compound eucalyptol) that can be accompanied by other aromas such as peppermint and strawberry. The leaves are used as a flavouring or ground as a spice but, in their whole, fresh form, are too fibrous to be digestible, so they are typically used to infuse flavour before being discarded. They are not true herbs, but are used as such. The two 'gum herbs' in this book are the peppermint gum (*Eucalyptus dives)* and strawberry gum (*Eucalyptus olida*). Both are endemic to the east coast of Australia. Eucalyptus oils, found in the leaves, have potent antibacterial, anti-inflammatory, antioxidant, and deodorising properties. They have long been a part of traditional medicine, and the strawberry gum is noted for its use by Indigenous Australians in the easing of digestive ailments.

Peppermint gum — *Eucalyptus dives*
The leaves of the peppermint gum have a peppery, eucalyptus, and minty flavour that pairs well with sweet dishes in need of a zing but, like other mint flavourings, it also combines beautifully with chocolate. The flavour is quite intense, so should be used sparingly, or it may become overpowering.

Strawberry gum — *Eucalyptus olida*
This extraordinary gum tree produces aromatic eucalypt leaves with strong hints of strawberry: a delicious and tantalising mix of sweet fruit notes with warm eucalypt flavours. The leaf is most commonly used, dried, as a herb in various dishes, or ground into a powder. It pairs well with fruit compôtes, jams and other dishes that complement its berry flavours.

'Using the gums delivers an unmistakable Australian character to so many dishes.'

peppermint gum

strawberry gum

The 'Myrtle Herbs'

The leaves of many myrtle trees emit tantalising, sometimes pungent, aromas, especially when rubbed or crushed, or after rainfall. The scents give hints of the flavours contained within. They are frequently used, in fresh or dried form, in the same way as herbs: to add piquant touches to various dishes, or to make herb-like teas, or dried and ground and used as a spice. Some are even used for antiseptic and deodorising purposes. In botanical terms, all myrtles are within the family Myrtaceae, which is said to include close to 6,000 species world-wide. Many are found in Australia, including several that are not native but, over thousands of years, have entrenched themselves within the natural environment and have flourished. Not all of the edible myrtles can be discussed here, but there are three that are readily available, take the term 'myrtle' in their common name, and are used in a similar way to herbs. They are anise myrtle, cinnamon myrtle, and lemon myrtle. Gums (eucalypts) are also a type of myrtle, as too are lillipillies and Geraldton wax, among many others, but are discussed separately (pp. 38, 122).

Anise myrtle — *Syzygium anisatum*

Anise myrtle has a strong, sweet aniseed flavour and scent and can be used in place of star anise, dill, or other anise-flavoured herbs. The leaves can be added to foods during preparation to impart the flavours, then removed when spent. They are also used in their dried form, as a herbal tea, or ground. Anise myrtle is one of the highest known sources of the compound anethole, which is responsible for its aniseed flavour and aroma but also has antifungal, antimicrobial, and antioxidant properties.

Cinnamon myrtle — *Backhousia myrtifolia*

The leaves have a pleasant but subtle cinnamon and nutmeg-like scent and aroma and can be used in place of cinnamon in various savoury or sweet dishes, in fruit pies, or added to crumbles, biscuit batters, and the like. It is also sometimes called 'nutmeg myrtle' and by other names. The leaves can be used fresh and also in dried form or ground. Traditionally, they have been used by Indigenous Australians for medicinal purposes, particularly for treating digestive ailments. The compound that gives the cinnamon flavour is elemicin, found also in nutmeg, and is known as a cause of delirium and disorientation but only if consumed in excess, as may occur with high levels of nutmeg consumption. It is a rich source of various vitamins and minerals and a little goes a long way so too much consumption is unlikely! It is high in calcium, iron and manganese, as well as antioxidants including Vitamin E. I find its flavour a little bland compared to lemon myrtle and anise myrtle, but that is a matter of personal taste and also flavour combinations.

cinnamon myrtle

Lemon myrtle — *backhousia citriodora*

This has a superb, intense, floral citrus flavour and aroma with hints of its rainforest origin. It can be used in place of lemon in almost any dish or beverage. It has a special use in milk-based preparations such as ice-cream and custard with less risk of curdling. It is sometimes called the 'Queen of lemon herbs' and is the world's richest source if citral, the compound responsible for its lemon-like flavour, and which is also used as an insecticide, deodoriser and antiseptic. It's a potent antioxidant and good source of calcium magnesium, lutein, zinc and various other antioxidants including Vitamin E.

'Anise and lemon myrtle deliver superb and powerful flavours.'

anise myrtle

lemon myrtle

Native Violet

This plant is native to predominantly eastern regions of Australia.

native violets

Native voilet — *Viola hederacea*

The subtly flavoured petals, used as an edible garnish, add a decorative splash of colour and soft, velvet-like texture to salads and other dishes, to contrast nicely with crisper ingredients.

Old Man Saltbush

Saltbushes are found globally and many are native to Australia, but it is 'old man saltbush' that has become increasingly popular. Fresh leaves are used as a vegetable, like baby spinach, while dried leaf flakes are used as a table seasoning, in place of salt, or as a salty spice in coatings, stuffings, and the like.

Old man saltbush — *Atriplex nummularia*

Old man saltbush provides a distinctive herbaceous and salty flavour that can negate the need for further seasoning. Early colonials likened it to a type of sage and appreciated its flavour and nutritional value. By contrast, it is said the leaves were not eaten by Indigenous Australians, although the seed was ground to a flour and used to make damper. In harsh wild conditions, the leaves can be very bitter and astringent, whereas when cultivated in lush conditions they become much softer and palatable, and can be eaten raw or cooked. Due to its ability to extract salt from soil, saltbush is also used to desalinise land. Saltbush is a good source of protein and also contains calcium and anti-oxidants. It has 20% less sodium than table salt.

old man saltbush

'Saltbush makes a natural seasoning to use as an alternative to salt, with less sodium.'

Pepperleaf

Both the leaves and the berries of the Australian peppertree provide a lovely peppery punch.

Pepperleaf — *Tasmannia lanceolata*

The recipes in this book use the leaves and berries of *T. lanceolata*, or Tasmanian peppertree, although they are similar to those of the Dorrigo peppertree (*T. stipilata*), which can used in their place. Both trees produce edible pepperberries, which can be ground and used as a seasoning, in the same way as peppercorns. The pepperleaves are used fresh or dried and ground as a herb and seasoning. The leaves and berries both produce an intense, peppery flavour, evocative of bush settings, and so only small amounts are needed. The heat comes from the compound polygodial, which builds intensity slowly on the palate, but it is denatured during cooking and loses its heat properties. Therefore, if you want the spice 'kick', it is better to add the ground spice or fresh leaf towards the end of the cooking process. Both leaves and berries contain anti-oxidants, and also have antimicrobial and antifungal properties, largely due to their significant amounts of polygodial.

ground pepperberries

pepperleaf

Rivermint

This is native to Australia but related to the other mints found the world over, including peppermint and spearmint. Along with its mint characteristics, it also has a powerful menthol flavour and aroma.

rivermint

Rivermint — *Mentha australis*

Like other mints, the leaves are used as a herb to add a fresh, slightly peppery and minty flavour with menthol notes to various foods. The Australian type tends to be quite pungent and sharper than most others, and also emits a menthol aroma. Fresh or dried, only a small amount is needed, and it can be used in place of other types of mint in any type of food, including salads, dressings, teas, sauces, jellies and jams. It works particularly well in yoghurt dishes such as tzatziki, where it provides a lovely contrast to the smoothness of the yoghurt and cooling ingredients such as cucumber. Traditionally, it has been used by Indigenous Australians as a flavouring in food but also as an insect repellent and in remedies for certain ailments. Like other herbs, rivermint is a source of various vitamins and minerals, including vitamin A, calcium, iron and antioxidants. It grows easily in home herb gardens.

Coastal Rosemary (Coastal Daisy)

This evergreen shrub grows from southern Western Australia right across to New South Wales.

Coastal rosemary — *Olearia axillaris*

This plant has some physical resemblance to the herb rosemary, but tastes nothing like it. It has a mellow yet almost sage-like and herbaceous taste. I use it occasionally with heartier meat dishes and starchy vegetables.

coastal rosemary

Rosella

This is not a true herb: it is a hibiscus, and the petals are used for flavourings.

Rosella — *Hibiscus heterophyllus*

Although closely related to other Asian species, the Australian rosella is endemic to Queensland and New South Wales. As is typical of the hibiscus (warm-climate plants with brightly coloured flowers), it has attractive petals. For culinary purposes, the flowers have a tart berry flavour with hints of rhubarb, which works well with fruit compôtes, jellies and other sweet dishes, and it is also said to have been eaten by Indigenous Australians as a vegetable.[1] In this book, however, the petals are used as a fruity floral addition to harissa paste in place of rose petals in the classic rose harissa. The attractive petals also make a lovely garnish. Rosella flowers are a good source of several vitamins and minerals, including vitamins C, D, B1 and B2, and calcium, among others. The red colouring also indicates the presence of potent antioxidants.

rosella flowers and leaves

Warning: rosella plants have long been consumed, but one adverse reaction has been reported, after consumption of rosella leaf tea over many days. Further investigation found: 'We suggest that native hibiscus leaves or flowers used as a food or beverage are unlikely to pose a health risk to healthy humans in terms of its oxalate content. . . we suggest that humans with poor kidney function should not eat this material or drink tea made from it.' (D. Harrison, R. McKenzie, C. Keena, G. Harvey, *Oxalate Analysis of Australian Native Hibiscus*, Hibiscus Organisation, 2011.) This book echoes that advice.

Sea Parsley

A lovely native herb related to celery, often found growing near the sea. It is used in the same way as flat-leaf (continental) parsley.

Sea parsley — *Apium prostratum*
Also known as 'sea celery', sea parsley is generally used like a herb, and occasionally blanched and served as a vegetable. It has a strong herbaceous flavour similar to a parsley celery-cross but with mild bitterness and, given the seaside environs in which it grows, carries subtle notes of the ocean. It is a native to the southern coastlines of Australia, and it's said it was eaten by Captain Cook and his crew to prevent scurvy. This suggests that, like other parsleys, it is a rich source of Vitamin C, along with other vitamins, minerals and antioxidants. It can be used in any dish to add flavour and nutrition, and also as an attractive garnish.

sea parsley

'Sea parsley is easy to grow at home — it is immensely versatile but has more punch than traditional parsley.'

White Kunzea

The leaves and flower of the white kunzea are generally used dried and whole, as a tea or flavouring, like a dried herb. The plant is endemic to the south-eastern coast of Australia.

White kunzea — *Kunze ambigua*
The tiny leaves as well as the flowers of the white kunzea emit a sweet honey-like fragrance and are used as a tea or a herb. The leaves and the flowers both impart surprisingly strong but elusive herb flavours with hints of eucalyptus, honey, and citrus. It is used mostly like a spice or seasoning to flavour sweet or savoury dishes, and as a direct infusion for cordials and herbal teas. Nutritional details for white kunzea are not yet widely available, but as a member of the myrtle family it is likely to share similar properties to that of related species and to be a good source of antioxidants and other nutrients. The essential oil contains many of the anti-oxidant compounds found in other myrtles. It can also be used as an antiseptic and has anti-inflammatory properties which have been used in the treatment of arthritis and other conditions.

white kunzea

'White kunzea has a calming aroma and warming flavour.'

Wild Basil

Wild basil is widespread all over the northern tropical regions of Australia and is also found in South East Asia. This species is known as *Ocimum tenuiflorum*, although another species, *Plectranthus graveolens*, is also commonly described as 'native' or 'wild' basil but is endemic to New South Wales and Queensland. Either one can be substituted for the other. Early European settlers called *Plectranthus graveolens* the 'five spice plant', on account of its herbacious notes of basil, mint, sage and other herbs.

Wild basil — *Ocimum tenuiflorum; Plectranthus graveolens*

Ocimum tenuiflorum is an aromatic herb with strong hints of sweet basil and an almost sweet, 'bubblegum-like' fragrance, along with other herbaceous flavours. It works very well with Mediterranean- and Asian-style dishes, but can also be used to add a piquant note to sweeter dishes. There are some claims it may have antidepressant and anti-anxiety properties. It is found in other parts of Asia as well as Australia and has long been a part of traditional Indian medicine.

Plectranthus graveleons is an Australian native with a similar flavour, and it is also commonly called 'wild basil' although it is actually a type of mint. Traditionally, wild basil has long been used by Indigenous Australians for medicinal purposes and, in colonial times, it was often boiled in hot water to make a pleasant-tasting 'bush tea'. Historically, it was noted that the basil found in the north of Australia had an aroma similar to that of anise, while that of east Australia more closely resembled cloves. All 'basils' are nutritious herbs, containing vitamins A and C, various minerals, and chlorophyll (an antioxidant).

wild basil

'Australian wild basil adds a unique pungency to many sauces and baked dishes.'

Wild Thyme

Wild 'thyme' is endemic to south-east Queensland, New South Wales, and Victoria.

Wild thyme — *Prostanthera incisa*

Australia's wild 'thyme' is closely related to another herb, wild 'oregano' (*Prostanthera rotundifolia*), so much so that the common names are often used interchangeably – and they are also interchangeable in some recipes. They are actually both from the Australian mint bush family, but dried *P. incisa* has been traded as a 'thyme' because of the similar appearance and aroma and flavour notes to conventional thyme. (Wild oregano, however, is not endemic to Queensland but rather is found further to the south, in the eastern states of New South Wales, Victoria, and Tasmania, as well as South Australia.) Australia's wild thyme has a powerful flavour that is 'thymey' and 'minty' and with savoury herbaceous notes, all at once. It is both strongly flavoured and aromatic, so a little goes a long way. It is used in both its fresh and dried forms, and its warm, earthy notes lend themselves to hot meat dishes such a roasts, braises and grills. It's traditionally been used by Indigenous Australians for various medicinal purposes. Detailed nutritional information is not readily available, but as a herb related to several mints and other herbs, it is most likely a good source of various vitamins and minerals. The green colouring of the leaves, is an indicator of chlorophyll, an antioxidant.

wild thyme

OYSTER RIVERMINT SHOOTERS

Light – 4-6 serves

You don't often see mint paired with fresh oysters, but I know you will love this when you try it. It just 'works', and makes an awesome start to any dinner or cocktail reception. This recipe covers plenty of oysters, so if you have left-overs, the zingy fresh salsa is also superb with grilled fish, chicken or lamb, and you can make it as hot or as mild as you like, depending on the type of chilli and how much is used.

INGREDIENTS

2-3 ripe, red roma tomatoes, or a similar weight of mixed coloured, large cherry tomatoes

---

100 ml (3⅓ fl oz) rice vinegar
210 ml (7 fl oz) tomato juice
50 g (1⅔ oz) white or light palm sugar
1-2 red chillies, finely chopped
1 tbs rivermint, stalks only, finely chopped (keep the leaves for the dressing base – see below)

---

4 tsp fish sauce, or to taste
zest and juice of 1 lime
1 tbs rivermint, leaves only, finely chopped
2-3 dozen oysters on the shell

SUBSTITUTIONS

rivermint:
mint.

METHOD

1. Cut the tomatoes into quarters, then slice off the seeds and flesh in the heart of the tomato and place these in a stainless-steel saucepan.
2. Dice the remaining tomato 'petals' of outer flesh into precise little cubes approximately 5 mm (about ¼ in.) in size. Put to one side.
3. Into the saucepan with the 'tomato hearts' (seeds and inner flesh), add the rice vinegar, tomato juice, palm sugar, chillies, and rivermint stalks.
4. Bring all to a gentle simmer, just enough to dissolve the sugar and infuse the flavours (about 2-3 minutes).
5. Chill completely, then strain through a sieve into a small bowl to remove the solids, which can then be discarded.
6. Now add the fish sauce, lime juice and zest to the strained sauce. Adjust to your taste: it should deliver a lively balance of hot, sour, salty and sweet flavours, all at once.
7. Stir through the chopped rivermint and diced tomato then allow to macerate for an hour or so.
8. Spoon over the top of the icy-cold fresh oysters on the shell, or, if you prefer, in shot glasses as I have done here. Wow!

CINNAMON *and* ANISE MYRTLE CRUMPETS

Makes 14-16 'egg-ring size' crumpets

These dainty little crumpets are a sweetly spiced delight. I like to serve them hot, together with grilled apricot and my Quandong Cômpote. You can also use other stone fruits such as peaches, nectarines when in season, as well as pears or apples — or even a colourful combination.

INGREDIENTS

7g (¼ oz) sachet of dried instant yeast
400 ml (13⅓ fl oz) milk, luke warm
2 tsp honey

300 g (10 oz) plain flour
½ tsp bicarbonate of soda
½ tsp salt
2 tsp ground cinnamon myrtle
2 tsp anise myrtle

1 batch quandong compôte (p. 157)
1 ripe apricot per person, cut in half and stone removed

neutral (flavourless) cooking spray

SUBSTITUTIONS

cinnamon myrtle:
cinnamon
anise myrtle
star-anise.

METHOD

1. Mix together the yeast, milk and honey then allow the mixture to sit in a warm place for an hour or so, to prove.
2. Separately, sieve the flour, bicarbonate of soda, salt, cinnamon myrtle and anise myrtle together into a bowl.
3. Whisk through the yeast mixture until smooth, then cover and allow to prove again for a further 30-40 minutes, or until the dough has almost doubled in size.
4. Spray the egg rings and a large non-stick frypan generously with cooking spray.
5. Working in batches, place a few egg rings in the frypan and heat them over a medium heat.
6. Using a jug with a spout, pour the batter into each ring until just up to the rim. Watch the heat carefully: you want the crumpets to cook to a crisp golden brown base with bubbles forming up through the dough, which should take 5-6 minutes. The tops should be soft and spongey.
7. Remove the rings with tongs, then flip the crumpets briefly to finish the cooking process. Remove the crumpets and keep warm while you cook the rest of the batter.
8. While the crumpets cook, heat a ribbed griddle pan or barbecue. Make sure the grill bars or ribs are brushed really clean. Oil with a paper towel just before using (see p.23 for notes on preparing your barbecue or grill).
9. Spray the apricots with oil. Grill for a couple of minutes or so on each side to caramelize and heat through.
10. Serve the crumpets hot with the grilled apricots and a warm quandong compôte drizzled over the top, together with yoghurt or whipped cream.

WOOD-FIRED CRAB, CHILLI *and* LEMON MYRTLE PIZZA

Main – makes 2 large pizzas | Light – makes 4 small single-serve pizzas

This is a spectacular pizza I've not seen elsewhere. It's not traditional and, quite frankly, not that easy to eat either (that becomes a 'labour of love' as you crack and pick through the crab, just like eating any whole crab dish). I developed it when I was a guest chef at Angove's Winery (McLaren Vale) some years ago, and it blew the guests away when they saw several very much alive-looking pizzas seemingly walk out of the oven — an amazing sight! (See also my notes on cooking in a wood oven, p. 267.) If you want show-stopping pizza, make it as I have, but if you like it easier to eat, forego the 'whole crab' bit and just fold all the crab meat into the sauce, without the shells. If you don't have a wood-fired oven, cook on pizza trays or a pizza stone for 5-8 minutes in your hottest possible fan-forced oven (to cook pizza properly and quickly with a crisp base, ideally the oven needs to be pre-heated to 350-400°C / 660–750°F).

INGREDIENTS

½ quantity of pizza dough (p. 267)

2 medium-sized cooked blue swimmer crabs
1½ cups Tomato, Lemon Myrtle and Ginger Sauce (p. 258)

½ bunch spring onions, trimmed and sliced on the diagonal
4-6 bocconcini, torn into pieces
extra flour for dusting

A show-stopping pizza!

METHOD

1. First, prepare your wood-fired oven (see notes on p.267) and then prepare the pizza dough.
2. Pick the crab meat from one crab and fold it into the Tomato, Lemon Myrtle and Ginger Sauce. Clean the other crab and cut into two halves. (Otherwise, if you prefer the crabs fully shelled, pick out all of the meat and fold all of it into the sauce, then discard the shells.)
3. On a floured workbench, roll out 2 large or 4 small pizza bases to 3-4 mm (⅛ in.) in thickness. Use lots of flour underneath so the base can slide easily, otherwise it's a challenge to slip the pizza peel (paddle) underneath it later.
4. Spread the sauce evenly all over the pizza bases. Sprinkle with spring onion and dot with small 'nuggets' of bocconcini.
5. Place a half a crab or a whole crab on top of each pizza (depending on how many you are making), spreading the legs and claws to help them stand up. If you like, add a cleaned carapace (head shell), to complete the picture.
6. Now, with a deft touch, quickly slide a pizza peel under each pizza, one at a time. Lift, then 'place and drop' onto the hearth, taking care not to let the crab fall over (don't worry if it does; you can always stand it back up later). Cook for 2-4 minutes, or until the pizza is crispy, puffed and golden. Slide onto a platter and serve immediately.

PEPPERLEAF BABBAGANOUSH

Accompaniment – makes about 2 cups

This classic Middle Eastern dish is spiced up nicely with Tasmania's native pepperleaf. One of the absolute 'must do's' is to really char the eggplant thoroughly, then cover immediately so it cools and traps all that wonderful smokiness.

INGREDIENTS

2-3 (about 500 g or 1 lb) eggplants

4-5 garlic cloves, peeled
1 tsp salt
5 g (⅙ oz) fresh pepperleaves stripped from the stem, or 1 tsp ground pepperleaf
zest and juice (about 100 ml / 3⅓ fl oz total) of 2 lemons
50 g (1⅔ oz) tahini
40 ml (1⅓ fl oz) extra virgin olive oil

1 tbs Pepperleaf Oil (optional, p.256)
sea parsley (for garnish, optional)
Davidson Plum Za'atar Flatbreads (optional, p.116)

SUBSTITUTIONS

pepperleaves:
green chilli or
green peppercorns
ground pepperleaf:
ground pepper
sea parsley:
flat-leaf or curly parsley.

METHOD

1. Set a wire cake rack over a gas flame hob on the stove, or crank up the barbecue grill outside to maximum heat.
2. Sit the eggplant directly over the flames and adjust so the flame is not so big that it's wasted up the sides. Instead, aim for a more even heat all over the base of the eggplant. Char over the flames, turning occasionally. It should be char-black all over, and the inside flesh soft and cooked right through. This can take 10 minutes or more.
3. Once completely charred, immediately place in a bowl and cover tightly with kitchen film. Allow to cool thoroughly.
4. Split the charred eggplant into quarters and scrape out all the cooked flesh and smoky juices with a knife. Discard the charred skins, but keep all the flesh and juices, which should now weigh about 300g (10 oz) net.
5. Using a food processor, pulse the eggplant, garlic, salt, pepperleaf, juice, zest, tahini, and oil into an even, chunky purée. Check seasoning and adjust as required.
6. Scrape the purée onto a large serving platter and spread in a rough circle about 2.5 centimetres (1 in.) thick.
7. I like to drizzle some Spicy Pepperleaf Oil generously over the babbaganoush to give an extra peppery zing and a lovely gloss to the dish, but you can also just drizzle with some more extra virgin olive oil. Sprinkle with fresh chopped sea parsley, if desired (as shown).
8. Serve with freshly baked Davidson Plum Za'atar Flatbreads.

CARROT, SWEET POTATO, LEMON MYRTLE *and* GINGER SOUP

Light – 5-6 serves

This healthy and vibrant soup can be made with varying quantities of carrot and sweet potato — or why not pumpkin? — it's up to you. If you are inter-changing the vegetables, remember to keep the quantity about the same or close. If you like it spicy, just ramp up the chilli. This soup is also lovely served chilled in hot weather — something we don't often do in Australian summers.

INGREDIENTS

30 g (1 oz) butter, diced
2 tsp sesame oil

200 g (7 oz) approx. onion, chopped
30 g (1 oz) ginger, peeled and grated
10-15 g (⅓-⅔ oz) chilli (mild, medium or hot, according to taste), sliced
3-4 garlic cloves, peeled and crushed

300 g (10 oz) sweet potato, peeled and diced into 5 cm (2 in.) cubes
450 g (15 oz) carrot, roughly chopped
1 litre (2 pints) vegetable or chicken stock
25 ml (1 fl oz) tsp fish sauce
10-12 fresh lemon myrtle leaves or 1-2 tsp dried
1 tsp ground pepperleaf

Geraldton Wax Coconut Cream (optional, p.253)

SUBSTITUTIONS

lemon myrtle leaves:
lemon verbena leaves, Geraldton wax leaves (chopped)
ground pepperleaf:
pepper, freshly ground.

METHOD

1. Gently melt the butter with the sesame oil.
2. Simmer the onion, ginger, chilli, and garlic in the butter and oil over a medium heat until they are only just beginning to colour.
3. Add the sweet potato, carrot, stock, fish sauce and lemon myrtle. Simmer for a further 30-40 minutes until the vegetables have softened.
4. If you are using whole lemon myrtle leaves, spoon them out now, before puréeing.
5. Purée finely with a stick blender. If you want a super-smooth soup, pass the purée through a fine sieve (but this is a lot easier if you have a Thermomix®, because it can cook and purée in the one utensil).
6. Serve the hot soup with a crusty sour dough or baguette. I also like to add a few dollops of Geraldton Wax Coconut Cream.

ZUCCHINI, SALTBUSH *and* RIVERMINT FRITTERS

Light – 4-6 serves

These golden fritters make for the perfect brunch, or a tasty side to serve up at a weekend barbecue. The saltbush and rivermint combine beautifully with the haloumi and zucchini, and they are delightfully crunchy on the outside while soft on the inside. I like to serve them with my Rivermint Yoghurt Sauce and salad, but they also work extremely well with poached eggs, smashed avocado, and even smoked salmon.

INGREDIENTS

4 spring onions

50 g (1⅔ oz) butter

2 packed cups fresh old man saltbush leaves
2 cups grated zucchini

2 eggs, beaten
150 ml (5 fl oz) water
2 cups besan (chickpea) flour
1½ tsp baking powder
1 tsp salt
1 tsp ground pepperleaf

½ red capsicum, diced into 5 mm (about ¼ in.) pieces
¼ cup fresh rivermint, chopped, or 3 tsp dried rivermint tea flakes
100 g (about 3½ oz) haloumi, grated

spray olive oil
Rivermint Yoghurt Sauce (p. 259), to serve

SUBSTITUTIONS

old man saltbush:
baby spinach, kale
ground pepperleaf:
pepper, freshly ground
rivermint:
rivermint flakes / dried mint flakes.

METHOD

1. I hate waste and the green tops of spring onions can often be discarded, but they make a beautiful, tasty garnish. So, before starting on this recipe, cut most of the green tops off the spring onions (reserve the white parts for use later). Hold together 2-3 pieces at a time flat on a chopping board and slice very finely on the diagonal. Drop them into iced water and allow to curl up over an hour or so.
2. Now heat a wide-based non-stick frypan. Drop in the butter and allow it to melt. (I personally love to get the butter to a foaming, golden brown before adding the vegetables.)
3. Add the saltbush and zucchini and cook for 4-5 minutes, stirring often, until wilted (but not overcooked). The wide pan allows for better and quicker evaporation of moisture.
4. Drain off any excess moisture, then tip the saltbush and zucchini onto a large, flat tray. Place in the fridge and allow to cool quickly. Meanwhile, whisk the eggs and water together, then add the flour, baking powder, salt and pepperleaf. Work into a smooth, thick batter.
5. Add the capsicum, the reserved white parts of the spring onions (finely sliced), rivermint and haloumi to the batter, as well as the cooled saltbush and zucchini. Mix thoroughly.
6. Spray a non-stick frypan (or barbecue hot plate) with the olive oil. Bring to a medium heat, then drop in large spoonfuls of batter, keeping them well apart in the pan. Cook for 3-4 minutes, flip and gently squash to flatten nicely, then cook for a further 3-4 minutes until golden brown.
7. Serve immediately with Rivermint Yoghurt Sauce, garnished with the spring onion curls.

CRISPY-SKIN BARRAMUNDI *with* LEMON ASPEN SKORDALIA

Large – 4 serves

I use barramundi for this dish, but Murray cod or salmon also produce a lovely, crispy-skinned fillet. To crisp-up the skin, it helps to 'air dry' it before cooking: just wipe the fillets dry with paper towels, then place on a plate in the fridge, uncovered, and leave to dry for a few hours or overnight. For a nice effect, cut a slash or two into the skin of each fillet (as I have done here). The fish combines perfectly with my adaptation of skordalia, which makes use of the fresh, citrus flavours of lemon aspen instead of vinegar.

INGREDIENTS

lemon aspen skordalia

360 g (12 oz) approx. potatoes (désirée or another red-skinned type)
4-5 garlic cloves, peeled
1½ tsp salt

---

50 ml (1⅔ fl oz) Lemon Aspen Juice (p. 242)
50 ml (1⅔ fl oz) extra virgin olive oil

fish

1 cup (about 60 ml / 2 fl oz per serve) Verjuice and Desert Lime Beurre Blanc (p. 250)

---

1 tbs (approx.) additional extra virgin olive oil, for frying
4 × 180 g (6 oz) approx. fresh barramundi fillets with skin dried (as described in notes above).

Note: this dish uses two native citrus flavours, lemon aspen and desert lime, but if only one is available, go that way (they are very interchangeable so one can easily be substituted for the other).

METHOD

to make the lemon aspen skordalia

1. Cover the unpeeled potatoes in water and bring to a gentle simmer. Cook until tender when pierced with a knife tip, then drain and allow to cool enough to be handled.
2. Peel off the skins using a small knife. Cut into rough chunks. You should be left with about 270 g (9 oz) net.
3. In a mortar-and-pestle, pound the garlic and salt to form a paste, or chop and grate very finely. Transfer to a saucepan.
4. Add the Lemon Aspen Juice and potatoes to the saucepan. Mash together while drizzling in the olive oil. When ready to serve, gently re-heat over a low heat (or microwave), stirring so it does not burn, or serve at room temperature.

to cook the fish and finish the dish

1. First prepare the Verjuice and Desert Lime Beurre Blanc and have it sitting in a warm spot with the skordalia.
2. Heat a non-stick, preferably heavy-based frypan over a medium heat and add a drizzle of the additional olive oil.
3. Season the fish skins and flesh generously with salt then cook skin-side-down over a medium heat for 8–10 minutes. Controlling the heat is critical: if too low, the skin will stew and not crisp up; if too hot, the skin will burn before the fish is cooked. Once almost cooked, flip them on to the flesh side for just 20–30 seconds, just before serving.
4. Serve the skordalia on plates then pour a generous amount (about 60 ml / 2 fl oz per serve) of the beurre blanc on top and around the sides before placing the crispy-skinned fish, crispy-side up, on top.

POTATO PEPPERLEAF GNOCCHI *with* MUSHROOMS, ASPARAGUS, SALTBUSH *and* SEA PARSLEY

Large – 4 serves | Light – 6-8 serves

These light little potato dumplings incorporate a uniquely Australian flavour. To cook the first time, I like to steam them, as I would Asian dumplings, but it's your choice: if you like, just cut the dough 'sausages' into pillows then simmer in gently boiling water as is traditional. Scoop them out as soon as they rise to the surface. Using an all-purpose 'floury' potato is essential; waxy/starchy varieties don't work as well.

INGREDIENTS

1 kg (about 2 lb) all-purpose potatoes

---

210 g (7 oz) flour
2-3 tsp truffle oil (optional)
1½ tsp sea salt (or to taste)
1-2 tsp ground pepperleaf

2-3 tbs extra virgin olive oil
handful of fresh saltbush leaves

---

2 tsp butter
2-3 asparagus spears per serve
4-5 broad beans per serve (optional)
1-2 small swiss brown mushrooms per serve
2-3 garlic cloves, peeled and crushed

---

4 tsp additional butter, cubed
8-10 sage leaves
8-10 fresh pepperleaves, shred super-thin across the leaf into a fine julienne

---

sea salt to taste
parmesan, freshly shaved, to serve
½ cup fresh sea parsley, chopped

SUBSTITUTIONS

ground pepperleaf:
pepper, freshly ground
pepperleaves:
green chilli
saltbush leaves:
baby spinach or kale
sea parsley:
flat-leaf (continental) parsley.

METHOD

1. Cover potatoes in cold water and bring to the boil. Simmer until tender, drain and peel, then pass them through a mouli or ricer, or grate on a box grater (easiest when still warm).
2. Keeping back a handful of flour, sift the rest into the potatoes, then add the truffle oil, salt, and pepperleaf.
3. Work the mixture quickly into a smooth mass (don't overwork it). If the dough doesn't bind and hold a nice shape, add just as much of the remaining flour as you need. Roll out into 30 cm (12 in.) long 'sausages' on a floured bench.
4. Line a bamboo steamer with baking paper and gently lay in the 'sausages'. Steam for 10–15 minutes, until they are just cooked through. Chill, then cut into 2 cm (about 1 in.) 'pillows'.
5. Simmer the olive oil and saltbush leaves in a pan, stirring frequently until the leaves go pale and crisp. Remove with a slotted spoon and drain on absorbent paper.
6. Using the same pan and oil, fry the gnocchi to a nice golden brown on both sides to reheat. Remove and keep warm.
7. Add the butter, asparagus, broad beans, mushrooms and garlic to the pan. Simmer for a few minutes until the vegetables are cooked through and the garlic just caramelized.
8. Plate up the gnocchi, vegetables and crisp saltbush leaves.
9. Increase the frypan heat and add the additional butter. Cook until the foaming subsides and the butter is a lovely dark brown (or even burnt). Remove from the heat and throw in the sage and pepperleaves (be careful: it will spit). Spoon the buttery herbs over the gnocchi and vegetables, then season with salt and garnish with parsley and parmesan.

SALTBUSH SCRAMBLED EGGS

Light – 4 serves

This is such a lovely and easy breakfast or brunch dish, which I developed while menu-consulting a few years ago for the superb Murray River Walks tours, where the food is very much of the river country (naturally, it's now a firm breakfast favourite with all the guests on the walking tours). There are plenty of spots around with old man saltbush shrubs. A word of caution, though: in wild, arid country, saltbush can live happily under very stressed and harsh conditions, but this makes its leaves particularly bitter and unpalatable (not for sheep, though — they love it!). But when it's growing in lush, well-watered environments, it is much softer and nicer to eat. You really should have one or two old man saltbush plants in your garden at home: they are a permanent and abundant vegetable supply from your garden if well watered, and almost impossible for the non-gardeners to destroy.

I have a pet hate of dry, over-cooked scrambled eggs; they are superbly creamy when slightly underdone. I also dislike the practice of many (including professional chefs) of adding milk or water to thin down the scrambled eggs (unless the aim is to stretch out the egg); all this does is dilute the flavour and texture. The other downside of adding liquid is that it can soon run out of the scramble and make the toast soggy.

INGREDIENTS

8-12 free-range eggs
black pepper, freshly ground

4 generous tsp of unsalted butter

2 generous cups of old man saltbush leaves
4-5 cherry tomatoes per serve
fresh crusty sourdough bread

Note: for a luxurious, textured dish, add a couple of teaspoons of cream at the end of the cooking process. This also helps arrest the cooking process at the right moment (it's a lovely treat, but cream doesn't need to be added each time — properly cooked scrambled eggs will still be delicious, and without the cream a little bit healthier, too).

SUBSTITUTIONS

saltbush leaves:
baby spinach or kale.

METHOD

1. Break the eggs into a bowl and grind in some fresh black pepper. Whisk thoroughly until smooth.
2. Separately, heat the butter in a large non-stick frypan and cook over a high heat until the foaming subsides and the butter is starting to turn a lovely golden brown.
3. Quickly add the saltbush and tomatoes. Stir-fry to wilt.
4. Add in the beaten eggs and stir briskly, still over the heat, with a small rubber spatula, to scramble the eggs as they firm up. But, as soon as the scrambled eggs are still a tiny bit runny and just holding their shape, take them off the heat. This is the perfect way to get a lovely creaminess in your eggs, and they will remain beautifully soft and moist.
5. Serve Immediately on hot, toasted, sourdough bread.

ROAST PUMPKIN *and* SALTBUSH LASAGNE

Main – 8 -12 serves

I first developed this lasagne with a pasta manufacturer, and it ended up on the Indian—Pacific train menus for a few years — it was very popular. Beautiful nut brown butter, or 'beurre noisette' as it's called in French ('noisette', meaning 'hazelnut', refers here to the colour of the butter; there are no hazelnuts in it!), is a classic combination with pasta and fried sage leaves. Old man saltbush leaves and sea parsley are great complementary additions, and make for a super vegetarian family meal that everybody, including die-hard carnivores that I have served it to, loves. It can be prepared a day ahead, chilled completely, then cut into portions and re-heated gently in the microwave or a low oven when ready to serve. You can also cook the pasta sheets the day before, lay them on a large tray with kitchen film between each layer to prevent sticking, and store them covered in the fridge, ready for assembling the lasagne the next day.

INGREDIENTS

1.5 kg (3 lb) Queensland blue pumpkin
1 large red onion
1-2 red capsicum
40 ml (1⅓ fl oz) extra virgin olive oil
1½ tsp salt
1 tsp ground pepperleaf

---

500 g (1 lb) dried lasagne sheets (or use my fresh pasta recipe, p. 268; just allow half again of the dry weight)
4 tsp additional salt
40 ml (1⅓ fl oz) additional olive oil

---

350 g (12 oz) mozzarella cheese, grated
150 g (5 oz) Italian parmesan, grated
300 g (10 oz) old man saltbush leaves

---

1 cup cream

---

2 batches Garlic Cream Sauce (p. 254)
2 batches Sage and Saltbush Beurre Noisette (p. 254, optional)
a few additional leaves of saltbush, shallow-fried in a little vegetable oil till crisp, then drained (optional)

SUBSTITUTIONS

old man saltbush leaves:
rosemary or thyme, salted to taste
sea parsley:
flat-leaf (continental) parsley.

METHOD

1. Pre-heat the oven to 200°C (390°F). Trim the pumpkin of seeds and skin and cut into large chunks about 5 cm (2 in.) in size. Then peel and cut the onion to the same size.
2. De-seed the capsicum and cut to similar-sized chunks.
3. Place all these vegetables in a large roasting tray and drizzle with the olive oil. Toss to coat, then sprinkle with the salt and pepperleaf.
4. Roast for about 40 minutes to caramelize lightly and barely cook through. Allow to cool.
5. Bring quite a large wide pot of water to a rolling boil over high heat and add the salt and olive oil. Slip in the pasta sheets one by one, ensuring they get a coat of oil as they sink. It's important to keep the water boiling rapidly and stir very gently (with a wooden spoon) to keep the sheets from sticking. Cook until they soften to 'al dente', then drain and rinse under cold running water to cool quickly. (This will be quicker with fresh pasta than dried, of course.)
6. Pre-heat your oven to 160-170°C (320-340°F), depending on how powerful it is. The heat needs to be moderate, or it will burn and dry out the pasta on the edges.
7. Take a small handful of each cheese and put to one side, to use later. Then, in a large bowl, mix together the remaining cheese and saltbush.

8. Stir the cheese mixture through the cooled vegetables.
9. Divide the vegetable mix into four roughly equal portions (to make four layers in the lasagne).
10. Oil a very large deep baking dish, at least 30 × 30 cm (12 × 12 in.). Alternatively, line it with silicone baking paper if you are planning to turn the lasagne out later, once cold, and slice into portions.
11. Begin building your lasagne by laying down about one fifth of the total amount of cooked pasta sheets on the base of the tray. It doesn't matter if the sheets overlap each other a bit – that's fine.
12. Layer about a quarter of the vegetable mix over the top, followed by another layer of the pasta (another fifth), and repeat until finishing with the last layer of pasta on the top.
13. Pour over the cream and sprinkle with the reserved cheese.
14. Cover with foil and bake for 1¼ hours, then allow to rest for 15 minutes, covered. When you are ready to serve, cut the lasagne into large squares. A 10 cm (4 in.) square is a generous portion.
15. Place the lasagne portions on each plate and pour over some hot Garlic Cream Sauce, then drizzle over warm Sage and Saltbush Beurre Noisette. Alternatively, before serving, shallow-fry the saltbush in a little vegetable oil to make crisp little saltbush 'chips' and sprinkle them over the lasagne instead of the beurre noisette (as shown).

PEPPERLEAF PARMESAN POLENTA

Side – 10-12 serves

I always found polenta a little underwhelming, until I made it with a rich chicken stock — what an amazing transformation! I don't know why anyone would make it with plain old water. Of course, you can also use vegetable stock for a vegetarian version. Then, use best-quality cheese and the fragrant spice of native pepperleaf to keep building the flavours. Cream isn't a traditional ingredient either, but it adds a luxurious finish. This recipe suggests cooling the polenta before cutting it into shapes then baking or frying, but it can also be eaten hot, when it's a thick 'porridge' consistency, and it's an equally delicious accompaniment to other dishes, such as my Bush Tomato Ratatouille on (p.189). Another personal favourite is to serve the polenta, either wet or in baked pieces, with the Kangaroo with Quandong Chilli Glaze (p.132).

INGREDIENTS

1 litre (2 pints) approx. chicken stock
1 tsp salt
35 g (1 oz) unsalted butter

200 g (7 oz) fine polenta

40 g (1⅓ oz) Italian parmesan, grated
1 tsp ground pepperleaf
100 ml (3⅓ fl oz) cream

1 tbs additional extra virgin olive oil or melted butter, or spray olive oil (optional), for baking, grilling or frying

SUBSTITUTIONS

ground pepperleaf:
pepper, freshly ground.

METHOD

1. Bring the stock, salt, and the butter to the boil in a saucepan, then reduce the heat.
2. Slowly add the polenta, whisking constantly, and return to a gentle simmer. Stir frequently with a wooden spoon or rubber spatula and cook over the lowest possible heat for 5-8 minutes (or longer if you are using a coarse polenta). Polenta will spit as it bubbles away, so keep it covered while it is simmering.
3. When cooked, stir through the parmesan, pepperleaf and cream, then spread the mixture out onto a baking dish lined with silicone baking paper. The mixture should be about 2-3 centimetres thick.
4. Smooth over the mixture with a wet spatula or scraper and allow it to cool completely in the fridge.
5. Cut the cooled polenta into shapes: triangles or rectangles or crescents and so on. A biscuit cutter works well for this.
6. When ready to re-heat the polenta, place the shapes onto a baking tray (again lined with silicone baking paper), and brush with melted butter or spray with olive oil. Place in a very hot pre-heated oven (about 230°C/440°F) and bake quickly for about 6-8 minutes to brown the edges and heat through. Alternatively, pan-fry the pieces with a little olive oil and/or butter in a non-stick frypan for a few minutes, turning once of twice.

HOT ROAST WILD BASIL TOMATOES *with* CHILLED LABNEH

Light – 4 serves, or can be served as a shared dish

I love this combination of hot roast tomatoes and the chilled tangy labneh. They are offset nicely by the sweet wild basil from the Northern Territory, which has an aroma vaguely reminiscent of sweet bubble gum – so unique!

INGREDIENTS

1 punnet of cherry tomatoes, mixed colours
½ cup extra virgin olive oil
2 tsp dried wild basil, crumbled

---

4 large slices of crusty baguette or sourdough

---

2 cups soft labneh (p. 244)

---

1 tbs fresh seablite, samphire, sea parsley or other fresh herbs (optional)

SUBSTITUTIONS

dried wild basil:
fresh basil

seablite, samphire, sea parsley:
flat-leaf (continental) parsley or other fresh edible succulents or fresh herbs of your choice.

METHOD

1. Cut the larger cherry tomatoes in half and mix together with the whole, smaller tomatoes. Add the oil and wild basil and allow to macerate for at least 1-2 hours.
2. Pre-heat your char-grill or barbecue. Once hot, brush some of the olive oil marinade over the bread, then grill both sides until nicely toasted and slightly charred.
3. Heat a non-stick, heavy-based frypan until it is quite hot.
4. While the frypan is heating up, spread a large spoonful or more of the soft labneh onto each of the four serving plates. Lay the grilled bread over the top.
5. Pour the marinated tomatoes into the pre-heated pan, carefully as it may spit! It is nice if you can char and blister the skins a little bit and just start to collapse the flesh. This will happen very quickly.
6. Once done, spoon the tomatoes and oil over the grilled bread and labneh.
7. Garnish with seablite, sea parsley, or other herbs of your choice, then serve immediately.

BLACK PEPPERBERRY CRAB

Light – 4 small serves

I love this dish which, like many of my favourites, evolved from my extensive travels as a chef. This time the inspiration came from Singapore, where their famous Black Pepper Mud Crab is legendary.

INGREDIENTS

2 medium-large fresh blue swimmer crabs or 1 mud crab

1 bunch spring onion

1½ tsp sesame oil

3 tsp peanut oil
3 tsp black peppercorns, crushed in a mortar-and-pestle to a medium kibble
12-15g (½oz) ginger, julienned
3-4 cloves garlic, peeled and finely slivered

100ml (3⅓ fl oz) oyster sauce
25ml (just under 1fl oz) sweet soy sauce (ketjap manis)
75ml (2½ fl oz) water, or seafood or chicken stock
50ml (1⅔ fl oz) rice vinegar
15g (½ oz) palm sugar
3 tsp pepperberries, freshly ground

1-2 large red chillies (optional)
Steamed Lemon Myrtle Rice (optional, p. 269)

SUBSTITUTIONS

ground pepperberries: ground black, green, white or pink peppercorns.

METHOD

1. Remove the head shell from the crabs. Cut each crab in half and cut away any gills and excess shell, and scrape off the stomach bits. Avoid over-rinsing, as you are just removing flavour, really.
2. Slice the white part of the spring onions into diagonal lengths of about 2-3 centimetres (about 1 in.) each. Put to one side. Also keep the green tops (sliced fine and soaked in ice water) to use as a garnish.
3. Heat the oils in a wok over medium heat then fry the crushed black pepper, ginger, and garlic for a few minutes, stirring constantly, until they are just starting to brown. Control the heat when you stir-fry, so the edges don't burn and the ingredients caramelize evenly.
4. Add the oyster sauce, sweet soy sauce, stock, vinegar and palm sugar to the wok. Bring to a simmer and add the crab, cover with the lid, then cook over a medium heat so the crab steams and is cooked through (about 6-8 minutes).
5. While it is cooking, crush the pepperberry in the mortar-and-pestle to a fine kibble. The pepperberry is added near the end of the cooking to retain its heat.
6. Add the white spring onion to the simmering sauce and fry for another minute. The sauce should now be reducing to coat the crab nicely.
7. Finally stir in the ground pepperberry, then arrange the crab on a platter with the rice (if using).
8. Garnish with the green spring onion tops.
9. If you like the sauce hot, add extra sliced red chilli.

LEMON MYRTLE 'BOUILLABAISSE'

Main – 4 serves

This is a wonderfully rich and aromatic soup where the 'heady' saffron flavour and lemon myrtle make it extra special. The seafood selection is really up to you, depending on the variety available – and super fresh is best. I always like to add the salmon last, so it is not over-cooked and stays pink. If you want succulent juicy seafood, not over-boiled and dry, it's all in the timing.

INGREDIENTS

1 generous pinch saffron threads
2 tsp water, boiling

3-4 cloves garlic, peeled and finely chopped
1 small fennel bulb, finely sliced
50 ml (1⅔ fl oz) extra virgin olive oil

---

1 litre (2 pints) approx. good quality fish stock
2 cups diced ripe tomatoes or 400 g (13⅓ oz) approx. diced tinned tomatoes
½ tsp wild basil leaves
8-10 fresh lemon myrtle leaves
1½ tsp sea salt
⅓ tsp ground white pepper
2 tsp sugar (optional)

---

1 large blue swimmer crab (head shell removed, quartered and cleaned)
1 × 50 g (1⅔ oz) approx. white fish fillet per serve
1 crayfish medallion and / or 1-2 prawn tails per serve

1-2 scallops per serve
1 x 50 g (1⅔ oz) approx. salmon fillet per serve
1 small squid, cleaned and cut into rings
3-4 mussels per serve

---

2 oysters per serve

---

favourite bread for grilling
1 tbs additional olive oil, for brushing
fresh herbs, chopped, to garnish
1 cup (approx.) Bush Tomato Rouille (p.177)

METHOD

to prepare the soup base

1. Well in advance of preparing the rest of the dish, cover the saffron in a couple of teaspoons of boiling water to draw out all the flavour. Leave it to sit for at least10 minutes.
2. In a wide braising pan, simmer the garlic and fennel in the olive oil over a medium heat for 2-3 minutes, until they are soft and translucent, but without colouring.
3. Add stock, saffron threads, tomato, basil, lemon myrtle, salt, pepper, and sugar, to taste. Simmer for 10 minutes.

adding the seafood in stages

4. First add the crab and simmer in the soup, covered, for about two minutes.
5. Add the white fish fillets, and the crayfish or prawns, then cook for another 2-3 minutes.
6. Add the scallops, salmon, squid and mussels. Cover and simmer for 1 more minute.
7. Add the oysters (in the shell) and cover again, turning off the heat. They will warm up as you prepare to plate the dish.

to finish the dish

8. While the seafood is cooking, grill the bread, brushing with a little oil. Serve the soup in large bowls with my Bush Tomato Rouille (an amazing accompaniment with the grilled bread to soak up all the juices) and garnished with herbs.

SUBSTITUTIONS

wild basil:
fresh basil
lemon myrtle leaves:
lemon verbena leaves, thai lime leaves.

CHAR-GRILLED SQUID, CHORIZO *and* LIMA BEANS *with* SEA PARSLEY SALSA VERDE

Light – 4 small serves

I love this summery dish, perfect for a light barbecue lunch or as a dinner-party entrée – it tastes so fresh and healthy. Of course, the chorizo is optional, and cuttlefish or prawns can also be used instead of or with squid.

INGREDIENTS

1 medium fresh whole squid or about 210 g / 7 oz squid tubes

½ red capsicum
½ yellow capsicum
extra virgin olive oil for brushing
1 tsp salt, or to taste
½ tsp pepperleaf, freshly ground

60 g (2 oz) spanish onion, peeled
½ continental cucumber
1½ cups lima or cannellini beans, drained
2 cups Sea Parsley Salsa Verde (p. 255)

a few slices of chorizo sausage, sliced thinly on the diagonal, to taste (optional)

SUBSTITUTIONS

pepperleaf:
pepper.

METHOD

1. Pre-heat and clean your barbecue grill (see p.23).
2. Clean and skin the squid in the usual way, while retaining the tentacles.
3. To cut the squid as I have done, lay the squid on its back (the flat side) and pinch the tube with one hand while cutting thin parallel slices through the tube, but not completely through the body.
4. Brush the squid and the capsicums with the olive oil, then season with the salt and pepperleaf.
5. Separately, slice or dice the onion and cucumber and mix together in a bowl with the drained beans and a little of the Sea Parsley Salsa Verde. Arrange on a large platter.
6. First, grill the chorizo (if using) and capsicums on high heat, turning regularly, for a few minutes until starting to caramelize, then add the squid. Continue cooking, turning all the time, until the chorizo is nice and crispy and the capsicums softened and charred. Watch the squid – it should be barely cooked through, but also nicely charred, to maximise the tenderness and flavour, so a high-heat grill is essential.
7. Remove from the grill, quickly slice the capsicum into smaller strips, and arrange all these hot ingredients over the salad. Top with a little extra salsa verde then serve.

SWORDFISH *with* YELLOW RIVERMINT CURRY SAUCE

Main – 4 serves

This is a delicious version of the classic Thai yellow curry that highlights the tart and sour flavour of tamarind and the freshness of mint (in the curry sauce). I like to use swordfish, but also snapper or barramundi wings, which are often discarded but so very flavoursome with an incredible gelatinous texture — you must try them! But, in fact, any firm white-fleshed fish or even chicken works just fine. Vegetarians will also love pumpkin and/or sweet potato simmered in this sauce (replacing the fish sauce with salt, of course).

INGREDIENTS

4 × 180 g (6 oz) swordfish steaks or other firm white fish or skinless chicken fillets, thighs or breast, per person
2 snake beans* or a few green or french beans per serve
2-3 cups Yellow Rivermint Curry Sauce (p. 263)

---

juice of 1-2 limes, to taste
small bunch thai basil, leaves torn
1 cup fresh rivermint leaves
2-3 chillies or to taste, sliced (optional)

Steamed Lemon Myrtle Rice (p. 269)

½ cup crispy fried shallots*
small bunch coriander (cilantro) to garnish

* *Snake beans grow to about 30–75 cm (1–2½ feet) in length and add a dramatic touch to the presentation of any dish. They can be found in Asian groceries and in other fresh produce stores at certain times of the year, but when not available ordinary green beans or french beans can be used instead.*

* *Crispy fried shallots, ready to use, can be purchased at Asian foodstores and some supermarkets and add a crunchy onion-flavoured garnish to many dishes. See also p. 107 on how to make your own, along with some garlic.*

METHOD

1. Simmer the fish and beans in the sauce for 3-4 minutes, or a little longer if the meat is thick.
2. Add some lime juice and check the balance of the sauce. You may like to thin it with a little more coconut milk, if desired.
3. Stir through the fresh herbs and chilli (if using).
4. Serve with Steamed Lemon Myrtle Rice.
5. Sprinkle with crispy shallots, garnished with fresh coriander (cilantro) leaves.

SUBSTITUTIONS

rivermint:
mint.

TOMMY RUFFS *with* LEMON ASPEN SALSA

Main - 2 large serves | Light - 4 small serves

A light, tangy and fresh seafood dish, complemented nicely by the crisp texture and the aniseed flavours of the fennel in the Fennel and Lemon Aspen Salad. 'Tommy ruff' is the local South Australian name for the native Australian herring.

INGREDIENTS

15g (½ oz) light palm sugar
30 ml (1 fl oz) Thai fish sauce

15 ml (½ fl oz) Lemon Aspen Juice (p. 242)

4 x 100g (3⅓ oz) medium fresh tommy ruffs or Coorong mullet fillets

1-2 tbs flour for dusting
1-2 tbs olive oil for grilling

Fennel and Lemon Aspen Salad (p. 112)

METHOD

1. Shave the palm sugar and place in a small ceramic bowl with the fish sauce.
2. Microwave for 20-30 seconds to dissolve easily, then allow to cool.
3. Mix in the Lemon Aspen Juice.
4. Cut diagonal slices into both sides of the fish and then marinate (or lightly sugar-cure) the fish in the sauce for 2-3 hours, turning once or twice.
5. Meanwhile, prepare the Fennel and Lemon Aspen Salad.
6. Once the fish has marinated for a few hours, pre-heat your char-grill on high, and brush down the grill bars with a wire brush so they are very clean. Oil the grill bars generously with paper towels or a clean rag cloth. This is important preparation for grilling food that can stick easily (see p. 23 for further notes on preparing your barbecue or grill).
7. Remove the fish from the marinade and pat dry with a paper towel. Dust generously with flour, then brush liberally with olive oil.
8. Oil your grill bars again before placing the fish on top. Barbecue for 2-3 minutes on both sides.
9. Serve immediately with the tangy salad.

CHICKEN *in* PAPERBARK *with* WHITE KUNZEA

Large – 4-6 serves

Cooking in paperbark is a superb way to bake food that also looks great when presented at the table. The other great joy is in the rush of steam and aromas when the parcel is opened, bringing diners right up to the action. It's one Indigenous cooking technique that adapts well to a modern home environment, as it works brilliantly cooked in the hot ashes of a campfire or in a kitchen oven. In this recipe, the white kunzea adds a subtle elusive flavour and aroma. Be aware that when cooking in ovens, barbecues, or traditionally in hot ash, the bark may start to smoulder. That's o.k., as it can add a lovely smokiness to your food, but make sure it smoulders only and does not catch alight (see notes on paperbark cooking on p.25).

INGREDIENTS

1 × 1.8 kg (4 lb) approx. free-range chicken

2 tsp butter
1 tbs extra virgin olive oil
1 tsp sea salt
½ tsp ground pepperleaf
2 tsp white kunzea leaves

1 recipe batch Bunya Nut and Muntries Stuffing (optional, p.231)

SUBSTITUTIONS

ground pepperleaf:
pepper, freshly ground
white kunzea leaves:
lemon grass, lemon myrtle leaves, or herbs of your choice.

METHOD

1. Remove excess fat from the bird's cavity and rinse clean. Pat dry with paper towels, then set the oven to 220°C (430°F) – or have plenty of hot coals ready in your campfire!
2. In a large pan, heat the butter and olive oil and lightly brown the chicken all over. Season generously with salt, pepperleaf and the kunzea leaves.
3. Fill the cavity with the Bunya Nut and Muntries Stuffing (if using) then wrap in generous layers of bark of paperbark cooking sheets (see p.25). Secure with string.
4. Place the parcel in a camp oven or on a baking tray in the oven and roast for 1 hour. Reduce oven heat to 80°C (180°F), the perfect resting temperature, and allow to rest for 15 minutes.
5. Place on a large platter before opening the parcel and carving. If opening at the table, lay out a large cloth to catch all the brittle bark shards. It can get a little messy, but the results are worth it. Transfer to a carving board to portion up.

ROAST WILD THYME KIPFLER POTATOES *and* ONIONS

Side – 4-6 serves

I like roasting kifplers in duck fat because of the great flavour but, for a vegetarian version, extra virgin olive oil works just as well. The bold flavours of pepperleaf and wild thyme go so well with the earthiness of onions and potatoes. This recipe is in fact two recipes combined, both wonderful, especially with roasts, but they can also be made separately, of course (just leave out the potatoes and adjust the amount of onion, or vice versa). The stuffed onions also makes a great vegetarian entrée with a rocket (arugula) salad and my Bush Tomato Balsamic (when making that version, I like to add a little goats cheese to the crumb mix). And remember, there's no need to peel kipflers: a good wash and scrub is fine.

INGREDIENTS

450 g (1 lb) kipfler or other 'waxy' potatoes

---

2 small-medium spanish onions

½ cup duck fat or extra virgin olive oil
2 tsp butter

---

1 heaped tbs high-quality parmesan (e.g. Parmigiana-Reggiano), grated
⅓ cup panko breadcrumbs
2 tsp fresh wild thyme, chopped, or 1 tsp dried, chopped

---

1 tsp ground pepperleaf
generous pinch of River Murray salt, to taste

3-4 whole garlic cloves per person

---

additional sprigs of fresh wild thyme, to garnish

SUBSTITUTIONS

ground pepperleaf: pepper, freshly ground
wild thyme: thyme.
River Murray salt: sea salt flakes.

METHOD

1. Pre-heat the oven to 180°C (350°F).
2. Cut the medium-sized potatoes length-wise into quarters. Larger ones are better sliced into sixths, and smaller ones into halves (they should all end up at about the same thickness for even cooking). Spread them out in a baking tray lined with silicone baking paper.
3. Trim the tops and tails of the unpeeled onions (to give them a flat base so later they can sit in the baking tray without toppling). Then cut them into halves crossways, across the grain.
4. In a small saucepan, gently melt the fat (or olive oil, if using) together with the butter.
5. Separately, mix the parmesan and breadcrumbs together. Add a pinch of the wild thyme and pepperleaf and moisten with about a tablespoon or so of the melted fats. Mix this in to make a slightly oily crumb, then spoon it over the onions.
6. Sprinkle the remaining melted fats, pepperleaf, wild thyme, and salt all over the potatoes to coat them evenly.
7. Add the crumbed onions to the tray with the potatoes.
8. Roast for 20 minutes then take out of the oven and reduce temperature to 140°C (285°F). Add the unpeeled garlic and gently stir through to coat (don't topple the onions!). Return to the oven and roast for a further 30-40 minutes to finish cooking. The garlic should have a lovely, nutty flavour and not be burnt. Serve garnished with a few sprigs of wild thyme.

NATIVE ANISEED FIVE-SPICE PORK *with* DAVIDSON PLUM HOI SIN

Shared entrée – serves 6-10

This beautiful pulled pork dish works brilliantly in bao buns, but is also great in wraps or served in sliders or burgers. You must make the effort to also prepare the crackling — it makes for incredible textural crunch and flavour with the soft bao buns and all the other elements.

INGREDIENTS

1 kg (2 lb) approx. pork shoulder
4 tsp Creative Native Anise Myrtle Five-Spice
⅓ cup shaoxing cooking wine
1 tsp salt
2 tsp sesame oil

½ bunch of fresh mint
1 large bunch coriander (cilantro)
3-4 fresh red chillies
1 bunch spring onions
pork crackling (see below)
2-3 bao buns per serve (p.266)
2 cups Davidson Plum Hoi Sin Jam (p.249)

To make the crackling:

Take 200-300g/7–10 oz pork skin. Slice off any excess white fat from the underside of the skin, wipe skin dry with a paper towel, then rub with salt. Leave in fridge (uncovered) for 4-5 hours or overnight. Pre-heat oven to 230°C/450°F. Wipe skin dry again, rub with a little oil, and salt generously again. Roast for 20 minutes, then reduce temperature to 175°C/350°F and roast for another 30-40 minutes until skin is completely crisp and dry. Drain and cool on absorbent paper. Place in a plastic bag and smash into a coarse 'crumble' (3–5 mm/1–2 in. chunks) using a rolling pin. Store in an air-tight container. It may be gently warmed in the microwave before use. Leftovers freeze well for later use.

SUBSTITUTIONS

Creative Native Anise Myrtle 5-Spice:
Chinese 5-spice.

METHOD

1. Rub the meat all over with the five-spice.
2. The pork needs to be slow-cooked, and there are a few ways. I like the sous-vide method, although it requires some special equipment (see p. 21). To cook this way, place the spiced meat, cooking wine, salt and sesame oil in a vacuum bag and seal. Cook in a water bath for 4½ hours at 85°C (185°F.). Alternatively, place the meat in a roasting tray and add the wine, salt and sesame oil. Cover tightly with foil (or seal in an oven bag) and cook in a 120-130°C (250-265°F) oven for 3-4 hours. Or, add the ingredients to a slow cooker and cook for several hours. Whichever way, the meat needs to cook slowly until it is falling apart.
3. Once the meat is cooked, carefully pour off all the juices and transfer to a wide-based pan. Reduce over a high heat, stirring occasionally, until it forms a syrupy glaze.
4. Allow the meat to cool to luke warm, then shred using your fingers or a fork. Fold the sticky reduction through the shredded meat. (The meat can be cooked and shredded a day or two ahead; just cover it well and store in the fridge. Alternatively, if vacuum-sealed in serving-size pouches, it will keep up for up to 12 months in the freezer).
5. Arrange piles of herbs, finely sliced chillies and spring onion (on the diagonal) and crunchy crackling onto a platter or individual bowls (easier to pass around the table).
6. Steam heat the bao buns, and microwave the pulled pork to hot, and place everything in the centre of the table with a couple of bowls of that addictive Davidson Plum Hoi Sin. Let the fun begin (you can't stop at just one!).

LAMB *with* RIVERMINT CHILLI PESTO *and* PEAS

Main – 4 serves (about 3 cutlets each)

I love to serve lamb after it has rested for at least 10–15 minutes, so that it is beautifully tender and moist. Resting cooked meats at the correct temperature is important, so take the lamb out of the oven, leave the door open for a few minutes to cool, re-set to 80°C (175°F), then return the lamb to the oven to rest. When cooking the peas, I like to use only a small amount of water. I have for many years favoured steaming vegetables with minimal liquid, rather than covering in boiling water — that just leaches out the flavour and a lot of the nutrients which end up being poured down the sink.

INGREDIENTS

2 racks of young spring lamb (about 12 ribs / cutlets)

salt to taste
½ tsp pepperleaf, ground

2 tsp extra virgin olive oil
1 tsp cold unsalted butter
1 small sprig rosemary, chopped

2 cups lamb, chicken or beef stock
2 additional tsp unsalted butter (optional)

2 generous cups of fresh or frozen peas
1-2 tbs water

1 cup Rivermint and Chilli Pesto (p. 261)
fresh pepperleaf, shredded (optional)

SUBSTITUTIONS

fresh pepperleaf:
green chilli, sliced
ground pepperleaf:
pepper, freshly ground.

METHOD

1. Pre-heat the oven to 230°C (445°F). You may like to trim the bones of your cutlets and scrape clean with a small knife.
2. Season the cutlets generously with salt and pepperleaf.
3. Heat the oil and butter in a heavy-based roasting pan. Brown the lamb on all sides, then sprinkle with the rosemary.
4. Roast for 5-8 minutes, depending on how well cooked you like it to be. Baste with the oils and juices. The timing is very dependent on the lamb's size and thickness, and I like to take it out at the rare stage when it is still very soft to the touch, then allow a good long resting. It's then ready to serve at a relaxed medium-well done – nice and pink.
5. For a simple pan jus while the meat is resting, deglaze the roasting pan with the stock and reduce down rapidly to about half a cup. If you like, add a teaspoon or two of cold butter at the end, swirling it into the jus over a low heat until it melts and emulsifies. This will give it a nice shine. Strain (if desired) and season to taste.
6. Also while the lamb is resting, prepare the peas by bringing them to a gentle simmer in a small, covered saucepan with only a tablespoon or two of water.
7. When the peas are just tender, stir in a generous amount of the pesto. Extra green chilli slices or finely shredded native pepperleaf may be added at this stage, if you like it spicy .
8. Carve the beautifully rested lamb and serve with the peas, and add more pesto if desired. This also goes beautifully with Crispy Saltbush and Vinegar Potatoes (p.114).

CRAB, COCONUT *and* LEMON MYRTLE PASTA

Light – 4 serves

This delicious sauce is based on the classic French lobster bisque but is uniquely transformed with the addition of lemon myrtle and Asian flavours. It's not typical of an Italian pasta dish either, but works superbly in unexpected ways. If you prefer a more traditional sauce, use dairy cream in place of coconut cream and omit the Asian flavours (sesame oil, ginger, chillies, fish sauce and palm sugar).

INGREDIENTS

1 large (or 2 small-medium) blue swimmer crabs, freshly cooked

---

30 g (1 oz) ginger, skin on, roughly chopped or grated
3-4 garlic cloves, peeled and crushed
1 small onion, peeled and chopped
2 tsp sesame oil
2 tsp vegetable oil

---

2 cups chicken or fish stock
400 g (13⅓ oz) coconut cream
1 small carrot, grated
1 red chilli, chopped
1 bunch coriander (cilantro) roots, chopped
8-10 large lemon myrtle leaves or 1-2 tsp ground lemon myrtle

---

1-2 tbs thai fish sauce, to taste
1-2 tbs palm sugar, to taste
extra virgin olive oil
1 quantity Sea Parsley Pasta (p. 268) cut into spaghetti, linguine or fettuccine
1-2 additional large red chillies, finely julienned
½ bunch of chives, sliced very finely

SUBSTITUTIONS

lemon myrtle leaves:
lemon verbena leaves,
thai lime leaves,
lemongrass.

METHOD

to prepare the sauce

1. Crack open the crabs. Remove and flake all of the meat and put in the fridge, covered, to use later. Keep the crab shell, juices and innards as this is where a lot of flavour is hiding.
2. In a saucepan, gently fry the ginger, garlic and onion in the two oils until fragrant and just starting to brown on the edges. Add the crab shell, innards and juices, and fry gently for another 3-4 minutes, stirring constantly.
3. Add the stock and coconut cream, followed by the carrot, chilli, coriander roots, and lemon myrtle. Simmer for 15-20 minutes. Remove from heat and allow it to cool a little, then strain through a sieve. Keep the stock and discard the shell and other solids.
4. Pour the stock into a wide frypan. Simmer over a medium heat until reduced to about 2-3 cups of sauce. Now season with fish sauce and palm sugar to balance the mild heat from the chilli, adding a little of each at first, and tasting as you go.

to finish the dish

1. Bring a large pot three-quarters filled with water to a rapid boil. Salt generously and add the olive oil. Drop in the pasta and cook for 3-4 minutes until 'al dente'. Drain immediately.
2. While the pasta is cooking, re-heat the sauce. Add as much chilli as you like (remove seeds if you don't like it too hot!).
3. Toss in the hot drained pasta and crab meat. Garnish with the chives and serve immediately.

WHOLE FISH *with* BLACK BEAN *and* LEMON MYRTLE

Main – 5-6 serves

A superb meal to share, quite special and spectacular served on a huge platter in the centre of a table. The rush of aromas certainly gets the saliva running in anticipation, and it more than delivers on flavour. I've used snapper, but any large whole fish (salmon, barramundi, Murray cod, mulloway, etc.) will work just as well.

INGREDIENTS

½ cup of peanut or vegetable oil

4-6 large garlic cloves, peeled and slivered

⅓ cup of salted black beans, rinsed and coarsely chopped

1 large whole snapper, 1.2-1.5 kg (2½-3 lb)

12-15 fresh whole lemon myrtle leaves

1 bunch spring onions, trimmed and sliced on the diagonal

⅓ cup best quality soy sauce

5-6 serves Lemon Myrtle Rice (p. 269)

* *To check whether the fish is cooked, quickly open the foil packet slightly and insert a sharp, thin knife into the thickest part of the flesh. Pull it apart a little, to see close to the bone inside. If the flesh is still just slightly translucent and under-done on the bone, it's almost ready. If it's still a touch too raw, bake for a bit longer.*

SUBSTITUTIONS

lemon myrtle leaves:
thai lime leaves.

METHOD

1. Set your oven to 220–230°C (430–445°C), then spread out a double layer of heavy-duty foil onto a large baking tray (enough to easily wrap the fish).
2. Heat the oil in a small pan and gently fry the garlic slivers until they are becoming crisp and a light golden brown.
3. Add the black beans and fry for another minute.
4. Cut four or five deep parallel slashes into each side of the fish with a sharp knife. This will help the flavours to be absorbed into the flesh.
5. Scatter some of the lemon myrtle leaves and spring onion in the cavity and over the foil, leaving enough to use on the top of the fish later. Scatter some of the garlic-and-beans oil mixture in the same way.
6. Lay the fish onto the foil and top with the remaining lemon myrtle and garlic-and-beans mix.
7. Pour over the soy sauce.
8. Fold the foil over the fish, crimping at the edges to make a sealed parcel. Place in the pre-heated oven and bake for approximately 1 hour (it will of course depend on the size and thickness of the fish).*
9. Once the fish is just cooked, rest it, out of the oven, for 5–10 minutes (in foil, which I cover with a clean folded bath towel) before serving. This allows gentle, continued cooking, through to the perfect almost well-done stage. Cooking fish of this type beyond well-done serves only to dry it out unnecessarily.
10. Serve with Steamed Lemon Myrtle Rice and a crisp salad.

SLOW-ROASTED LAMB SHOULDER *with* ANISE MYRTLE

Main – 4-6 serves

This slow-cooked roast produces a flavoursome and tender meat that is perfectly complemented by its sticky, anise-and-lamb flavoured glaze. I like to throw in some extra sliced chillies and a few fresh, glossy anise myrtle leaves just at the end, to add some brilliant colour and extra kick. I usually favour cooking this 'sous vide' style, but here I have detailed the traditional way.

INGREDIENTS

1 × 1.25-1.5 kg (about 2½-3 lb) lamb shoulder on the bone

100 ml (3⅓ fl oz) extra virgin olive oil

1 tsp ground coriander
1 tsp ground fennel seeds
½ tsp ground cardamom
½ tsp ground cumin
1 tsp ground pepperleaf
2 tsp sea salt

2 large handfuls of whole anise myrtle leaves, or 2-3 tsp dried
3-4 large, mild red chillies, thinly sliced
1 lt (2 pints) quality lamb stock (beef or chicken will also work)

Roast Bush Tomato Spanish Balsamic Onions (optional, p.193)

SUBSTITUTIONS

ground pepperleaf:
pepper, freshly ground
anise myrtle:
star anise.

METHOD

1. An hour before cooking, take the lamb from the fridge and bring to room temperature – a good practice when roasting all meats. Pre-heat your oven to 130°C (265°F).
2. Choose a heavy-based roasting pan that's large enough to hold the meat nicely, and heat it on the stove top. Rub the shoulder with the olive oil then seal the lamb over a medium-high heat until it is nicely browned on all sides.
3. Mix together the coriander, fennel seeds, cardamom, cumin, and pepperleaf with the salt. If you are using dried anise myrtle, add this now. Sprinkle this spice mix all over the lamb.
4. Surround the lamb with the anise myrtle (if using) and chillies (save a few to garnish, if you like) then pour over the stock.
5. Cover the pan with a double layer of foil, crimping down on all sides to lock in steam. Roast for about 2½-3 hours, or until the lamb is just falling off the bone. If it is not ready after 2½ hours, reduce heat to 110°C (230°F) and cook for another hour or more. Cooking times will vary, depending on the age and quality of the lamb, so keep an eye on it.
6. Remove the cooked lamb from the oven. Pour off and reserve the juices. Cover the lamb with the foil and allow to rest in a warm spot for about 20 minutes until ready to serve (my tip is to cover with a clean, thick folded bath towel over the foil to help keep in the heat).
7. Skim off the excess fat from the juices and strain through a super-fine sieve (or clean Chux®) into a wide pan. Bring to the boil and reduce to a superb sticky, 'lamby' glaze.
8. Serve the lamb with vegetables of your choice (I suggest Bush Tomato Balsamic Onions) together with the glaze. (about 30-50 ml / 1-1⅔ fl oz per serve is perfect).

MUSSELS *in* COCONUT *and* TOMATO LEMON MYRTLE CHILLI JAM

Light – serves 4-6

This is a nice variation on the classic Asian dish, Chilli Jam with Mussels (or clams). Lemon myrtle gives it a superb floral and lemony fragrance and flavour.

INGREDIENTS

50 ml (1⅔ fl oz) vegetable oil
15 g (½ oz) galangal or ginger, finely julienned
2-3 garlic cloves, peeled and crushed

400 g (13⅓ oz) coconut cream
8-10 fresh lemon myrtle leaves

½ cup – or to taste – Tomato Lemon Myrtle Chilli Jam (p. 257)
20 ml (⅔ fl oz) fish sauce, to taste

1 kg (about 2 lb) mussels, or pippies or clams

1 small bunch thai basil leaves, torn into 2 cm chunks
Steamed Lemon Myrtle Rice (p. 269)

SUBSTITUTIONS

lemon myrtle leaves:
lemon verbena,
lemon \grass.

METHOD

1. Heat the oil in a large wok over medium heat, then add the galangal (or ginger) and garlic.
2. Cook for 2–3 minutes, stir-frying continuously until they start to caramelize, then add the coconut cream and lemon myrtle leaves.
3. Bring to a simmer, then stir in the Tomato Lemon Myrtle Chilli Jam, according to your taste. Use more if you like it hot. Add the fish sauce, to taste, remembering that the shellfish also have a saltiness.
4. Add the shellfish. Cover tightly, and bring to a brisk simmer for 2-3 minutes, or until the first few shells just begin to open. When this happens, remove from the heat immediately and allow to sit for 2-3 minutes, still covered, to equalize the heat and complete the cooking process. Continued boiling beyond this point only toughens the shellfish unnecessarily.
5. Stir in the thai basil and serve with bowls of steamed Lemon Myrtle Rice.

WILD LEMON HERB-STEEPED CHICKEN

Main – 6-8 serves

This is a wonderful way to serve a whole chicken as a family meal. Cooked in the style of Hainanese or 'white cut' chicken, it is simmered very briefly and then steeped in a fragrant stock. It is important to use the correct ratio of bird-to-water weight, which makes it easier to control the timing and temperature. It's such an easy thing to cook, but what incredible moisture and texture! It also makes lots of lovely excess stock to put into soups, stews, risottos and so on; just freeze in tubs to use at a later date.

INGREDIENTS

1 × 1.8-2 kg (about 4 lb) fresh free-range chicken

double the weight of the chicken in water

50 g (1⅔ oz) fresh ginger

1 bunch spring onions

4-5 garlic cloves
10-15 large fresh lemon myrtle leaves
10 g (⅓ oz) fresh Geraldton wax leaves and stalks
20 g (⅔ oz) lemongrass stalks
50 ml (1⅔ fl oz) fish sauce

6-8 serves Lemon Myrtle Steamed Rice (p. 269)
Geraldton Wax and Spring Onion Salsa (p.251)
Sunrise Lime and Chilli Black Vinegar (p.257)
additional Geraldton wax leaves (for garnish, optional)
toasted saltbush seeds (for garnish, optional)

SUBSTITUTIONS

lemon myrtle leaves:
thai lime leaves
Geraldton wax:
lemon or lime zest.

METHOD

1. Bring the chicken to room temperature over 30-60 minutes.
2. Add the correct amount of water (for example, a 1.8kg / 4lb chicken needs 3.6 kg / 8 lb of water) to a suitably sized pot that will fit the bird snugly.
3. Peel the ginger and add the peel to the pot. Keep the ginger flesh for making the salsa.
4. Wash the spring onions. Reserve the white parts for the salsa, then add the stems and roots to the pot.
5. Smash the garlic and add to the pot with the fragrant lemon myrtle, Geraldton wax, lemongrass and fish sauce. Bring to a gentle simmer.
6. Carefully lower in the chicken, making sure the cavity fills with boiling stock. Put on the lid and bring it back to a gentle simmer for exactly 10 minutes only (use a timer).
7. When the timer goes off, push a carving fork through the back/ribcage area of the chicken and lift it out of the stock. Drain the cavity of stock back into the pot, then submerge it again, to re-fill the cavity with boiling stock. Put the lid back on and bring briefly back to the simmer. Turn off the heat.
8. That's it! All that needs to be done now is leave the chicken to poach incredibly gently in that latent heat (with lid on) for at least 2 hours until luke warm (room temperature), leaving plenty of time to prepare your accompaniments.
9. Lift onto a chopping board and remove legs and breasts with a carving knife, cutting into smaller pieces in Chinese style. Arrange on a large platter or in individual bowls, on a base of steamed rice together with the salsa and vinegar, and garnishes (if using).

CHAR-GRILLED MARRON *with* WILD TAMARIND *and* LEMON MYRTLE 'BEURRE BLANC'

Light – 4 serves

Grilled marron was a big seller at my Red Ochre Restaurant for many years in the 1990s and featured on the front cover of another cookbook to which I contributed: simple, spectacular and superb!

INGREDIENTS

1 batch Orange, Ginger, and Lemon Myrtle Beurre Blanc (p.250)

½ cup wild tamarind fruit, seeds removed

4 × 250-300g (about ½ lb) fresh marron or 8-12 large yabbies, or 1 small-medium lobster)

70g (2⅓ oz) unsalted butter

salt and freshly ground pepper, to taste

1 cup assorted beach succulents (karkalla, samphire, sea blight, etc.)

SUBSTITUTIONS

wild tamarind:
rainforest lychee

beach succulents:
salted asparagus.

METHOD

1. Prepare the Lemon Myrtle Beurre Blanc sauce first.
2. Add the tamarind to the Lemon Myrtle Beurre Blanc and keep in a warm place while you prepare the shellfish.
3. If you have live shellfish, the easiest and most humane way to prepare them is to 'put them to sleep' in the freezer for a few hours before cooking. Split each one down the middle, piercing the head first with a very sharp knife. Use a spoon to clean out the stomach cavity, as washing only helps remove flavour.
4. Melt about half of the butter, reserving the rest for cooking the succulents in later. Brush the melted butter over the cut surface of the shellfish, then lightly season with salt and pepper if you wish, keeping in mind that the accompanying native succulents are salty.
5. Pre-heat your clean char-grill or barbecue (see p. 23). Grill the shellfish over a medium-high heat for 3-4 minutes on each side until just barely cooked through. I like to grill the flesh side first, then turn and leave the flesh facing up to finish, so I can baste it with a little sauce.
6. While grilling, heat the butter in a frypan until the foaming subsides and the butter starts to go a deep golden colour ('beurre noisette' or 'brown butter'). Quickly toss the succulents in the butter and stir-fry for 30-40 seconds to warm through. Season with pepper if you like.
7. Arrange the grilled marron on a plate and sprinkle with the succulents and the tamarind and beurre blanc. Serve immediately

SALTBUSH SCHNITZEL

Main – 4 serves

Who doesn't love a freshly crumbed schnitzel, especially when pan-fried in butter and olive oil? It's the only way to cook them in my book (please don't deep-fry - nowhere near as good!). Here I like to use saltbush in the crumbs, because it gives the crust a lovely herbaceous and salty flavour, without added salt. Many people overcook chicken and miss out on how juicy it can be. Instead, time your cooking carefully and, when you take the schnitzels from the pan, expect them to be very marginally pink on the inside - almost well done (make a small cut on the side of one to check). By the time you sit down to eat, the latent heat will have cooked them through and the meat should be white and ready to eat.

INGREDIENTS

2-3 large or 4 small free-range skinless chicken breasts

1 cup panko breadcrumbs
⅓ cup saltbush seeds
⅓ cup saltbush flakes
⅓ cup grated Italian parmesan
¼ cup sea parsley, finely chopped

1 egg, lightly beaten
½ cup milk
1 cup plain flour

2 tsp butter
¼ cup extra virgin olive oil
lemon wedges
Braised Red Cabbage with Malted Wattleseed Crisps (p. 228)

SUBSTITUTIONS

saltbush seeds:
rolled oats, salted to taste
saltbush flakes:
dried herbs or vegetable flakes of your choice
sea parsley
flat-leaf (continental) parsley.

METHOD

1. Lay the chicken breasts on a chopping board and remove the inner fillets (or 'tenderloins'). Place your spare hand over one chicken breast to hold it in position, then carefully slice through the thickest part horizontally, to make a second thin, 'escalope' (or slice) from the top of the breast.
2. Now cut the remaining piece into two (maybe three) further pieces of roughly the same thickness each. From one large breast, you can get 3-4 slices of chicken (below).
3. Repeat with the remaining breasts. The objective, really, is to get pieces of even thickness.
4. Cover each slice, one at a time, with baking paper or kitchen film.

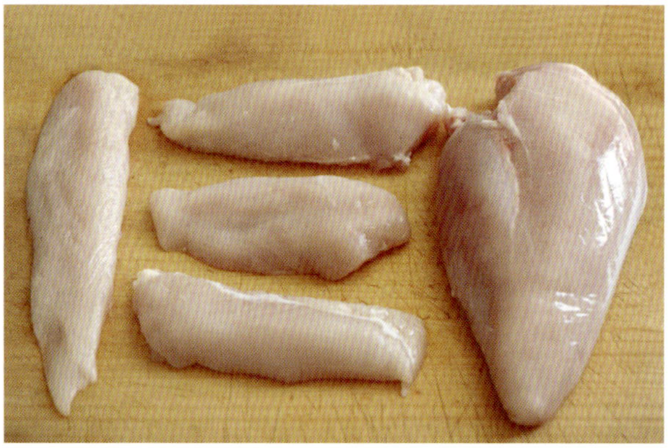

5. Using a meat mallet or heavy-based saucepan, beat each slice to about 5 mm (¼ in.) in thickness. Shape is not important as equal thickness (for even cooking).
6. Mix together the breadcrumbs, saltbush seeds, saltbush flakes, parmesan and parsley to make the coating.
7. In a separate bowl, whisk together the egg and milk.
8. Spread the flour in a shallow dish. Dredge each slice through the flour to coat, then shake off any excess.
9. Dip the slices in the egg and milk, then in the coating mix. Place on a tray in single layers, (or separated by baking paper). Chill uncovered for 10–20 minutes, time permitting.
10. Heat the oil and butter in a frypan over medium heat until they start to foam up. Working in batches (don't crowd the pan), fry the schnitzel for 2-3 minutes on each side until golden. Stay with them, shaking the pan gently as you go. You may need to top up the oil and butter a little along the way.
11. Quickly drain the schnitzels on a paper towel, then serve hot with lemon wedges and the braised cabbage or fresh salad.

VEGETARIAN EGGPLANT OPTION

1. Replace the chicken with eggplant: top-and-tail each eggplant, then cut through the length to make 'schnitzel' slices of about 12 mm (½ in) in thickness each. Discard the first and last slice which will have skin on one side and will be more difficult to crumb – and less enjoyable to eat!
2. Depending on the size of the eggplant, you can expect to get 5-6, maybe more, slices from one eggplant, so 3 eggplants should make enough to serve 4, but use your judgement here. Note, too, that some people like to salt the eggplant before cooking to remove some bitterness, but this won't be necessary if using young, fresh fruit. These schnitzels may take a little longer to cook than chicken schnitzels but are ready when the vegetable flesh inside is soft and cooked through and the crumbing crisp and golden. If they seem to be taking a while, you may need to reduce the heat a little so as not to over-fry the crumbing.

ROSELLA-FLOWER HARISSA ROAST CHICKEN

Main meal – 4-5 serves

Harissa is a spicy North African paste or sauce made mainly with chilli, red capsicum, garlic, salt, and olive oil. There are many variations, depending on the region and even family preferences. Some are very basic, while others include a vast array of herbs and spices and other exotic ingredients. When I first discovered harissa, I loved the rose variety so much I wanted to make my own native 'tangy flower' version. The rosella flower was a great fit, where the sharp rhubarb/berry flavours perfectly complemented the floral rose notes. Leaving some of the flowers in petal segments in the finishing stages adds a lovely tart flavour and lifts the presentation. This recipe makes enough paste for two chickens, but it is addictive, as it also makes a superb dip or spread to use on wraps and in sandwiches and burgers.

INGREDIENTS

2 medium/large red capsicums

100 ml (3⅓ fl oz) extra virgin olive oil
8 large, long red (mild) chillies, sliced, or to taste
6-8 large garlic cloves, peeled
1 tsp salt
100 g (3⅓ oz) rosella flower petals*

2 tsp sugar
5 tsp rose water

2 tsp cumin seeds
2 tsp caraway seeds

1 large free-range chicken, about 1.8 kg (4 lb), cut into 8-10 pieces

spanish onions, outer skins removed, and cut into wedges (optional)
cauliflower florets (optional)
zucchini slices (optional)

* *This recipe uses the petals only, which are also included in many other published recipes and have been consumed for thousands of years. Please, however, refer to page 41 for a caution concerning excessive consumption of rosella tea brewed from the stems, leaves, and petals.*

SUBSTITUTIONS

rosella flower petals:
rose petals, other edible flowers.

METHOD

to make the harissa paste

1. Over a direct gas flame or very hot barbecue, blacken and burn the capsicums, turning regularly to cook them evenly. Place in a suitably sized bowl and cover immediately, allowing them to steam and cool completely. Then, taking care to reserve the smoky juices, peel and de-seed them.
2. Blend the oil, capsicum flesh and juices, chillies, garlic and salt with half the rosella flower petals into a coarse purée. Note that you can easily adjust the heat of the paste by varying the number and/or variety of chillies used.
3. Separately, tear the remaining rosella flowers into individual petal segments. Add the sugar and a sprinkle of the rose water and mix. Cover and put to one side, to allow the rose petals to macerate.
4. Heat a frypan and add the cumin and caraway, shaking continuously until they start to become aromatic and toasted (about 1–2 minutes). Do not leave them, and remove them as soon as they are ready as they can burn very quickly. Crush the toasted seeds in a mortar-and-pestle or spice grinder.
5. Return the ground seeds to the pan, together with the purée and remaining rose water. Bring to a simmer and allow it to cook for a few minutes, stirring occasionally, to make a nice, thick sauce.

6. Remove from the heat and allow to cool. Note, you only need half the paste for this chicken recipe, so transfer the unused harissa into a sterilized jar and top with a generous layer of extra virgin olive oil. This will act as a barrier to oxygen and the paste will keep for longer. Cover and refrigerate for a week or two. It can also be frozen for later use.

rosella flower

to roast the chicken

1. Use a roasting tray big enough to hold the chicken pieces comfortably in a single layer. Slash the thicker parts of the joints with a sharp knife to allow more flavour penetration. Smear half the harissa blend over all over the pieces, and ideally allow the chicken to marinate for a few hours (or overnight) in a refrigerator before cooking.
2. Pre-heat the oven to 220°C (430°F) and bring the chicken to room temperature. Roast for about 20 minutes. Turn the pieces over once, then roast for a further 20 minutes. (For a tasty option, place some thick wedges of red onion and some cauliflower florets under the chicken before you begin the roast).
3. Carefully remove from the oven, then sprinkle over with the macerated rosella petals. At this point, you can add some thinly sliced zucchini if you want. Stir, then roast for another 5–10 minutes.
4. Remove the roasted chicken from the oven, cover with foil, and keep warm. Rest for 10 minutes before serving with cous cous or perhaps a rice dish.

VEGETARIAN OPTION

For vegetarians, rosella flower harissa works superbly when roasted with potatoes, pumpkin, and eggplant pieces – in fact, most vegetables – in place of chicken.

SALTBUSH DUKKAH-CRUSTED CHICKEN

Main – 5-6 serves

With its golden-textured crust, this is a very attractive dish to serve whole on the family table, but great care is needed to control the oven temperature (a convection oven works best for this recipe), simply because the spice-and-nut coating can easily burn if it's too hot. This dish has a distinctive Middle-Eastern flavour with a superb Aussie twist and works particularly well served with a freshly made Wattleseed and Sea Parsley Tabbouleh (p.209). You can always make this dish a little quicker to cook and easier to serve by using individual chicken legs (marylands) or breasts if you like.

INGREDIENTS

1 × 1.8-2 kg (about 4 lb) fresh free-range chicken
4 tsp extra virgin olive oil

---

1 tbs dijon mustard

½ cup Creative Native Saltbush Dukkah

---

3 cups fresh old man saltbush leaves
⅓ cup Preserved Desert Lime Oil (p. 252)
2 cups natural Greek-style yoghurt

SUBSTITUTIONS

Creative Native Saltbush Dukkah:
any other quality dukkah spice blend
old man saltbush leaves:
kale or baby spinach leaves.

METHOD

1. Pre-heat the oven to 220°C (430°F).
2. Pat the chicken dry with some paper towels then rub all over with the extra virgin olive oil.
3. Roast the chicken for 20 minutes exactly (use a timer for accuracy) then remove it from the oven and reduce the heat to 170°C (340°F).
4. Next, brush the bird with a coating of dijon mustard, which will act as a very tasty 'glue'.
5. Now sprinkle the dukkah all over the bird, gently patting it on (so that it sticks) to make a lovely, even crust. There should be no need for additional seasoning – Creative Native Saltbush Dukkah already has a nicely seasoned and balanced flavour.
6. Using a carving fork, lift the chicken through the cavity and pat more of the spice blend around the sides.
7. Return the chicken back to the oven and continue to bake for another 30-40 minutes, then allow to rest for 5-10 minutes before serving.
8. While the chicken is resting, stir-fry your saltbush or spinach leaves in a drizzle of the desert lime oil – just enough to wilt them. Arrange the wilted leaves on a platter with dollops of the chilled yoghurt, place the whole chicken in the centre and drizzle the desert lime oil all around.

OCTOPUS *with* SOY ANISE MYRTLE DRESSING

Light – 4-6 serves

Soy and anise are a lovely pair of flavours, and when combined with a quality red wine vinegar reduction, they become an excellent dressing for octopus. Crunchy shallot and garlic 'chips' together with native celery add depth and texture, to complete the dish. If you love it, you might make a big batch and increase the vinegar dressing a little, to turn this into an amazing pickled octopus that will last many months in your fridge — if you can hide it well!

INGREDIENTS

75 g (2½ oz) shallots

4-6 garlic cloves, sliced very finely on a mandolin or with a sharp knife
1 cup peanut or vegetable oil

1 kg (2 lb) approx. octopus tenticles, cleaned and surface-dried on absorbant kitchen paper.

2 tsp ground anise myrtle

1 batch Soy Anise Myrtle Dressing (p. 242)

3-4 wild celery stalks (reserve the leaves for the garnish) finely diced or cut into diagonal slices
1-2 large red chillies (optional)

2 tbs Carrot and Geraldton Wax Oil (p. 251)
reserved celery leaves
15 leaves fresh anise myrtle leaves (optional)

SUBSTITUTIONS

ground anise myrtle:
dill or star anise
anise myrtle leaves:
fresh dill
wild celery:
pale inner-most celery stalks and leaves.

METHOD

1. Peel and slice the shallots finely.
2. Heat the oil to about 150°C (300°F) in a large, wide, pot, then gently deep-fry the shallots and garlic in the oil until they are a light golden brown (about 5-8 minutes). Then, using a slotted spoon or skimmer, lift from the oil and drain on aborbant paper. Put to one side.
3. Increase the heat of the oil until it just begins to smoke, then slowly lower in the octopus (be careful: it will spit).
4. Fry the octopus for 3-4 minutes, then add the anise myrtle.
5. Cover the pot, then turn down the heat to a very slow simmer. Braise the octopus for 15-20 minutes, or until tender.
6. Use a large sieve to drain the octopus, and reserve the strained liquid for use in the dressing (see below).
7. Now whisk the strained liquid through the Soy Anise Myrtle Dressing.
8. To finish, slice the octopus diagonally into short pieces, then toss in a bowl with the dressing. At this stage you can store the octopus in the fridge if you have made it a day or so in advance – it will keep for about a week.
9. When ready to serve, add the celery, chillies (if using) and the crisp, fried garlic and shallots.
10. Arrange a on plate. Drizzle around the Carrot and Geraldton Wax Oil.. Serve garnished with celery leaves, additional fresh anise myrtle leaves if available, and a little more dressing.

PEPPERMINT GUM CHOCOLATE FONDANT PUDDING

Sweet – 10-12 serves

This is a superb, rich and gluten-free chocolate dessert, and the better the quality of chocolate you use, the better the result will be. The lovely peppermint flavour comes from the peppermint eucalypt. I always prefer to make a full batch, and then freeze any uncooked individual puddings I don't need to use at the time. Then, for a quick and easy treat, they can simply be taken out the day before needed and then defrosted in the refrigerator. Always cook these puddings straight from the refrigerator, so that they all have the same starting temperature of 3–4 °C (about 40 °F). This is important, because achieving the runny, molten centre is all about timing and temperature. The more elements that can be controlled precisely, the more predictable the outcome will be.

INGREDIENTS

210 g (7 oz) dark couverture chocolate (55%), small buttons or chopped into small pieces
210 g (7 oz) unsalted butter

3 eggs
3 additional egg yolks
120 g (4 oz) castor sugar

60 g (2 oz) gluten-free cornflour (cornstarch) or tapioca flour
40 g (1⅓ oz) best-quality dark cocoa powder
2 tsp ground peppermint gum

neutral (flavourless) cooking spray or macadamia oil

gluten-free icing sugar, for dusting (optional)

SUBSTITUTIONS

ground peppermint gum:
peppermint or mint essence.

METHOD

1. Melt the chocolate and butter using a warm double-boiler (see p. 22), stirring occasionally.
2. Separately, whisk together the eggs, egg yolks and sugar until the mixture is thick, pale and creamy (at least 5-7 minutes). It's important the sugar is completely dissolved.
3. Fold the melted chocolate and butter through the egg-and-sugar mixture.
4. Finally, sieve the flour, cocoa, and peppermint gum into the mixture and fold through.
5. Spray 10 or 12 ramekins (or use a muffin tray) with baking spray. Spoon all of the mixture, in approximately equal amounts, into the ramekins.
6. Chill in the fridge for at least 2-3 hours before baking.
7. Allow about 10 minutes before baking to pre-heat your oven to 220°C (430°F). The correct temperature and time is critical. Take the ramekins (or muffin tray) straight from the fridge and into the pre-heated oven. Bake for 10 minutes exactly (use a timer to be sure).
8. Once baked, remove from the oven and allow to stand for 5 minutes before serving. Dust with icing sugar and serve with cream or ice-cream, if desired. You may want to experiment with your oven and the times, as many ovens may not be as accurate as we'd like to think.

COCONUT, SAGO *and* LEMON MYRTLE PUDDING *with* PINEAPPLE, PALM SUGAR *and* LEMON MYRTLE SYRUP

Sweet – 6-8 serves

This is a lovely light summery dessert where one feature is the wonderful 'old-fashioned bounciness' (texture) of sago . The coconut creaminess of the chilled pudding contrasts beautifully with the sticky sweetness of the hot grilled pineapple, and the lemon myrtle palm sugar syrup gives the dish a lovely tangy contrast. I developed this desert for the new Great Southern Train menus in the summer of 2019/20.

INGREDIENTS

puddings

½ vanilla bean
1½ cups milk
275 g (9 oz) coconut cream
6-8 fresh lemon myrtle leaves or 1 tsp ground lemon myrtle

100 g (3 ⅓ oz) sago

100 g (3 ⅓ oz) sugar

sauce

250 g (½ lb) light palm sugar, chopped or grated
150 ml (5 fl oz) pineapple juice
4-5 additional fresh lemon myrtle leaves or ½ tsp additional ground lemon myrtle
1 fresh ripe pineapple wedge per person, with tops on (fresh lychees and mango also work very well)

neutral (flavourless) cooking spray oil or macadamia oil

SUBSTITUTIONS

lemon myrtle leaves: thai lime leaves, lemongrass.

METHOD

to make the puddings

1. Split and scrape the seeds out from the vanilla bean.
2. Place the seeds and pod in a saucepan together with the milk, coconut cream and lemon myrtle.
3. Bring to the boil, watching carefully.
4. Add the sago while stirring and simmer very gently, stirring regularly (so it doesn't stick) until the sago is soft (about 10 minutes).
5. Once the sago is completely cooked (check and make sure it is tender), stir through the sugar until it dissolves. Scoop out the lemon myrtle leaves and bean pod.
6. Spray 6-8 ramekins or other suitable moulds with the cooking spray. Pour the mixture in and allow it to set completely in the fridge.

to make the sauce and complete the dish

1. Simmer the palm sugar, pineapple juice and lemon myrtle very slowly (over a low heat) for about 20 minutes to make a nice syrup. Allow to cool then strain.
2. Brush the pineapple wedges with some of the syrup. Grill for 4-5 minutes on each side on a clean barbecue or in a griddle pan (at a moderate heat). They should caramelize nicely.
3. Turn the puddings out from the ramekins onto serving plates and place the pineapple wedges to the side. Drizzle with the syrup.

FENNEL *and* LEMON ASPEN SALAD

Side – 2-4 serves

The dressing for this salad is sour, sweet, tangy and salty, all at once, and provides a lovely contrast to the chilli and anise flavour of the fennel. The native celery and the wild tamarind adds a definitely unique touch that is offset by the sweetness of the apple.

INGREDIENTS

dressing

25 g (1 oz) light palm sugar, or to taste
30 ml (1 fl oz) of fish sauce

4-5 cloves of garlic, peeled and crushed
100 ml (3⅓ fl oz) Lemon Aspen Juice (p. 242)

salad

1 small (about 200g/7 oz) fennel bulb
1 crisp, red apple
3-4 large fresh green chillies (less if you want a milder dressing)
1 small red onion, peeled
½ cup native celery, leaves and stalks

SUBSTITUTIONS

native celery:
celery, inner stalks and pale leaves
wild tamarind berries:
other sour fruit of your choice like green mango.

METHOD

to make the dressing

1. Prepare the tangy dressing first, so it's ready before you cut the salad ingredients (it will prevent the apple from discolouring). Shave the palm sugar with a knife and microwave with the fish sauce for 30-40 seconds, until it dissolves easily.
2. Allow to cool, then add the crushed garlic and Lemon Aspen Juice and mix together well. Check the sour, salty and sweet balance and adjust to taste.

to make the salad

1. Slice the fennel very finely or shave on a mandolin.
2. Finely julienne the apple (leave the skin on, but remove the core and pips), tossing it straight away into the dressing.
3. Julienne the chilli.
4. Finely slice the onion and celery (leaves and stalks).
5. Toss everything together with the dressing and allow to macerate for at least 30-40 minutes.
6. When ready to serve, sprinkle over with the tamarind berries. It is lovely served with light seafood meals, such as Tommy Ruffs (p.76).

WILD THYME RÖSTI

Sides – makes 4-6

I fell in love with 'rösti' (Swiss fried potatoes) during my first international job as a young chef working in Switzerland and, ever since, I have enjoyed creating many variations by adding herbs, speck, prosciutto and other flavoursome ingredients. It's a very versatile dish, brilliant for a brunch or served as a breakfast dish, along with bacon and eggs, fried mushrooms, tomatoes and wilted greens. Rösti also works really well pre-cooked and then re-heated later in a very hot oven or under a grill, to crisp up just before serving.

INGREDIENTS

600 g (about 20 oz) all-purpose potatoes (e.g. désirée)

25 ml (1 fl oz) extra virgin olive oil
3 tsp butter
1 large onion, peeled and finely sliced

1 tsp salt
½ tsp dried wild thyme
½ tsp ground pepperleaf

SUBSTITUTIONS

wild thyme:
thyme
ground pepperleaf:
pepper, freshly ground.

METHOD

1. Peel the potatoes then grate with a box grater. Wrap the grated potato in a clean tea towel or Chux® cloth and squeeze out all the excess water (or squeeze out with your hands).
2. Heat the oil and butter in a medium-sized non-stick frypan and add the sliced onions. Simmer gently for 4–5 minutes until they are translucent.
3. Add the grated potato, salt, thyme and pepperleaf to the pan. Stir or toss until nicely mixed, then, using a rubber spatula, compress the mixture to a large, thick pancake shape.
4. Cook over medium heat for 5–10 minutes until a lovely golden crust forms on the underside of the 'pancake'. Sometimes the potato can absorb a lot of the butter and oil, so I always have more on hand so I can add a little extra if required to 'lubricate' the rösti. It should always be able to move freely when you shake the pan. Check regularly by gently turning up an edge, to make sure the crust is not burning or sticking: controlling the heat is critical.
5. If you are confident, you can now toss the rösti to cook the other side for about the same amount of time, so that both sides are golden brown and the rösti is cooked through. Otherwise, turn the rösti out onto a plate (so it lands with the crust on top), then slide it back into the pan to cook the other side.

CRISPY SALTBUSH *and* VINEGAR POTATOES

Side – 4-6 serves

This is a bit of a take on the commercial salt-and-vinegar packets of potato crisps, but, boy, is it tasty and tangy! Having lots of roughed-up edges and exposed surfaces on the potatoes is the key for getting that amazing crunchy crust.

INGREDIENTS

1 kg (about 2 lb) large potatoes

½ cup duck fat or extra virgin olive oil
2 cups fresh old man saltbush leaves

4 tsp Creative Native Saltbush and Vinegar Seasoning

SUBSTITUTIONS

saltbush:
rosemary and/or thyme (adjust salt to taste)

Creative Native Saltbush and Vinegar Seasoning:
other salt-and-vinegar seasoning.

METHOD

1. Peel the potatoes and cut them into halves or quarters, so the pieces are all a similar size (for even cooking). Cover with cold water in a saucepan and bring to a gentle simmer.
2. Cook for 5-8 minutes until just tender when pierced with a knife tip, then drain and spread out on a tray to cool.
3. You may cut them into large fat chips, or other shapes. Next, use a fork to scrape and rough up the surfaces of the potatoes; this helps provide more surface area to make the potatoes super crunchy!
4. Pre-heat your oven to very hot (230-260°C/450-500°F).
5. Gently heat the duck fat or olive oil in a frypan and carefully shallow-fry the saltbush leaves, stirring slowly, until they start to dry and crisp, then lift them out with a slotted spoon (keep the duck fat/oil).
6. Drain the saltbush on absorbent kitchen paper.
7. Drizzle the duck fat/oil over your potato chips and toss lightly to coat.
8. Roast the potatoes in the oven, stirring gently every 10-15 minutes, until they are a lovely golden brown. This will take 30-40 minutes, depending on the strength of your oven.
9. Remove from the oven and transfer them to a serving platter. Sprinkle over the crisp saltbush leaves and season very generously with the Saltbush and Vinegar Seasoning. Serve immediately.

CARROT, CHICKPEA *and* HONEY LEMON MYRTLE SALAD

Side – 6-8 serves

This salad has become a family favourite, and we often serve it at large gatherings, such as barbecues in summer. Cooking the carrots in the 'dressing' is a great way of intensifying the flavours, as the liquid reduces to a syrupy, tangy and sweet dressing infused with the stunning flavour of lemon myrtle.

INGREDIENTS

1 kg (about 2 lb) carrots
1 generous tbs honey
juice of 1 large lemon (about 50 ml / 1⅔ fl oz)
40 ml (1⅓ fl oz) water
10-14 lemon myrtle leaves
1 tsp whole cumin seeds
2 pinches River Murray or sea salt

400 g (about 13⅓ oz) canned chickpeas, rinsed and drained

⅓ cup extra virgin olive oil

1 cup thick Greek yoghurt

herbs for garnish: fresh coriander (cilantro) leaves, rivermint, additional lemon myrtle leaves (optional)

SUBSTITUTIONS

lemon myrtle leaves:
thai lime leaves,
lemon verbena leaves
rivermint:
mint.

METHOD

1. Peel and cut the carrots into thick 1 cm-wide (about ⅓ in.) diagonal slices.
2. Place the carrots in a stainless-steel saucepan with the honey, juice, water, lemon myrtle leaves, cumin and salt.
3. Cover tightly with the lid and bring to a gentle simmer. On low heat, steam in the juices for about 6-8 minutes, stirring often, until the carrots are just tender. The juice should now be nice and syrupy.
4. Stir through the chickpeas.
5. Simmer again for another minute or two to infuse the flavours.
6. Remove the lid and allow to cool to room temperature or, if not using immediately, refrigerate until ready to serve.
7. Once cooled, add the olive oil to dress the salad and remove the spent lemon myrtle leaves.
8. Place the salad in a large salad bowl or arrange on a serving platter.
9. Garnish with generous dollops of yoghurt and fresh herbs when ready to serve.
10. Note that this salad is best served at room temperature, or luke warm, so don't add the cold yoghurt until you are just about to serve.

DAVIDSON PLUM ZA'ATAR FLATBREAD

Accompaniment – makes 4 flatbreads

These flatbreads are quite easy to make but, if pressed for time, Greek yiros wraps work nicely as well, baked quickly with the za'atar and oil. The method is similar to making pizza, but if you're not confident using a pizza peel and sliding the dough onto a hot oven tray or stone surface, I recommend you roll each flatbread out on a sheet of silicone baking paper. This will make it easier to lift and slide it onto a hot baking tray or pizza stone.

INGREDIENTS

7 g (¼ oz) sachet dried yeast
1 tsp sugar
¾ cup water, luke-warm

75 g (2½ oz) wholemeal flour
210 g (7 oz) plain flour
1 tsp salt
30 ml (1 fl oz) extra virgin olive oil

8 tsp Creative Native Davidson Plum Za'atar or other za'atar blend

METHOD

1. Whisk the yeast, sugar, and water together in a small bowl and sit in a warm place for 10 minutes to prove.
2. Place the flours, salt and half the oil in a bowl and add the yeast mixture. Using a mixer with the dough hook attached, work for 5–10 minutes on a slow-medium speed to form a smooth, silky dough. If it's too sticky, add a little more flour; if too tight, add a dash more water. It should be very soft, not too sticky, and stretch a little when pulled. Or, knead by hand for at least a similar amount of time to develop the 'stretchy' quality.
3. Cover the bowl with kitchen film and leave in a warm place to prove, until doubled in size (about 20–30 minutes).
4. Meanwhile pre-heat the oven to about 230–240°C (445–460°F). If using a pizza stone, place in the oven now.
5. Once the dough has doubled in size, use your fist to firmly punch it down (once or twice), to remove air bubbles.
6. Turn the dough onto a floured workbench, knead briefly, then divide into four even pieces. Roll out into round discs, about the size of a dinner plate and 3 mm (⅛ in.) thick.
7. Use your fingertips to push into the dough all over to make dimple-like depressions. Brush with the remaining olive oil and sprinkle with the za'atar. Cover with kitchen film and prove in a warm spot for a further 10–15 minutes.
8. Slide a pizza peel under each piece of dough (one at a time) then slide them onto the pizza stone (if using) or a baking tray. Cook for 10–15 minutes, until golden brown and puffed. Remove from the oven and serve immediately.

Australia's
Wild Fruits

Sunrise lime — *Citrus australasica x*

AUSTRALIA'S WILD FRUITS

Summary

This table is a summary of the notes on Australia's native and wild fruits and is intended as a brief introduction to their use in home cooking. A list of suppliers and wild food stores is included on page 280. The table includes information about the commonly eaten parts ('edible parts'). It should be noted that some plants might include other edible parts but only those that are used in this book and tested in the recipes are listed here.

Common name	Botanical name	Edible part	Form	Preparation and use	Flavour	Sourcing
LEMON ASPEN						
lemon aspen 	*Acronychia acidula*	fruit	fresh	*The raw fruit can be eaten whole, including its thin skin and apple-like core, but the flavour is quite intense. It works best if the entire fruit (skin, flesh and seeds) is puréed then strained to extract a juice, or the pulp infused in liquid to extract the flavour before straining out the solids. The tiny black seeds are either pulverized or strained out.*	*Citrus lemon flavours with tropical 'camphor' notes.*	*The powder and fruit, generally fresh or frozen, are available through various native food stores and on-line suppliers, subject to seasonal availability.*
			dry, powdered	*Used as a flavouring in food preparation.*		
THE LILLIPILLIES (RAINFOREST BERRIES)						
riberry satinash  *riberry*  *satinash*	*Syzygium luehmannii* *Syzygium fibrosum*	fruit	fresh	*There are many lillipilly fruits, or berries, and the flesh and skin can be eaten raw but are more commonly used in cooking to make jams, coulis, compôtes and other fruit dishes. Some riberries have a very small seed which may be eaten. The satinash has a larger, firm seed which is removed before eating.* *Lillipillies are native Australian rainforest plants, although they are now grown widely around Australia.*	*riberry: spicy, fruity, with notes of cinnamon and cloves.* *satinash: quite tart berry flavours that soften when sweetened and cooked.*	*Riberries are available fresh or frozen from various stores and on-line suppliers, subject to seasonal availability. Satinash and other lillipillies are less common.*

Common name	Botanical name	Edible part	Form	Preparation and use	Flavour	Sourcing
THE LIMES						
blood lime desert lime finger lime sunrise lime  blood lime  finger lime	*Citrus australasica var. sanguinea* *Citrus glauca* *Citrus australasica* *Citrus australasica x*  desert lime  sunrise lime	fruit	fresh or frozen	*Blood lime: the skin and juicy flesh are used to add bursts of flavour to salads, beverages, and many cooked foods. There is no need to peel this fruit.* *Desert lime: the entire fresh, raw fruit — skin and tiny seeds included — are edible and they are very versatile sliced, chopped or puréed in many sweet and savoury dishes.* *Finger lime: the crunchy juicy vesicles (flesh) of the finger lime is used to add bursts of flavour to salads, beverages, and some cooked foods. The skin is not generally eaten.* *Sunrise lime: the flesh and skin of the sunrise lime can be eaten raw, but more usually is cooked in jams, fruit dishes, etc.*	*Blood lime: has a tart 'blood orange' and lime flavour with mildly bitter notes.* *Desert lime: tangy lime and grapefruit notes.* *Finger lime: intense, fresh lime flavours.* *Sunrise lime: sweet, orange-like citrus flavours with floral notes.*	*The fresh fruits are occasionally available from various stores and on-line suppliers. More commonly frozen fruit is available.*
NATIVE CURRANT						
native currant 	*Acrotriche depressa*	berry	fresh or frozen (but are mostly available frozen)	*The entire berry is edible and eaten fresh.*	*Strong, tangy, wild currant flavour.*	*The frozen berries are available from various stores and on-line suppliers, subject to seasonal availability.*
MUNTRIES						
muntries 	*Kunzea pomifera*	fruit	fresh or frozen	*Can be eaten fresh (raw) and whole — flesh, skin and tiny seeds — but is also used in prepared foods such as pies, flans and jams. It loses its soft crunchy texture on cooking.*	*Sweet, tart, apple-like flavour.*	*Frozen muntries are available from various stores and on-line suppliers. Fresh muntries may also be offered, subject to seasonal availability.*

Common name	Botanical name	Edible part	Form	Preparation and use	Flavour	Sourcing
THE PLUMS						
davidson plum Illawarra plum Kakadu plum  *davidson plum*  *Illawarra plum*  *Kakadu plum*	*Davidsonia spp.* *Podocarpus elatus* *Terminalia ferdinandiana*	fruit	fresh	*davidson plum: the flesh and skin but not the seed can be eaten raw but is very acidic so is usually cooked.* *Illawarra plum: the flesh and skin can be eaten raw and cooked but the seed, which grows outside of the fruit, must be removed before eating — which is easily done.* *Kakadu plum: the flesh and skin can be eaten raw or cooked. The flesh clings to the stone, in a similar way to that of mango.*	*davidson plum: is very acidic when raw but once cooked develops tangy, plum-like flavours.* *Illawarra plum: raw or cooked, has sweet plum-like flavours.* *Kakadu plum: the flavour is sour and slightly sweet, with stewed apple and pear notes.*	*Available fresh through various stores and on-line suppliers, subject to seasonal availability. Some suppliers may offer frozen plums.*
QUANDONG						
Quandong 	*Santalum acuminatum*	fruit	fresh	*The flesh and skin are 'one' and can be consumed raw, once the inner seed has been removed. They can also be poached or stewed.*	*The flavour is sweet and tangy, with hints of peach and rhubarb.*	*Available from native food stores and on-line suppliers when in season. Also available in dried form, and should be reconstituted before use.*
			dried	*Dried quandongs are re-constituted in water before use.*		
RAINFOREST LYCHEE or NATIVE TAMARIND						
Rainforest lychee (native tamarind) 	*Diploglottis australis* *D. bracheata* *D. cambellii*	fruit	fresh frozen	*The flesh is edible but both the hard outer casing and the inner seeds are removed before consumption.*	*Sweet-sour tangy flavours reminiscent of apricot and mandarin.*	*Available from native food stores and on-line suppliers when in season. Some suppliers also offer frozen rainforest lychee.*

AUSTRALIA'S WILD FRUITS

Australia is home to an abundance of delicious, nutritious and visually spectacular native and wild fruits, many of which have been used by Indigenous Australians for sustenance and medicinal purposes for thousands of years. Australian fruits (both Indigenous and some cultivars) include plums, berries and limes, among others. They are easily used in place of their non-Indigenous cousins to produce familiar foods such as compôtes, pie fillings, jams, chutneys and other condiments, or used as a flavouring in beverages, foods, and oil infusions. They each, through their taste and aromas, carry a tantalising hint of their place in the wild. Some, including the finger lime, are considered to be among the finest of their type in the world in terms of textural crunch and flavour, and are also leaders in nutritional value. The intense and vibrant colours of many – the deep reds, pinks and purples; the golden oranges and greens – indicate the presence of certain powerful antioxidants (such as anthocyanans and chlorophyll) that are associated with particular hues. It is not possible to include all of Australia's wonderful array of fruits here, but below is a list of those found in this book, together with some background notes.

Lemon Aspen

There are a few native varieties of lemon aspen that are used for culinary purposes, but it is the species *Acronychia acidula* that is considered the 'true' lemon aspen.

Lemon aspen — *Acronychia acidula*
The fruit of this tree has strong but refreshing citrus flavours of lemon together with tropical 'camphor' notes, and it is really quite unique. It can be eaten whole (the skin is very thin and the fruit does not need to be peeled), but it's best puréed to extract the flavour for use in various prepared foods and beverages. The dried powder is also excellent. Lemon aspen is a rich source or antioxidants (higher than the 'super-food' blueberries) and a good source of various vitamins and minerals including folate, zinc and iron.

'The best way to extract that wonderful unique, lemony flavour is to purée the whole fruit and infuse it into liquid preparations, vinegars and sauces, as the spongy flesh and apple-like core with its seeds is not as pleasant to eat whole.'

lemon aspen

The Lillipillies

Lillipillies belong to the Myrtaceae, or myrtle, family, along with eucalypts, the herb-like 'myrtles' (anise, cinnamon, and lemon myrtle) and thousands of other species globally. They all have edible fruit, or berry, of which two are most commonly used for Australian culinary purposes: the riberry (*Syzygium luehmannii*) and the satinash (*S. fibrosum*). Other Australian lillipillies include the brush cherry (*S. australe*), the blue lillipilly (*S. coolminianum*), and the sour cherry (*S. corynanthum*). Due to their similarities there is some overlap and interchanging of their common names. They are native Australian rainforest plants but are now grown widely around Australia.

Riberry — *Syzygium luehmannii*

Perhaps the most well-known of culinary lillipillies, this tree bears small, rounded, sometimes slightly pear-shaped fruit of about 1.5 cm (about ½ in.) in length. The fruit is a beautiful, deep cerise pink on the tree but fades to a softer shade upon cooking. It has the spicy, earthy notes of cinnamon and cloves that complement other foods, especially fruit when used in jams, conserves, coulis, chutneys, compôtes, and the like. As suggested by its rich and deep colours, it contains powerful antioxidants but is also a good source of other nutrients, most notably folate, calcium, and Vitamin C.

Satinash — *Syzygium fibrosum*

This lillipilly bears medium-size pink to red berries of about 10–18 mm (4–7 in.) in diameter, with a succulent but sour flesh that when cooked becomes enjoyably tart. As the botanical name suggests, the flesh is very fibrous and clings to the stone, and is easiest removed after cooking. It is a rich source of antioxidants, as indicated by its deep colour. Specific nutritional information is not readily available but likely to be similar to the riberry (left) and to include anthocyanans, thought to have inflammatory properties that can be particularly useful in the treatment of painful conditions such as arthritis, along with other benefits.

riberries

satinash

The Limes

Australian limes are considered amongst the finest in the world, revered for their superb flavour, unique structure, nutritional qualities, and vibrant colours. They are all true citrus fruits, of the genus *Citrus*. The limes used in the recipes in this book include both wild and cultivated native species.

Australian blood lime — *Citrus australasica var. sanguinea*

This exquisite, egg-shaped fruit, sometimes referred to as the 'Red Centre lime', is a hybrid of the Australian finger lime and a particular variety of the mandarin lime (a type of lime that has similarities to a mandarin but is categorised as a lime, leading to some confusion on this point). It was developed by the CSIRO. It does, in fact, look just like a deep red-coloured lime and, inside its richly coloured skin, it is filled with juice and small 'pearls' (vesicles) of pink and red that release additional intensely flavoured juice. The flavour is a very tart 'blood orange' with a hint of grapefruit bitterness, and both the juice and pearls work well in any number of sweeter dishes. Although its nutritional properties are subject to further research, it can reasonably be assumed that, as a citrus fruit, it is a good source of Vitamin C, and its rich blood red colours indicate the presence of antioxidants.

Desert lime — *Citrus glauca*

These small, grape-like fruits (in size and shape) have a sour, tangy lime-grapefruit flavour. They can be used in place of lemons in conserves, compôtes, jams, and jellies as well as other cooked foods, savoury and sweet, that require a sharp citrus tang. They are also used to infuse wonderful concentrated lemon flavours into oil, or preserved like a tasty pickle. They don't require peeling (the skin is very thin and the entire fruit is edible) but if eaten raw, they are sour with a mild grapefruit-bitter aftertaste. They also freeze well, without loss of shape of flavour. The fruit is particularly rich in Vitamin C and a source of potent antioxidants, and is said to offer anti-fungal and anti-inflammatory benefits.

Australian blood lime

desert limes

Finger lime — *Citrus australasica*

On first glance, the unique, long finger shape belies the exquisitely beautiful, delicately shaped and coloured flesh within. It is also a joy to consume, because of the way juice-filled pearls (vesicles) pop open on the tongue to release an intense burst of fresh, rainforest lime juice, considered superior to that of other limes. The pearls, or 'caviar' as they are sometimes called, are generally pink, green or lemon in colour. The fruit itself is small, slender, and cylindrical, and its outer skin can be green, yellow, red, purple or black. When cut open, the pearls burst forth intact, or can be gently squeezed out from the skin. I find the easiest way to extract the crunchy pearls from the lime it to cut it in half, across the lime, not lengthwise. Then, starting half-way along each half, firmly squeeze to push the flesh out, just like squeezing toothpaste from a tube. Then finish by squeezing further back from the very end tip of the fruit. It's an amazing sight to see! And you will also know if your limes are super fresh and in season if you cut them as described and leave them to sit on a plate. They will literally seem to 'come alive' as they slowly start to expel the pearls (vesicles) all by themselves. This is because those tiny vesicles are so tightly packed inside the fine skin that they have to escape to freedom. It's a great 'magic' trick to perform for young kids.

Although delicate in appearance, those pearls are hardy, and they hold their shape very well until they pop open in the mouth. They can also be used in place of lime juice in any number of sweet or savoury recipes, working equally well in salads, desserts, drinks, seafood and chicken dishes, or to make an exciting garnish and a surprise ingredient in salad dressings. Like all citrus fruits, the finger lime is a rich source of Vitamin C, and also contains Vitamin A, Vitamin E, potassium, antioxidants, and other nutrients.

Sunrise lime — *Citrus australasica x*

This delectable fruit was developed by the CSIRO, as a cross between the Australian finger lime and the calamondin, itself a cross between a mandarin and cumquat. With this heritage, as can be expected the fruit is beautifully coloured in hues of golden orange, while juicy and sweet in flavour, with subtle floral notes. The fruits themselves are shaped like small rounded pears. They can be eaten fresh (including the skin, which is edible) or used in fruit dishes, beverages, and preserves. The rich orange colours suggest the presence of beneficial antioxidants and, while nutritional details are not yet readily available, it can reasonably be expected, given its close relationship to the finger lime, to be a rich source of Vitamin C and a good source of Vitamin A, Vitamin E and various other vitamins and minerals.

sunrise limes

finger limes

finger limes

Native Currant

There are a few different native currants. This one is endemic to South Australia and Kangaroo Island.

Native currant — *Acrotriche depressa*

About the size of a small pea, these dark purple berries are eaten fresh (not dried) and have a strong, tangy wild currant flavour with a unique 'tannin' dryness that lends itself to both sweet and savoury culinary fare. They are fleshy and juicy with a small hard seed that must be removed, and were traditionally enjoyed by the local Indigenous people.

native currants

Muntries

These are also commonly known as 'native apples', 'cranberries', or 'emu apples'.

Muntries — *Kunzea pomifera*

These sweet and tart little berries have a mild apple-like flavour. They are generally about a centimetre or so (or a little under half an inch.) in diameter, and they grow in tight clusters on low-growing, sprawling, ground cover. Initially, they are green in colour, but tend towards brown with red and pink tinges as they ripen. Like an apple or a berry, they can be eaten whole when fresh — no need to peel — but also work well cooked in compôtes, pies, jams, and similar dishes. Nutritionally, they are exceptionally high in antioxidants, said to have four times that of the renowned 'superfruit', blueberry.

'Muntries are the ultimate healthy superfruit that you can eat whole, and when fresh have a lovely soft spongy crunch, not crisp like an apple crunch. The seeds are so tiny you hardly notice them (unlike raspberry seeds). When frozen, they lose the crunch but are excellent in pickling and cooked dishes — and are so easy to use!'

muntries

The Plums

There are several native Australian plums, and some are discussed below. Like all plums, they are stone fruits, or 'drupes', with inedible stones that house their seeds. The stones of the davidson and Kakadu plums are found in the middle of the fruit in the usual place. Unlike the other two plums, however, the davidson plum has two unusual, flat stones (or seeds) that are soft rather than hard and sit side by side inside the fruit. The Illawarra plum has its own unique feature: an external stone attached to its outer skin.

Davidson plum — *Davidsonia spp.*

Of the several types of davidson plums, the 'ooray' or 'Queensland davidson plum' (*Davidsonia pruriens*) and the 'davidson plum' or 'Mullumbimby plum' (*Davidsonia jerseyana*) are the most commonly available for use as fruit or as a flavouring in food. They are endemic to the tropical north of Australia as well as northern New South Wales. A third species, commonly known as the 'smooth davidson plum' (*Davidsonia johnsonii*), is rare in the wild but also bears edible fruit. All the fruits of the davidson plums are, however, very acidic and not usually eaten raw. Once cooked they provide a wonderful sour and tangy plum flavour, a deep earthy aroma, and rich colour. They can be stewed to make compôtes or used to make jams, chutneys and sauces. They have been described as having a taste similar to satsuma plum with both fruity and sour notes. The plums themselves grow in clusters of deeply coloured blue and black fruit of around 5 cm (2 in.) in diameter, although the ooray's is larger than that of the 'Mullumbimby'. Inside the thin but generally tough skin, the flesh is a deep dark red. As a carbohydrate, this plum is a good source of energy, and is also rich in Vitamin C. Its deep colour is evidence of the presence of anthocyanans, powerful antioxidants also found in other purple-hued fruits and vegetables, such as blueberries and beets. It is also a good source of other nutrients, including potassium, Vitamin E (an antioxidant) and magnesium.

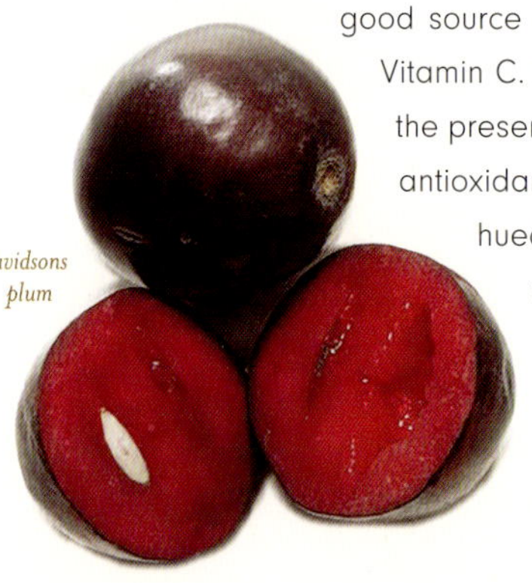

davidsons plum

Illawarra plum — *Podocarpus elatus*

The dark, juicy, purple pulp of the Illawarra plum has a subtle sweet, plum-like flavour with hints of pine and a grape-like luscious texture. It can be eaten raw, but its subtle flavour is enhanced by cooking. It is very unusual in that its stone, or seed, grows outside of, yet is attached to, the fruit (as shown below) but is easily removed during harvesting. This plum is well suited to jams and pickles but is also delicious poached and served as a dessert. It is about the size of a large grape, growing to about 2.5 cm or so in diameter (1 in.), and it is also very high in antioxidants, even more so than blueberries, noted for their antioxidant properties.

Illawarra plum

Kakadu plum — *Terminalia ferdinandiana*

This pale green, oval-shaped fruit grows to about 3 cm (a little over an inch) in length and about a third of that in width. Like all drupes (stone fruits) it has a small, woody stone, which (unlike that of the unusual Illawarra plum) is found at its centre. The edible, fibrous flesh clings hard to the stone and has a sour, slightly sweet flavour and an aroma

Illawarra plums

reminiscent of stewed apples and pears with some citrus notes. It is claimed the Kakadu plum has the highest level of Vitamin C found in any fruit around the world. Not surprisingly, this has led to its use, in the form of a concentrated powder, in various nutritional supplements. Like other Australian plums, it is high in antioxidants, as well as in iron and folic acid, hence its reputation as the greatest of the Australian superfoods

Kakadu plums

'Australian native plums are a joy to cook with and so easy and versatile to use in a multitude of applications.

Quandongs

There are many variants of quandongs found in the wild. It is known by many names, including 'wild peach', 'native peach', 'desert peach', 'sweet quandong', or simply 'quandong'.

Quandong — *Santalum acuminatum*

These lovely stone fruits grow to about 2-2.5 cm (¾-1 in.) in diameter, and have a shiny, crimson edible exterior (the 'skin' and 'flesh' are eaten as 'one' and is thin compared to the stone). Further inside, a large stone takes up the rest of the room. The flesh is sweet and tangy, reminiscent of peaches and rhubarb, and the aroma is warm, fruity and earthy. They can be used in a similar way to rhubarb, too: poached to make compôtes, with the sweetness adjusted according to taste; used in pie fillings, jams, and preserves; or as a flavouring in various sauces and beverages. The flesh can be eaten fresh, but has a naturally dry texture and is more commonly obtained frozen or dry. The dried form can be stored for several years, without deterioration to its flavour. It is very easily re-constituted, by simmering in water (the fruit is too leathery to be eaten dry).

dried quandongs

The quandong is a very nutritious fruit, said to contain twice as much Vitamin C as an orange and to be an excellent source of Vitamin E, folate, magnesium, and calcium, as well as a good source of iron and zinc. It's also rich in antioxidants, as suggested by its deep, crimson colours. Traditionally, the stones have been used by Indigenous Australians for medicinal purposes and also as a food, but as with all drupe stones they may contain certain toxins.

quandongs

'Quandong is the most famous and beautiful native desert fruit — like decorative baubles on a tree, but in the springtime.'

Rainforest Lychee *or* Native Tamarind

The most commonly available native Australian rainforest lychees are, botanically, of the genre *Diploglottis* and are generally referred to as 'native tamarinds'. The flesh has sour, intense flavours.

Rainforest lychee — *Diploglottis spp.*

There are a few types of rainforest lychee, or native tamarinds, used in Australian native cuisine, including *D. australis* (the 'native tamarind'), *D. bracheata* (the 'boonjie tamarind'), and *D. cambellii* or 'small leaf tamarind', so named because it has a smaller leaf than that of the 'boonjie'. They have yellow or bright orange fruit inside a hard outer casing, and the firm, orange-hued flesh has a sweet-sour tang described as reminiscent of tropical apricot and mandarin, but it is quite intense, so only a little needs to be used. Peeling open the flesh layer will reveal the hard seed within. In savoury dishes, tamarind pairs well with poultry and seafood and as a souring agent in curries but can also be used in jellies, jams and fruit dishes. Specific nutritional information is not yet readily available but, like so many other native fruits, the vibrant colours of the fruit indicate the presence of potent anti-oxidants, and most likely other phyto- (plant) nutrients.

rainforest lychees (native tamarind)

Wattleseed pavlova with rainforest berry compôte

SEVICHE *of* MURRAY COD

Light – 4-6 serves

This is an exquisitely pretty as well as delicious dish, based on the cured seafood cuisines of South America. The seafood is cured rather than cooked, so it is important that it is prepared and eaten fresh.

INGREDIENTS

dressing

100 ml (3⅓ fl oz) Lemon Aspen Juice (p. 242)
100 ml (3⅓ fl oz) coconut cream
⅓ tsp salt
30 g (1 oz) spanish onion, finely chopped (about 1 small onion)

cure

400 g (13⅓ oz) fresh Murray cod fillets (or other white fish fillets such as Barramundi)

serve

½ bunch chives, chopped fine
1-2 tbs fine dill sprigs
50 g (1⅔ oz) wild tamarind or rainforest lychee fruit segments
⅓ cup satinash (or riberries or other edible lillipillies, or finger lime pearls)
3-4 native violets (betony) per serve
few drops of Sea Parsley Oil (p. 255)

1 continental cucumber (optional)

SUBSTITUTIONS

Lemon Aspen Juice:
lemon or lime juice
satinash:
riberries or other edible lillipillies, or finger lime pearls
wild tamarind:
Asian tamarind.

METHOD

to make the dressing

1. Mix together the Lemon Aspen Juice, coconut cream, salt, and onion, to make a dressing.

to cure the fish

1. Remove the skin from the fillets and dice the flesh into 5 mm (2 in.) cubes.
2. Gently but thoroughly mix the fish with the dressing.
3. Place in the refrigerator and allow to 'cure' for 2-3 hours prior to serving.

to serve

1. Once cured, remove from the fridge and add the chives. Arrange the seviche in nice piles in small bowls. Garnish with the dill sprigs, fruit, and berries, then drizzle just a few drops of sea parsley oil over the top. Serve immediately.

SERVING OPTION

1. Another option is to serve this seviche piled into cute little cucumber cups as a super fresh and healthy starter for cocktail parties. Simply cut the cucumber into thick 1-2 cm (¼-½ in.) slices and, using a small knife or melon baller, hollow out a 'cup'. Follow the recipe above but, at step 4, instead of putting the seviche into bowls, place small spoonfuls into each cup. Garnish as above and serve on a platter.

KANGAROO *with* QUANDONG CHILLI GLAZE

Main – 4 serves

I couldn't do my cookbook without including this dish. For me, it symbolizes the pivotal moment in my career when, at Mount Lofty House (Adelaide Hills) in 1985, I first combined two native ingredients: kangaroo and quandong. The recipe was later refined at the Red Ochre restaurant in the '90s to include the braised tail, and it became the signature dish that couldn't be taken off the menu.

The braised kangaroo tail is a wonderfully rich dish that freezes exceptionally well under its own stock so, for a hearty, delicious meal that's ready to serve in a flash, double the quantities and keep a tub or two in the freezer (note that you may need to order the kangaroo tail in from a specialist butcher, but otherwise ox tail can be used). Either way, some recipes that call for braising start with water, but I always use stock instead for the flavour and richness it provides. My cooking philosophy has always been about depth and clarity of flavour.

The glaze itself is based on one of the most amazing sauces I ever learnt to make — Sauce Poivrade — while working at the Savoy in London in 1984. It is a lovely sweet-sour reduction that pairs superbly with game meats. At the Savoy, we would serve it with pheasant, grouse or venison.

This is quite a complex recipe with many stages: first, braising the tail (optional); second, making the quandong chilli glaze; third, making the polenta (optional — but one of the nicest ways to mop up the sauces); fourth, preparing the fillets; and finally, putting it all together — but it is worth the effort!

If short for time, you can omit the braised tail and instead serve the fillets only; if so, for this version you will then need to make the glaze using a rich beef gravy or store-bought stock, but it will lack that depth of flavour and 'gelatinous stickiness' so loved in dishes like braised shanks, ox or kangaroo tail.

INGREDIENTS

kangaroo tail (optional)

1 small onion
1 carrot
1 stick of celery
¼ cup extra virgin olive oil

1 kg (2 lb) jointed kangaroo tail

1 litre (2 pints) beef or chicken stock
1 tsp ground pepperleaf
1 sprig of native thyme
1 bayleaf

quandong chilli glaze

60 g (2 oz) quandong halves, fresh or frozen, or about 15 g (½ oz) dried
60 ml (2 fl oz) orange juice
60 ml (2 fl oz) water
⅓ cup sugar

60 ml (2 fl oz) red wine
40 ml (1⅓ fl oz) red wine vinegar
30 g (1 oz) quandong jam
400 ml (13⅓ fl oz) kangaroo-tail glaze (see above), or 1 litre (2 pints) of beef gravy or stock reduced to 400 ml (13⅓ fl oz) of glaze

METHOD

to braise the kangaroo tail and make the kangaroo tail glaze

1. Pre-heat the oven to 220°C (430°F).
2. Coarsely chop the onion, carrot and celery (just wash them quickly beforehand; no need to peel anything).
3. Place the vegetables on a baking tray with the jointed tail pieces, drizzle with the olive oil, and toss to lightly coat. Roast in the oven for 30–40 minutes, to caramelize.
4. Place the stock, peppercorns, thyme and bayleaf in a large saucepan. Add the roasted meat and vegetables and bring to a gentle simmer. Cook for 2–3 hours, very slowly, until the meat is very tender but not quite falling off the bone. While cooking, make sure the meat is always covered with liquid, and top up with a little extra stock or water, if needed.
5. Using a slotted spoon, lift the meat out of the stock. Place on a tray, cover and allow to cool.
6. Using a fine sieve, strain the stock into a smaller saucepan and simmer gently, skimming occasionally, until reduced to approximately 400 ml (13⅓ fl oz) of superb, rich kangaroo-tail glaze. This will be used to make the quandong chilli glaze (see below).

to make the quandong chilli glaze

1. Place the quandongs, juice, water, and sugar in a medium-sized stainless steel saucepan and bring briefly to the boil.
2. Turn off the heat immediately and allow the syrup and fruit to cool. The fruit should be nice and tender without falling apart.
3. Using a slotted spoon, lift out and reserve the stewed fruit.
4. Add the red wine, vinegar and quandong jam to the syrup.
5. Bring to a fast simmer to reduce to about one third of its original volume, to become a nice, rich syrup. Stay close and keep an eye on it, as it can easily burn.
6. Add the 400 ml (13⅓ fl oz) of kangaroo tail glaze, if using, or substitute with 400 ml (13⅓ fl oz) of the reduced gravy or stock.
7. Simmer for another five minutes or so, skimming as needed. You may choose to strain the liquid through a fine sieve to make a clear, shiny glaze, but it's not essential.

polenta

Pepperleaf Parmesan Polenta (p. 65)

kangaroo fillets

4 × 150g (⅓ lb) approx. kangaroo loin (saddle) fillets; if omitting the kangaroo tail from the recipe, use larger fillets, about 200g (7oz) each

1 tsp sea salt
1 tsp ground pepperleaf

1 tsp additional olive oil

2-4 chillies, finely sliced (optional)

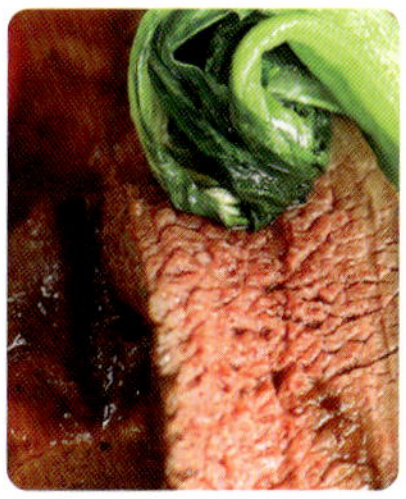

SUBSTITUTIONS

kangaroo tail: ox tail
native thyme: thyme
quandong halves: dried peach halves
ground pepperberry: ground black pepper
pepperleaf: ground black pepper
quandong jam: red currant jelly.

8. Meanwhile, prepare the polenta, baking it until caramelized and a nice golden brown in colour. Reduce the oven temperature to about 80°C (175°F) – this is also the perfect temperature for resting grilled meats. Open the oven door slightly to help then reduce the heat, but leave the polenta in the oven so it stays warm until ready to serve.

to prepare the fillets

1. Trim the kangaroo fillets of any sinews.
2. Season them with salt and ground pepperberry, to your taste.
3. Moisten the fillets with the additional olive oil, then barbecue or char-grill to rare or medium-rare over a high heat, turning once or twice as needed. This will take 5-8 minutes, depending on the thickness of the meat.
4. Place the fillets on a plate, then rest in the cooled 80°C (175°F) oven (with the polenta) for 5-10 minutes, covered with foil.
5. While your meat is resting, add one or two pieces per serve of braised kangaroo tail (if using) to the quandong chilli glaze and gently warm up the glaze and meat over a low-medium heat.
6. Just before you are going to serve, add the reserved stewed quandong fruit and fresh chillies (if using) to the hot glaze, to add a lively zing.
7. If you want to carve the fillets, look carefully at the pieces so you can see which way the grain runs: always carve across the grain.
8. Serve the fillets with the polenta, braised tail (if using, and green vegetables of your choice (I have used stir-fried bok choy).

TAGINE *of* RABBIT *with* PRESERVED DESERT LIME

Main – 4 serves

Rabbit lends itself beautifully to this classic Moroccan-style dish, but because the loin can become very dry if over-cooked, I like to braise the other cuts first, which remain succulent after slow cooking. Then, when close to serving the dish, I quickly sear the loin fillets, keeping them pink in the middle. Please invest in quality Spanish smoked paprika — most supermarket brands are very disappointing!

INGREDIENTS

rabbit

1 × 1.5 kg (3 lb) approx. rabbit

rabbit legs

40 g (1⅓ oz) butter
3 tsp olive oil
1 large onion (about 200 g/7 oz), skinned and thinly sliced
2-4 garlic cloves,, peeled and chopped
1 bunch coriander (cilantro), roots (reserve leaves for garnish)
1½ tsp ground ginger
generous pinch of saffron
2 heaped tsp smoked paprika
1 tsp black pepper, ground
1-2 red chillies and sliced on the diagonal
1 tsp ground pepperleaf
½ tsp salt
1 litre (2 pints) approx. rabbit or chicken stock

dash of extra olive oil for searing

Date, Cinnamon and Sandalwood Cous Cous, hot (p. 230)
Preserved Desert Limes (p. 252)
Carrot, Chickpea and Honey Lemon Myrtle Salad (p. 113)

To make a simple stock:

Simply simmer the bones (chopped into approximately 5cm / 2 in. pieces) slowly with 2 litres of water and a sliced celery stick, carrot and onion for 2–3 hours, skimming occasionally. Allow to cool slightly then strain through a fine sieve. Alternatively, substitute store-bought chicken stock.

METHOD

to prepare the rabbit

1. First, with a boning knife, remove the forelegs and hindlegs. Cut the large hindlegs into two or three pieces using a heavy knife or meat cleaver.
2. Next, cut the forelegs into two.
3. Finally, bone the loin fillets from the back of the carcass and reserve them for cooking later. (If you prefer, your butcher may bone out the meat for you on request.) You can also use the bones to make the stock that is needed for the braise (see below left).

to braise the rabbit legs

1. Heat the butter and oil in a heavy-based braising pan and add the leg portions. Brown the meat on all sides, then remove from the pan and set aside.
2. Add the sliced onions and garlic to the pan and simmer for 10-15 minutes over a gentle heat, stirring regularly until they are a light golden brown.
3. Next, add the finely chopped coriander (cilantro) roots. Follow with the ginger, saffron, paprika, pepper, chillies, pepperleaf and salt.
4. Now return the browned meat, together with the stock, to the pan. At this point, you may transfer the meat and sauce to a traditional earthenware tagine if you wish.
5. Bring to the boil and simmer gently for 1-2 hours, until tender (this varies considerably depending on the age and quality of the rabbit).

SUBSTITUTIONS

ground pepperleaf: pepper, freshly ground
desert lime: preserved lemon.

6. I like to reduce the sauce, so remove the meat, set aside in a dish, and cover with kitchen film. Leave the pot or tagine on the stove and continue to simmer the sauce down to about a third of its original volume. You want to concentrate those amazing flavours to about 400 ml (13⅓ fl oz) —perfect for four main serves.
7. Return the braised meat, cover and turn off the stove and keep warm until ready to serve.

to finish

1. In a hot frypan, quickly sear the reserved loin fillets in a dash of olive oil for about two minutes, turning on all sides. Season to taste, and when cooked to medium, remove from the pan and rest the meat in a warm place covered with a lid or foil for 5 minutes.
2. Meanwhile, bring the sauce and braised rabbit back to a gentle simmer to reheat.

to serve

1. Reheat the Date and Sandalwood Cous Cous.
2. Slice both of the pink rabbit fillets into 2–4 pieces and scatter over the tagine.
3. Garnish with the reserved coriander (cilantro) leaves and additional sliced chillies (if desired), just as you are about to serve.
4. Serve with the Carrot, Chickpea and Honey Lemon Myrtle Salad and Preserved Desert Limes on the side and allow your guests to help themselves. Sometimes, with tagines, I chop the preserved limes coarsely and mix through when re-heating

RED BRAISED KANGAROO TAIL *with* SUNRISE LIME CHILLI CARAMEL

Main – 4 serves

Kangaroo meat is one of the most nutritious and lean meats available. Many think it may be quite 'gamey', but I disagree: it has a wonderfully rich and mild meat flavour (to achieve real gaminess, it would need to be hung whole like pheasant or venison in the traditional way). Slow-braised, the tail is delicious and meltingly tender. If you love lamb shanks, you will love 'roo tail! You may need to pre-order the tail from a specialist butcher and, if only frozen is available, defrost it for at least a day in the fridge — or try this recipe with ox tail.

INGREDIENTS

braising and the master stock

1 kg (2 lb) approx. kangaroo tail, jointed
40 ml (1⅓ fl oz) vegetable oil

---

40 ml (1⅓ fl oz) shaoxing wine
60 g (2 fl oz) dark soy sauce
30 g (1 fl oz) sweet soy sauce
4 tsp sesame oil
1 litre (2 pints) approx. beef stock
20 g (⅔ oz) brown sugar
2-3 cloves garlic, peeled and crushed
15-20 anise myrtle leaves or
 2 whole star anise
½ cinnamon stick
peel of 1 orange (peeled with a peeler)
2-3 large red chillies, split

caramel sauce

4-6 tsp water
250 g (½ lb) dark palm sugar, shaved
50 ml (1⅔ fl oz) fish sauce
100 ml (3⅓ fl oz) orange juice
1 red chilli, finely sliced

finish

1 litre (2 pints) vegetable oil for frying
2 tsp Creative Native Anise Myrtle 5-spice
1 cup plain flour
50 ml (1⅔ fl oz) lime juice
5-6 sunrise limes
1 red chilli, finely sliced
coriander (cilantro) and wild basil,
Steamed Lemon Myrtle Rice (p. 269)
¼ cup Sunrise Lime and Chilli Black Vinegar
 (p. 257)

METHOD

to braise the meat and make the 'master stock'

1. Pre-heat the oven to 240°C (460°F).
2. Rub the tail pieces with the vegetable oil, then place in a baking pan. Roast for 15-20 minutes, to caramelize.
3. Place the meat in a large cooking pot and cover with the wine, soy sauces, sesame oil, and stock.
4. Follow with the sugar, garlic, anise myrtle, cinnamon, orange peel and chillies.
5. Bring the pot to a gentle simmer (uncovered) and cook very slowly for 2-3 hours, until the meat is very tender but not quite falling off the bone yet.
6. Lift out the meat with a slotted spoon and place it on a tray, then cover and allow to cool.
7. Skim off the fat from the 'master stock' then strain and reserve 1 cup for your caramel sauce (see below). The rest may be frozen for later use (I love to use it for an Australasian-style soup or pho).

to make the caramel sauce

1. In a saucepan, simmer the water and palm sugar to dissolve, and cook to a dark caramel over a high heat, until it is just beginning to smoke.

SUBSTITUTIONS

kangaroo tail:
ox tail
anise myrtle:
star anise
anise myrtle five spice:
five-spice powder
wild basil
thai basil
sunrise limes
orange zest.

2. Quickly add the fish sauce, orange juice and reserved master stock.
3. Simmer gently to reduce down to a syrupy honey-like consistency. Keep warm until ready to serve. (The lime juice, sunrise lime, and chilli will be added a little later.)
4. Cut the sunrise limes into quarters and slice finely, or chop coarsely.

to finish

1. Heat the vegetable oil in a deep fryer or a deep pot to 190°C (375°F). Use caution: this is very hot.
2. Mix the ground Anise Myrtle 5-Spice and flour together thoroughly.
3. Take the cooked, jointed kangaroo tail and dredge the pieces through the flour-and-spice mix. The meat should be moist, so the flour should stick well.
4. Shake any excess flour off the meat, then carefully slide the kangaroo pieces into the oil, a few at a time.
5. Deep-fry until they are a dark golden colour and very crispy (about 3–5 minutes).
6. Scoop out with a slotted spoon or skimmer, drain quickly on paper towels, then lay out on a large platter or, even better, a big, fresh banana leaf.
7. Quickly heat the caramel sauce. Once it has heated through, stir through the fresh lime juice, some sunrise limes, and chilli.
8. Drizzle the sticky, fruity and spicy sauce over the hot, crispy meat. Garnish with torn basil and coriander (cilantro) and additional sunrise limes.
9. Serve with Steamed Lemon Myrtle Rice with Sunrise Lime Chilli Black Vinegar on the side.

OYSTERS *with* KAKADU PLUM VINAIGRETTE

Light - 4 serves

This could possibly be the world's healthiest aphrodisiac, combining the Kakadu plum's incredible Vitamin C attributes (with its antioxidant and bio-active compounds) with oysters — sure to get you going! I think six oysters per person is really under-estimating it . . . Note, too, that grating the plums only really works if they are frozen, but that's perfect for chilled oysters.

INGREDIENTS

50 g (1⅔ oz) or about 1-2 golden shallots, peeled and finely diced
juice of 1 lime, about 30 ml (1 fl oz)
½ tsp white pepper, freshly ground
2 tsp sugar
4 tsp best-quality white wine vinegar

5-8 (depending on size) medium to large frozen Kakadu plums
24 oysters, freshly shucked
3-4 tsp red or pink finger lime 'caviar' (the 'pearls' or 'vesicles')

METHOD

1. Whisk together the shallots, lime juice, pepper, sugar and wine vinegar until the sugar is dissolved.
2. Using a microplane grater, grate the plums into a fine 'snow' then mix into the vinaigrette.
3. Arrange the oysters on plates, over crushed ice.
4. Spoon over a little of the dressing and top with a tiny amount of the finger lime 'caviar'.

SUBSTITUTIONS

Kakadu plums:
other sour plums or green mango
finger lime:
lemon or lime juice.

PORK, SAGE *and* MUNTRIES BURGERS *with* RIVERMINT *and* ONION CHILLI JAM

Main – 4 serves | Light – 6-8 serves

This is a great recipe that you can use to make burgers, koftas, or even as a filling in sausage skins. Here I have used it for making burgers, paired with pepperberry brioche buns and the very moreish Onion and Rivermint Chilli Jam.

INGREDIENTS

meat

500 g (1 lb) minced pork or pork shoulder
1 tbs sage leaves, chopped
1 tbs sea parsley leaves, chopped

1½ tsp salt
1 tsp ground white pepper
2-3 tsp rice flour
1 tsp garlic granules (or 2 tsp fresh garlic, crushed)
4 tsp dried onion flakes or fresh onion, chopped
50 g (1⅔ oz) muntries

burgers

1 large sprig coastal rosemary (optional)

20 ml (⅔ fl oz) extra virgin olive oil
20 g (⅔ oz) unsalted butter

4 large brioche buns (p. 266)
1 cup Rivermint and Onion Chilli Jam (p. 262)
lettuce and tomato, to taste
cheese slices, to taste (optional)

SUBSTITUTIONS

muntries:
try dried currants or chopped dried apple

sea parsley:
flat-leaf (continental) parsley

coastal rosemary leaves:
lesser amount of rosemary leaves.

METHOD

to prepare the meat

1. Keep all the ingredients as cold as possible, removing the meat from the refrigerator only when you are immediately ready to use it. Cold ingredients helps the meat, fat and salt to bind together really well.
2. Mince together the pork with the sage and parsley (if you are using pre-minced pork, just add the chopped herbs).
3. Mix through the salt, pepper, rice flour, garlic granules, onion flakes and muntries until the mixture is tacky.

to make the burgers

1. Shape the meat-mix into nice round patties, about 10 cm (4 in.) in diameter, and weighing about 120 g (4 oz) each.
2. Strip the coastal rosemary leaves from the stems and sprinkle them over both sides of the patties. Gently press them into the patties to make them stick. (Note, this is an optional step, which gives a rustic, textured crust to the patty, but it is not a strongly flavoured addition.)
3. Place the oil and butter in a non-stick frypan and heat until foaming. Add the patties (don't crowd the pan) and cook over a moderate heat until the crust is lovely and golden. Flip the patties over and cook for a further 3-4 minutes on the other side. Control the temperature carefully, so the crust doesn't burn, and reduce the heat if necessary.
4. Meanwhile, gently toast the pepperberry brioche buns. Be careful: this sweet bread can burn quite easily.
5. Fill the buns with sliced tomato, lettuce leaves, maybe a slice of cheddar, and Rivermint and Onion Chilli Jam.

CARAMELIZED MUNTRIES *and* ONION PIZZA *with* GOATS CHEESE

Main – makes 2 large pizzas | Light – makes 4 small single-serve pizzas

This is a fabulous vegetarian pizza and I really like the sweetness of muntries and caramelized onion balanced with the creamy tang of a good chèvre — but it also works brilliantly without cheese as a vegan option. Try a pinch of wild thyme also mixed into the jam, and asparagus in season will also work a treat.

INGREDIENTS

½ quantity of pizza dough (p. 267)
extra flour for dusting

1½ cups of Caramelized Onion and Muntries Jam (p. 262)
75-100 g (2½-3¼ oz) best quality goats cheese (chèvre)

---

2 cups lightly packed baby rocket leaves (arugula)
1 tbs extra virgin olive oil

---

2 tsp Spicy Pepperleaf Oil, or to taste (optional, p. 256) or fresh chillies, if you like a little spice
additional flour for dusting

METHOD

1. On a heavily floured workbench, roll out the pizza bases to 3-4mm (about ½ in.) in thickness. Always use a generous amount of flour underneath so the base can slide easily, otherwise it's a challenge to slip the pizza paddle underneath when you want to lift the pizza and place it in the oven.
2. Spread the onion and muntries jam all over the bases, then liberally sprinkle the finely crumbled goats cheese over the top.
3. Make sure your oven is pre-heated to the absolute maximum – 250°C+ (480°F+). If using a wood-fired oven, allow a few hours for it to heat up properly (see notes on p. 267).
4. Now, deftly slide a pizza peel under each pizza, one at a time. Lift, then 'place and drop' onto the hearth if using a wood-fired oven, or drop onto a baking tray and place in the oven.
5. Cook the pizza in the oven for 2-4 minutes, until crispy, puffed and golden (this may take longer in a standard convection oven).
6. Once cooked, slide the cooked pizza onto a chopping board and cut into portions.
7. Quickly toss the rocket in a light coating of extra virgin olive oil and scatter all over the pizza. If desired, fresh pepperleaf oil or chopped chilli may be added at this point. Serve immediately of course!

DUCK *with* NATIVE CURRANT GLAZE *and* WILD THYME RÖSTI

Side – 4 serves

In my restaurant days, I would cook this dish in the French confit style, where the duck legs are simmered, very slowly, while submerged in duck fat. Braising in stock is just as delicious and much healthier!

INGREDIENTS

4 large duck legs
1 tsp salt
½ tsp pepperberry, freshly ground

1 litre (2 pints) chicken stock.

150 ml (5 fl oz) quality port wine
40 g (1⅓ oz) native currants

Wild Thyme Rösti (p. 113, optional)
stir-fried broccolini, saltbush or other green vegetables of your choice (optional)

SUBSTITUTIONS

pepperberry:
peppercorns
native currants:
red or black currants
saltbush:
spinach or kale.

METHOD

1. Pre-heat your oven to 230°C (445°F).
2. Place the legs into a deep baking tray and season with the salt and ground pepperberry, then roast in the oven for 20–30 minutes until caramelized nicely.
3. Remove from the oven, allow to cool a little, then carefully pour off or scoop out the excess duck fat. (If you like, you can freeze this cooked duck fat in ice-cube trays and store in the freezer, in zip-lock bags for use with recipes such as duck-fat potatoes.)
4. Pour the chicken stock into the tray, over the duck. Cover with foil or a lid and return it to the oven. Reduce the oven temperature to 150°C (300°F) and allow the legs to braise in the stock for a further 45 minutes, or until quite tender.
5. Meanwhile, begin to make the glaze. In a small stainless-steel saucepan, gently simmer the wine and currants until reduced to a syrupy glaze. Put to one side. (You can also use this time to prepare side dishes, such as my Wild Thyme Rösti. Stir-fried broccolini and saltbush also work well.)
6. Once the legs are tender, remove the tray from the oven again. Very carefully pour off the stock and strain it into a suitable heat-proof bowl and allow it to settle. Leave the legs in the baking tray, cover again with a lid or foil, keeping them warm while you finish the glaze.
7. Return to the syrupy glaze and bring it back to a gentle simmer. Skim off any excess fat from the strained stock then add the stock to the glaze.
8. Continue simmering the glaze until it reduces to about 210ml (7 fl oz); 60 ml (2 fl oz) per serve is a good rule of thumb..
9. Return the legs back to the sauce, gently re-heat and serve immediately with your preferred accompaniments.

ROAST MURRAY COD CUTLETS *in* SUNRISE LIME MISO GLAZE

Light – 4 serves

This is a wonderful savoury marinade with great 'umami', that elusive savoury quality — just be sure to marinate for at least a few hours. I have used Murray cod here, but other white fish and chicken also work nicely. High heat is the key here, to achieve the beautiful golden colours and blackened edges.

INGREDIENTS

marinade

50 g (1⅔ oz) sunrise limes, sliced

½ cup light palm sugar
1 cup white miso paste
juice of 1 large lemon
juice of 1 large orange
⅓ cup mirin (rice wine)

4 × 250 g (½ lb) approx. white fish cutlets (Murray cod, kingfish, snapper or barramundi)

finish

4 bok choy or other green vegetables
1 tbs extra virgin oil
1 tsp salt, or to taste
½ tsp ground pepperleaf, to taste

SUBSTITUTIONS

sunrise limes:
try orange zest
ground pepperleaf:
ground pepper.

METHOD

to make the marinade

1. Halve the sunrise limes (no peeling required), and remove any seeds if you wish. Slice into thin, half, or quarter rounds.
2. Separately, shave the palm sugar finely and whisk together with the miso, lemon and orange juices, and mirin in a stainless steel or glass bowl, until the sugar has dissolved.
3. Stir through the sliced sunrise limes.
4. Add the fish, coating it generously with the marinade. Cover and marinate in the fridge for at least two hours.

to finish the dish

5. Pre-heat the oven to a very hot 250°C (480°F). Meanwhile, place the marinated fish in a large baking dish (lined with baking paper, if you wish, to make cleaning up easier).
6. Bake in the pre-heated oven for 8–12 minutes, depending on the thickness of the cutlets, until barely done. To check, use a sharp knife to slice into the thickest part, or that part closest to the bone. The flesh should still be slightly translucent (not opaque) on the bone. Allow to rest for about 5 minutes. (When cooking fish, I like to cook the flesh until its 'barely done', then allow it to rest and let the latent heat complete the cooking. This ensures the fish remains beautifully moist.)
7. Meanwhile, stir-fry the vegetables in some olive oil over a medium heat until wilted. Season to your liking.
8. Plate the fish and vegetables and drizzle over any extra roasting juices. Serve immediately. Steamed Lemon Myrtle Rice (p. 269) also makes a nice additional accompaniment.

MULLOWAY *in* DESERT LIME CHERMOULA

Main – 4 serves

This is spectacular presented as a whole baked fish on a huge platter, but fillets also work and cook much more quickly. Snapper, barramundi or, in fact, any fresh white flesh fish, can also be used. If using a whole fish, allow roughly 400g (14 oz) per person for a main meal, because with most fish you will lose about half of it to bone. The chermoula is also great with baked pumpkin or chicken pieces.

INGREDIENTS

chermoula

- 100g (3⅓ oz) fresh or frozen desert limes
- 3-4 peeled garlic cloves
- 3 tsp ground cumin
- 2¼ tsp ground coriander
- 2¼ tsp sweet paprika
- 10g (⅓ oz) medium-heat red chillies, to taste
- 1 heaped tsp Murray River salt or sea salt
- 1 generous pinch saffron threads
- 15g (½ oz) rivermint leaves
- 15g (½ oz) coriander (cilantro), leaves and stalks, coarsely chopped
- 30g (1 oz) sea parsley leaves and stalks, coarsely chopped
- 1 small (150g / 5 oz approx.) spanish onion, peeled and coarsely chopped
- 75 ml (2½ fl oz) extra virgin olive oil

- 1 whole fish, approx. 1.5 kg (3 lb)*
- additional coriander (cilantro) and red chillies, to garnish (optional)
- lemon and lime wedges (optional)

* *If you prefer, you could substitute 4 × 180–200g (6½ oz) of fish fillets, skin on or off according to your preference.*

METHOD

1. Partially defrost the desert limes then slice into 2.5-3 mm (⅛ in.) rings (they're easier to slice when still partly frozen).
2. Using a food processor, process all the ingredients (except the desert limes, fish and garnishes) to a smooth purée. Fold the sliced desert limes through the purée.
3. Marinate the fish in the purée for at least 2-3 hours.
4. If you are cooking fillets, place them on a baking tray lined with baking paper and roast at 250°C (480°F) for 6-8 minutes. They should be nicely browned and cooked medium to well done, but the cooking time will vary depending on the thickness of the fillets.
5. If you are cooking a whole fish, bake at a lower temperature, about 220°C (430°F) for approximately 45 minutes. You can check the cooking progress by using a knife to gently pull apart the flesh at it thickest part, towards the head. If it's still a little raw on the bone, cook for a little longer. Ideally, you want to take it out of the oven when it is almost well done, but not quite. Then, allow the fish to rest, covered by foil in a warm place for about 5-10 minutes. This will allow the latent heat to complete the cooking process so that the fish is only just cooked through. This will give you the most wonderful moist fish imaginable.
6. Garnish with coriander (cilantro) and chillies. Serve with lemon and lime wedges if desired.

SUBSTITUTIONS

desert limes:
lime or lemon zest and juice

sea parsley:
flat-leaf (continental) parsley

rivermint:
mint or spearmint.

SMOKY SLOW ROAST BRISKET *with* ILLAWARRA PLUMS

Main – 5-6 serves

Slow-roasted brisket makes a delicious slow braise when prepared in a braising pot. Alternatively, it can also be cooked in a covered, roll-top barbecue roaster but needs regular basting to keep it moist while it develops its lovely crust. What makes this recipe special is the light curing and smoking of the meat over native pepperleaf wood chips (if you're into home smoking). But, if you're not able to smoke at home, skip the smoking step and you will still have a lovely result. (You can also add a sprinkle of the commercially available 'liquid smoke' at the marinating stage). The pickled Illawarra plums (liquid and fruit) are delicious served with all kinds of grilled and roast meats.

INGREDIENTS

curing

1.5 kg (3 lb) approx. piece of beef brisket
45 g (1½ oz) salt
2¼ tsp smoked paprika
2¼ tsp ground coriander
2¼ tsp ground pepperleaf
1½ tsp garlic powder
45 g (1½ oz) brown or white sugar

smoking

1½ cups Creative Native Pepperleaf Wood Chips (optional)

braising

40 ml (1⅓ fl oz) extra virgin olive oil
1 litre (2 pints) beef stock
1 cup Pickled Illawarra Plums (p. 253) in their juice

METHOD

to cure the brisket

1. Mix the dry spices and the sugar and rub into the meat, then vacuum-pack and chill for 2–3 days. If you don't have a vacuum machine, simply put the meat into a large, clear, zip-lock food bag and try to push out most of the air before sealing it. Turn the bag once or twice a day so it cures evenly.

to smoke the brisket (optional)

1. Skip the two steps below if you don't have proper smoking equipment and are not familiar with the process.
2. Prepare a smoking cabinet with the native pepperleaf woodchips, or other fine smoking chips or sawdust.
3. Remove the cured meat from the bag and 'cold smoke' for 3–4 hours. There's no need to rinse the meat first: I use a low-percentage of sugar and salt in the cure and it becomes part of the seasoning.

to braise the brisket

1. In a suitably-sized braising pot, heat the oil until smoking and nicely brown the brisket on all sides, turning regularly. This will take about 5 or so minutes.
2. Add the stock and bring to a gentle simmer, lid on. If using a roll-top barbecue, place the meat and stock in a roasting tray. Cook very slowly for 3–4 hours, until meltingly tender. Use a timer and check and turn the meat every hour.

Crispy Saltbush and Vinegar Potatoes, p 114

3. When the meat is almost falling apart, turn off the heat and pour off all of the stock into a suitable bowl, while keeping the meat covered in the pot to stay warm.
4. Allow the liquid to settle, so you can scoop or pour off the excess fats.

for the sauce

1. Strain the Illawarra plums while catching the liquid in a small stainless-steel saucepan.
2. Bring the liquid to a rapid simmer over a medium heat and reduce down to a quarter of the original volume. Keep an eye on it and watch and control your heat (you don't want to burn it).
3. Add the lovely rich brisket stock and cook down further, to about 300 ml (10 fl oz), to make a superb, rich syrupy glaze.
4. Add the plums back in and warm through to serve.

to serve

1. Carve the warm brisket and serve with the sauce and fresh greens such as asparagus. Crispy Saltbush and Vinegar Potatoes (p. 114) also make a delicious accompaniment, as shown.

QUANDONG COMPÔTE

Savoury or sweet - makes 1½-2 cups, depending on the liquid content.

I've always used orange juice instead of water in this recipe, as it helps build flavour and complements that of quandong so well (but you can use water, if you prefer). It makes a lovely sweet treat on its own, but can also be mixed with various other ingredients to make savoury sauces. The amount of liquid can be adjusted to vary the thickness, depending on how you will use it, and depending on the moisture content of your fruit, which can vary from year to year. The compôte can be thickened even further with some starch and water to make a quandong pie filling.

INGREDIENTS

1 cup orange juice
75 g (2½ oz) castor sugar
½ cinnamon quill

30 g (1 oz) dried quandongs, or 120 g (4 oz) frozen quandongs

METHOD

1. Bring everything except the quandongs to the boil.
2. Add the quandongs and re-boil briefly. Remove from the heat immediately. Allow to cool, covered, to 'plump up' before use. (You can adjust sugar to taste, as the amount of natural fruit sugar will vary. Using honey instead also works).

SUBSTITUTIONS

quandongs:
dried peaches.

* *If using frozen quandongs, halve the amount of orange juice.*

* *If making a pie filling, mix about 50g (just under 2 oz) of cornflour (cornstarch) or tapioca starch with a tablespoon or two of water to form a paste, and stir through at the final stages of cooking to thicken.*

PORK SPARE RIBS *with* DAVIDSON PLUM *and* CHILLI SAUCE

Main – 4 serves

Pork spare ribs are very popular, enjoyed with many types of sauces such as smoky barbecue-style and spicy plum. This recipe has the incredible sharp and rich plum flavour of the huge davidson plum, from our east coast rainforests.

INGREDIENTS

1.5 kg (3 lb) approx. pork spare ribs, whole racks
2 cups Davidson Plum Chilli Sauce (p. 248)

---

1 large red chilli, finely julienned (optional)
1 large green chilli, finely julienned (optional)

---

lime cheeks or wedges
Steamed Lemon Myrtle Rice (p. 269)

METHOD

1. Place the pork ribs in a deep roasting tray that fits them neatly. Pour over the sauce and rub it all over the pork. Cover the tray with foil.
2. Bake at 175°C (350°F) for about an hour, or until the meat is nice and tender when pierced with a knife. Timing may vary a little depending on the size and quality of the ribs.
3. Allow the ribs to cool a little then pour off the juices into a small saucepan. Simmer gently until reduced to a syrupy glaze.
4. 15 minutes before serving, pre-heat your clean char-grill or barbecue (see p. 23).
5. Cut the ribs into 4 sets, or individual ribs if you like. (It will mean there are a lot more pieces to turn and manage on the grill, but it gives a lot more of the delicious, sticky, caramelized surfaces.)
6. Brush the rib pieces generously with reduced glaze and briefly grill for about 3-4 minutes on each side, basting with more glaze as you go.
7. Just before taking the ribs off the grill, I like to add finely julienned strips of red and green chilli to the final basting, for a nice, hot kick.
8. Serve with lime and Steamed Lemon Myrtle Rice.

RICH CHOCOLATE *and* RIBERRY CAKE

Sweet – up to 12 serves

This is a superb, rich and flourless chocolate cake. One of the nice things about it is the fragile crust, which crumples and cracks and looks irresistible. This is due to the aeration of the eggs and the rising and falling of the crust during the cooking and cooling processes. Make sure you use a high quality dark couverture chocolate: the higher the quality, the better the final result.

INGREDIENTS

2 cups frozen riberries
60 g (2 oz) castor sugar

---

225 g (7½ oz) dark couverture chocolate
180 g (6 oz) unsalted, butter, diced
30 ml (1 fl oz) cognac or brandy
30 ml (1 fl oz) espresso coffee
or 2 heaped tsp of instant coffee dissolved in 30 ml (1 fl oz) of boiling water, then cooled

---

6 eggs yolks (reserve the whites, see below)
180 g (6 oz) ground almond or macadamia meal

---

6 (reserved) eggs whites

---

180 g (6 oz) additional castor sugar
cocoa powder, for dusting

SUBSTITUTIONS

frozen riberries:
other stoned lillipillies in season, or blueberries or raspberries.

METHOD

1. Over a gentle heat, simmer the riberries with the sugar for approximately 10 minutes, stirring regularly, until the liquid is quite syrupy and almost gone.
2. Allow to cool, then set aside a heaped tablespoon of these 'glacéed' riberries to use as a garnish later.
3. Heat the chocolate gently together with the butter, brandy and coffee using a double-boiler (see p. 22), until completely melted and the mixture is luke warm.
4. Remove from the heat and whisk in the egg yolks and almond or macadamia meal.
5. Separately, whisk the egg whites with the additional castor sugar until medium peaks form (not too stiff, otherwise it becomes more difficult to incorporate into the batter).
6. Fold the egg whites through the riberry mixture, then pour into a lined, round 20 cm (8 in.) spring-form cake tin, or run a few folded strips of baking paper along the base of the tin and up the sides until they overlap the edges to make 'paper handles' to use when lifting out the cake (see p. 190, where paper strips are used to lift pie shells out of ramekins – it's basically the same technique).
7. Bake in a pre-heated oven at 160°C (320°F) for 45 minutes.
8. Remove from the oven and allow the cake to subside and cool to room temperature.
9. Cut the cake into even wedges and dust with cocoa powder. Serve with rich cream, if desired, or perhaps my 60-second Riberry and Raspberry Sorbet (p. 170), as shown here. The reserved glacéed riberries will make an attractive garnish.

BOILED ORANGE, BLOOD LIME *and* MACADAMIA CAKE

Sweet – 12 serves

This cake is based on the classic flourless boiled orange and almond cake but has that unique blood orange tang and subtle bitter notes. It works really well with chocolate icing, but here I have served it with strawberries macerated with Pickled Illawarra Plums and some rich cream.

INGREDIENTS

1 large whole orange
200 g (7 oz) blood limes

250 g (8 oz) ground macadamia nuts (macadamia meal)

50 g (1⅔ oz) almond meal
6 eggs
250 g (8 oz) sugar
1 tsp (3 g) ground lemon myrtle
2 tsp (6 g) baking powder

2-3 strawberries per serve (optional)
Pickled Illawarra Plums (optional, p. 253)
icing sugar, for dusting
rich cream, to serve

SUBSTITUTIONS

blood limes:
limes; blood oranges
macadamias:
cashews.

METHOD

1. Cut the whole, unpeeled orange into quarters.
2. Cover the oranges and blood limes with water and simmer gently for approximately 45 minutes, until all the fruit is very tender. Drain and allow to cool (discard the water).
3. In your food processor, blend the boiled fruit with the ground macadamias, almond meal, eggs, sugar, lemon myrtle and baking powder.
4. Pour the mixture into a baking tin lined with baking paper.
5. Bake for 1 hour at 165°C (330°F). Once cooked, remove from the oven and cool to room temperature.
6. While the cake is cooling, cut the strawberries into halves or quarters and mix in with the Pickled Illawarra Plums and syrup (if using). Allow to macerate for an hour or so. If you like, add a little sugar to sweeten the syrup to your taste.
7. Once the cake has cooled, remove it from the cake tin. Dust the cake generously with the icing sugar, then cut into portions.
8. Swirl rich cream onto serving plates, and then spoon over the strawberries and Illawarra plums and syrup. Finally, add the slices of cake.

MUNTRIES *and* CARAMEL APPLE FLAN

Sweet – 12 serves

The apples, muntries and cinnamon combine perfectly in this unique and delicious dessert. It takes a bit of effort, and it's a long slow cook, but it is worth it!

INGREDIENTS

150 ml (5 fl oz) water
600 g (20 oz) white sugar

3.5 kg (7½ lb) approx. green apples (granny smiths)
300 g (10 oz) fresh or frozen muntries, coarsely chopped

250 g (½ lb) dark brown sugar
1 tsp cinnamon
1 tsp strawberry gum

double or rich cream, to serve
Finger Lime Sweet and Sour Crunch (optional, see below)

neutral (flavourless) cooking spray

SUBSTITUTIONS

muntries:
try diced dried apple or sultanas

strawberry gum:
few drops strawberry essence

Finger Lime Sweet and Sour Crunch:
This is a winner for a superb 'crunchy-sweet, crunchy-sour' last-second garnish on a multitude of sweets. Just mix equal quantities of the crunchy pearls of flesh from finger limes (the 'vesicles') with a crunchy, larger grain sugar like raw sugar or coffee crystals in equal amounts (e.g. 1 teaspoon of pearls to 1 teaspoon of sugar). You must mix it just before serving the dish, so the sugar does not have time to dissolve in the moisture of the finger lime pearls.

METHOD

1. Select a 28 cm (11 in.) solid, square or round cake tin (not one with moveable parts, as it won't work for the water bath). Next, make a 'collar' for the tin to extend its height: simply line the sides with a wide strip of silicone baking paper cut 6 cm (about 2½ in.) taller than the tin itself. Lightly spray with cooking spray on one side so it sticks to the inside of the tin.
2. To make the caramel, simmer and stir the water and sugar until clear and bubbling. Do not stir the syrup after it has gone clear. Cook to a medium-gold colour (stay close; it can easily burn and become black and bitter), then pour immediately into the cake tin and allow to cool and set hard.
3. Peel, core, and cut the apples into thin 2–3 mm (about ⅛ in.) slices (a mandolin works best for this). Arrange a layer of overlapping apple slices over the caramel, enough to completely cover the base. Reserve the rest.
4. Mix together the sugar, cinnamon and strawberry gum, then sprinkle about 2 tablespoons of the mixture and about 2 tablespoons of the muntries over the top of the apple slices.
5. Repeat the layering steps, until all the apple, sugar, cinnamon, and muntries have been used and the flan is made up of several layers of roughly equal portions. The flan may be about 4-5 cm (about 1½-2 in.) taller than the tin.
6. Cover the flan with foil and place the tin in a larger baking tray with hot water as high as you can reasonably go (to make a water bath). Bake very slowly at 120°C (250°F) for 8–10 hours or overnight. Remove from the oven and water bath, allow to cool completely and set in the fridge overnight.
7. When ready to serve, sit the tin in a bath of hot water for a few minutes to warm the edges (and melt the caramel sauce). Turn the flan out of the tin by placing a platter on top, then quickly flipping it. Reserve the caramel syrup, and if it's thin, you may reduce it to a sticky consistency over a gentle heat (if desired). Pour over the sliced flan to serve.

QUANDONG *and* RIBERRY SUMMER PUDDING

Sweet – 10-12 serves

This delicious and vibrant dessert is refreshing and not too sweet. Based on the traditional English 'Summer Pudding', it's actually become a family favourite for Christmas in our house as a light chilled dessert after a big Christmas lunch — so suited to our Australian summers. I add a little gelatine to the filling to help set the pudding slightly firm, just so it holds a better shape when cut, but this is optional. The natural pectin always seems to vary depending on the selection of berries used, and if they are fresh or frozen. Agar agar can be used in place of gelatine for a vegetarian option.

INGREDIENTS

pudding sides and top

½ loaf thick sliced white sandwich bread (1-2 day-old bread works best)

pudding filling

210 g (7 oz) quandong halves, (fresh or frozen)
210 g (7 oz) fresh or frozen riberries
300 g (10 oz) sugar
1 cup orange juice

3 leaves gelatine (optional) soaked for 20 minutes in ice-cold water
500 g (1 lb) raspberries
250 g (½ lb) strawberries
250 g (½ lb) blackberries or mulberries

crème fraiche or whipped cream, to serve

SUBSTITUTIONS

quandongs:
dried peaches or apricots
riberries:
try dried cranberries.

METHOD

to make the pudding sides and top

1. Line a medium pudding bowl, about 20 cm (8 in.) in diameter with kitchen film. Make sure the film overhangs the bowl edges, with at least10-15 cm (4-6 in.) of excess.
2. Cut all the crusts off the bread slices.
3. Cut one slice into a circle. This will be used to make the pudding top. Place this in the middle of the bowl's base.
4. Cut the remaining bread slices in half diagonally to produce long, wedge shapes. Arrange these (with the pointy ends overlapping the circle of bread at the base) around the sides of the bowl, pressing into place one after the other. This forms the sides of the pudding. Make sure they also overlap each other by about a centimetre (about ½ in.) each time (this adds some strength to the pudding structure).

to make the pudding filling

1. Place the quandongs, riberries, sugar and orange juice in a stainless-steel saucepan.
2. Bring to the boil, stir once, then simmer for 1-2 minutes. Turn off the heat and allow to cool, covered.
3. Once cool, remove about 5-6 tablespoons of the stewed quandongs and riberries and reserve to use as a garnish later.

4. Add the softened gelatine leaves (if using), raspberries, strawberries and blackberries to the remaining quandong and riberry mixture, then bring all to a gentle simmer. Cook for 3-4 minutes then turn off the heat.

5. Pour the fruit into a fine sieve over a bowl, to drain off and catch the juices. Allow the juices and fruit to cool a little.

6. Pour all the drained fruit filling into the bread-lined bowl, together with enough of the juice to moisten and soak into the bread. Add the remainder to the reserved fruit, as this will become your sauce and garnish.

7. Cover the top of the pudding (which will later become the base) completely with more bread slices. Now drizzle more juice over the top – it needs to be fully soaked.

8. Cover the pudding bowl with the excess kitchen film, and use more if needed so it is securely wrapped.

9. Next, place a plate (or other flat-based item, such as a saucepan) that fits the size of the pudding base perfectly. Place on top, then put all in the fridge and weigh down further with a heavy object such as a can or two of food. Chill overnight.

10. Next day, invert the pudding, out of the bowl, onto a serving platter and remove the kitchen film. Pour over the reserved juice and garnish with the reserved riberries and quandongs. If the juice has set into a light jelly, simply warm very gently before serving.

11. Serve with some crème fraiche or whipped cream.

RAINFOREST BERRY COMPÔTE

Sweet – 6 or more serves

This compôte works with pavlova, ice-cream, with cheesecake or even over yoghurt. You can vary the berries, and for more tartness use less sugar, or add a squeeze of lime or some Lemon Aspen Juice (p. 242).

INGREDIENTS

1 cup rainforest cherries
1 cup riberries
1 cup Illawarra plums, halved
1 cup davidson plums, cut into 2 cm (½ in.) diced and de-seeded
1 cup (100 g) Kakadu plums, de-seeded
1 cup apple juice
1 cinnamon quill

1.5 cups sugar

25 g (just under 1 oz) cornflour (cornstarch) or tapioca starch

* *If making a pie filling, increase the starch by a lot — double or more and adjust as needed — the compôte needs to be really thick .*

SUBSTITUTIONS

rainforest cherries:
cherries
riberries
dried cranberries
Illawarra plums
plums
davidson plums
plums
Kakadu plums
try green grapes.

METHOD

1. Bring all the fruits, apple juice and cinnamon to a gentle simmer, then cook for 5 minutes.
2. Add the sugar, stir to dissolve, and return the mixture to a gentle simmer.
3. Mix the starch together with a little water to make a smooth paste.
4. Add to the compôte, stirring to thicken, and bring briefly back to a simmer, then transfer to a storage container. Allow to chill thoroughly before use.

davidson plums

60-SECOND RIBERRY *and* RASPBERRY SORBET

Sweet – 4-6 serves

This can be whipped up in a few seconds, using a Thermomix®, to be enjoyed on its own, or paired with a heavier, richer dessert to give lovely refreshing contrast (see 'Rich Chocolate and Riberry Cake' on p. 160, and the accompanying photograph). If you don't have a Thermomix® don't despair — the sorbet can still be made in the more traditional way, even if it takes a little longer — it will be worth the effort. A little cream at the end will turn it towards an ice-cream.

INGREDIENTS

100g (3⅓ oz) sugar

1 cup (3⅓ oz) frozen riberries
⅓ cup orange juice

200g (about 1½ cups) frozen raspberries

⅓ cup cream (optional)

SUBSTITUTIONS

riberries

frozen cranberries.

METHOD

1. Using the Thermomix®, grind the sugar to a find powder on speed 9 for 10 seconds.
2. Add the riberries and juice. Process for 15 seconds, then scrape down.
3. Now add the raspberries and purée for 30 seconds on high speed, stirring with the spatula.
4. For a lovely, creamy texture, add the cream and process while stirring with the spatula for 10-20 seconds on a medium speed (speeds 4-6). You can vary the amount of cream to your liking: less cream will produce a stronger fruit flavour and a firmer texture, while more cream will give you a softer and creamier texture.

Australia's
Wild Vegetables

Warrigal spinach — *Tetragonia tetragonoides*

AUSTRALIA'S WILD VEGETABLES

Summary

This table is a summary of the notes on Australia's native and wild vegetables and is intended as a brief introduction to their use in home cooking. A list of suppliers and wild food stores is included on page 280. The table includes information about the commonly eaten parts ('edible parts'). It should be noted that some plants might include other edible parts but only those that are used in this book and tested in the recipes are listed here.

Common name	Botanical name	Edible part	Form	Preparation and use	Flavour	Sourcing
BUSH TOMATO						
bush tomato 	*Solanum centrale*	fruit	dried	*Small amounts of the whole dried fruit can be added to slow-cooked or baked foods for intense bursts of flavour. It can also be ground to make an intense savoury spice (see 'Bush Tomato', on p. 37). It is not usually available fresh.*	*Robust flavours reminiscent of tamarillo and sun-dried tomatoes. It is quite strong — but 'moreish' — and only small amounts are used.*	*The dried fruit (whole or powder) is available through various native food stores and on-line suppliers.*
THE SUCCULENTS						
samphire seablite karkalla  *samphire*  *seablite*  *karkalla*	*Sarcocornia spp.* *Suaeda australis* *Disphyma crassifolium*	leaves	fresh	*Australia's succulents hold water in their stems and leaves to enable their survival in dry conditions. They are generally best eaten when they are young, fresh or cooked, as they tend to become 'woody' as they mature.*	*All the succulents have crisp, fleshy textures that soften on cooking, along with 'briney', salty flavours, and samphire is said to develop an asparagus-like flavour on cooking.*	*The fresh leaves are available through various native food stores and on-line suppliers. Some suppliers and stores also offer frozen succulents.*

Common name	Botanical name	Edible part	Form	Preparation and use	Flavour	Sourcing
WARRIGAL SPINACH						
warrigal spinach  *warrigal spinach*	*Tetragonia tetragonoides*	leaves and stalks	fresh	*Warrigal spinach grown in lush, well-watered conditions is fine to eat raw in salads; otherwise, it may need to be blanched briefly before use. It can also be wilted, steamed or stir-fried, and used as a side dish or in pies and other dishes in the same way as spinach.*	*This vegetable has a grassy, spinach-like flavour and texture that becomes mildly and pleasantly bitter upon chewing.*	*Available fresh through various stores and on-line suppliers. Warrigal spinach is also suitable for growing in a home vegetable garden.*
WILD CELERY						
wild celery  *wild celery*	*Apium insulare* *Apium annuum*	leaves, stalks	fresh	*The leaves and stalks can be eaten raw, in salads and juices, but is also used in cooking in the same way as conventional celery. The stalks tend to be quite thin and can become tough, so younger leaves and stems are best for consumption.*	*This vegetable has a strong, celery flavour and some bitterness.*	*Available from native food stores and on-line suppliers. Dried conventional celery is often used as a seasoning but dried wild celery is not yet readily available.*

AUSTRALIA'S WILD VEGETABLES

Warrigal spinach, karkalla (beach bananas), samphire and native celery are just some of the nutritious and flavoursome vegetables that grow in the wilds, on land and even in the seas, of Australia. Additionally, bush tomato, a fruit, is regarded here (like tomatoes) for culinary purposes as a vegetable. They each contain various vitamins and minerals, and some are also good sources of protein and carbohydrate. Most have helped sustain Indigenous Australians for thousands of years. Two other vegetables include old man saltbush, used as both a vegetable and a herb, and sea parsley, used mainly as a herb. Both are discussed in the Herbs and Spices section (starting on p. 31).

Bush Tomatoes

The type discussed below, *Solanum centrale* (also known as the 'desert raisin') needs to ripen then dry naturally on the bush before consumption. There is at least one other variety that is eaten fresh. All told, there are over 100 species of bush tomatoes but, importantly, only a small number are edible.

Bush tomato — *Solanum centrale*

The bush tomato, once dry, develops a strong, slightly sweet and tangy flavour, reminiscent of sun-dried tomatoes and tamarillo but, after an initial caramel-like sweetness – which, along with its size, texture and colour, accounts for its comparison to a raisin – may tend towards bitterness on the finish. A little goes a long way, so it should be used sparingly so the bitter notes don't dominate. It has been a staple food of Indigenous Australians for thousands of years, who are said to have gathered the dried tomatoes before grinding them into a powder and mixing that with water to form a paste. From the paste, patty-like balls were formed and allowed to 'bake' in the hot sun. Containing their own natural preservatives, including Vitamin C, they were then stored in caches (in tree forks and cavities and the like), for later use. Young fruits on the shrub grow up to 1-2 cm (¾in) in diameter, changing in colour from a green to a creamy yellow when ripe. As they dry, they shrink to almost half their original size, causing the flavours to intensify, while developing a chewy, raisin-like, texture and changing to a dark brown in colour. They add intense bursts of flavour to slow-cooked or baked foods, including soups and casseroles, as well as sauces and other condiments. Nutritionally, they are a good source of carbohydrate, protein and potassium, and they also contain Vitamin C (a powerful antioxidant, among other benefits) and various other phyo- (plant) nutrients. As well as their use as a dried, whole vegetable, they are also ground to make a richly coloured and intensely flavoured spice, known by various Indigenous names, including 'akudjura' (see p. 37).

bush tomato

'Bush tomato (of the true tomato family) is intensely flavoured and nutritious — it is used mostly like a spice.

bush tomatoes and dried ground bush tomato powder

The Succulents

Australia is home to hundreds of 'succulents', plants that store water, usually in their stems and leaves, to enable their survival in semi-arid or dry conditions when water is scarce – although they are also found in wetlands and tidal coast areas. Many can be eaten as tasty vegetables, raw or cooked, with the crisp outer leaf or stem giving way to fleshy and briney interiors. Three are discussed below: karkalla, samphire, and sea blight.

samphire

Samphire – *Sarcocornia spp.*

Some other curious names for this succulent include 'chicken claws' and 'beaded glasswort', and the reason soon becomes clear: it comprises leafless stems of a green or dark-reddish colour, generally 10-20 cm (6-9 in) tall, 3-4 mm (about an eighth of an inch) in diameter, and segmented, to appear beaded or, less attractively, to resemble chicken claws. It is also called 'sea asparagus'. Raw, it has a crisp, fleshy texture and sea-salty, mineral-like flavour. On cooking, it becomes soft and develops a more subtle salty asparagus-like flavour. It is best to use the younger stem tips, as the older stems develop a woody core. It contains many minerals (magnesium, potassium, calcium, and sodium), vitamins (A, B, and C), and various antioxidants.

Seablite – *Suaeda australis*

Seablite, although a herb, is eaten as a vegetable, raw or cooked. In colonial times, the edible leaves, which grow up to 4 cm (about 1½ in.) in length, were used as a vegetable or a pickle. Like other succulents, they have a crisp exterior and a watery flesh that softens when cooked – steamed or sautéed – to make a naturally salty accompaniment to other fare. Not surprisingly, given its origins, it pairs well with seafood.

Small amounts of raw seablight can be added to salads, in place of capers, to add some salty bursts. It's high in

seablight

iodine and, given its salty flavour, it can be assumed to also contain sodium. Although subject to further research, it is likely to have antioxidants as well as a wide variety of vitamins and minerals, similar to those of other succulents.

Karkalla – *Disphyma crassifolium*

Also known as 'beach bananas' (because of the young, green or reddish leaf clusters, shaped a bit like a small hand of bananas), or 'round-leaf pigface' (due to its horned, deep-pink fruit), both the fruit and the leaves have long been part of traditional Indigenous diets. They're a source of antioxidants and carbohydrates, and have been used in traditional medicine as an antiseptic. Other succulents are also called 'karkalla', but *D. crassifolium* is preferred for the crisp yet fleshy texture and salty flavours of the its leaves. They can be enjoyed raw in salads, or quickly sautéed, blanched or steamed, and served without added salt.

right: karkalla

samphire

Warrigal Spinach

It is said that warrigal spinach is the only Australian native vegetable to be cultivated internationally although, traditionally, it was rarely eaten by Indigenous Australians.

Warrigal spinach — *Tetragonia tetragonoides*

Warrigal spinach (or 'greens') has a spinach-like texture and a grassy flavour that becomes mildly and pleasantly bitter upon chewing. Its nutritional properties were highly valued in colonial times, and it was used by Captain Cook to ward off scurvy among his crew. It contains protein as well as vitamins A, B, and C, and the minerals magnesium, calcium, phosphorous and potassium. Its green colouring indicates the presence of antioxidants. It is eaten in much the same way as conventional spinach: the delicate, crescent-shaped leaves are wilted, steamed, or stir-fried as a vegetable; used as a filling in pies; and added to various salads. Warrigal spinach grown in lush, well-watered conditions is also fine to eat raw, but otherwise might need brief blanching and rinsing before consumption. Bower spinach is a close relative (they are both of the same genus *Tetragonia*) with very similar properties, and can be used in place of warrigal spinach. They are both suitable for growing in home vegetable gardens.

warrigal spinach

Wild Celery

Celery grows in many places around the globe, both as a cultivated crop and in the wild. Perhaps the most widespread, *Apium graveolens*, or simply 'celery', originated in the Levant and southern Europe thousands of years ago. Australia's wild celeries include 'Flinders Island celery' (*A. insulare* and 'annual celery' (*A. annuum).*

Wild celery — *Apium insulare, Apium annuum*

Wild celery is quite different to the cultivated crop, and tends to have thinner and tougher stalks and to be a lot smaller overall. It has an intense celery-and-parsley like flavour, stronger than cultivated and conventional celery, and may also be bitter, depending on the growing conditions. Yet, it is highly nutritious and has a long history in traditional medicine around the world, with all parts of the plant – including bulb, stems, leaves, and seeds – being used in this way. For culinary purposes, the focus is on the fresh leaves and stalks, although they and the seeds can also be dried to make celery-flavoured seasonings. The presence of antioxidants in conventional celery (*Apium graveolens*) is well documented and, while subject to further research, it can reasonably be assumed that they are also present in Australia's native celery. Both the fresh leaves and stalks can be used in salads, in a mirepoix, or juiced. As a juice, celery pairs well with cucumber, carrot, apple, and mint, to make a cooling and refreshing beverage.

wild celery

wild celery

BUSH TOMATO ROUILLE

Accompaniment – makes 12-15 serves

This is my version of the classic emulsion sauce from Provence in France, often served with bouillabaisse (see my recipe on p. 71). It is rich and pungent and goes so well with the bush tomato flavour, and can also be used on sandwiches and wraps, or as a dip with crudites (raw vegetables).

INGREDIENTS

6 egg yolks

pinch of saffron threads

50 g (1⅔ oz) dried bush tomatoes

50 g (1⅔ oz) tomato paste
5-6 garlic cloves peeled and chopped
75 ml (2½ fl oz) lemon juice
30 g (1 oz) red chillies
30 g (1 oz) dijon mustard
30 g (1 oz) anchovy fillets
pinch of saffron threads
⅓ tsp pepper, ground
1 heaped tsp cooking salt

450 ml (15 fl oz) extra virgin olive oil

METHOD

1. Place three of the egg yolks in a small ceramic dish and cover with kitchen film. Microwave for 20-30 seconds until just set, like hard-boiled eggs. Allow to cool.
2. Cover the saffron threads with a couple of teaspoons of boiling water. Allow to sit for at least 10 minutes.
3. Grind or chop the bush tomatoes to a coarse kibble.
4. In a blender or Thermomix®, process all the ingredients except for the oil into a smooth purée.
5. Slowly drizzle in the olive oil while still blending, to form a smooth emulsion.

SUBSTITUTIONS

dried bush tomatoes:
sun-dried tomatoes.

SMOKY BUSH TOMATO SHAKSHOUKA

Light - 4-6 serves

This richly flavoured and satisfying light meal is based on the tantalising tomato-and-egg shakshoukas of the Mediterranean, Middle East and Africa. In my version, the traditional flavours are perfectly complemented by pepperleaf and bush tomatoes, to give a uniquely Australian twist. I enjoy it most when served as a breakfast on a chilly winter morning camping or houseboating on the River Murray overlooking magnificent ochre-coloured cliffs in the sweet light.

INGREDIENTS

sauce

30 ml (1 fl oz) extra virgin olive oil
1 small spanish onion, peeled and chopped into 1 cm (½ in.) approx. chunks
2-3 garlic cloves, finely chopped
1 red capsicum

eggs

3 cups passata, or about 800 g (1¾ lb) tinned chopped tomatoes (for a chunkier sauce)
2 heaped tsp chopped dried bush tomatoes
1 tsp salt
2½ tsp raw sugar
1 tsp dried pepperleaf
2 heaped tsp best quality Spanish smoked paprika

2 eggs per person

* *There are many cheap 'smoked' paprikas in Australian supermarkets - stay clear of these and buy the genuine Spanish type.*

SUBSTITUTIONS

ground pepperleaf:
pepper, freshly ground

sea parsley:
flat-leaf (continental) or curly parsley.

METHOD

to prepare the rich sauce

1. Using a large, non-stick frypan with a tight-fitting lid, gently heat the oil and fry the onion, garlic and capsicum for 3-5 minutes, stirring often until softened but not coloured. The onion should be almost translucent.
2. Add the passata (or tinned tomatoes, if using), together with the bush tomatoes, salt, sugar, smoked paprika and pepperleaf.
3. Bring to a simmer and cook gently for 5-10 minutes to reduce the sauce to a nice, thick consistency. Adjust seasoning to taste.

to poach the eggs

4. While the sauce is still slowly simmering, gently break in the eggs then cover with the lid. Allow the eggs to slowly poach for 5-6 minutes, until cooked to your liking (soft or firm).
5. Serve on crusty toasted ciabatta or wood-fired bread, sprinkled with chopped sea parsley.

OPTIONS

1. For a meaty version, brown-off some diced or sliced chorizo sausage in the olive oil before adding the onion and other vegetables.
2. To bring on the heat, add some chillies when frying.
3. Another option is to include a handful of warrigal spinach (see p. 176) when adding the eggs.

GRILLED HALOUMI *with* ASPARAGUS, CHERRY TOMATOES *and* BUSH TOMATO BALSAMIC

Light – 4 serves

My family love this dish, and ever since the sticky bush tomato balsamic was developed at the Red Ochre in the '90s it's been in our home pantry. It's great drizzled all over many grilled foods, but pairs especially well with this 'squeaky cheese' (as my kids used to call it when young).

INGREDIENTS

- 240 g (8 oz) haloumi (about 60 g / 2 oz per serve)
- 1 punnet of cherry tomatoes, assorted colours
- 2 bunches of asparagus
- ⅓ cup extra virgin olive oil
- ground pepperberry, to taste
- 4 tbs Creative Native Bush Tomato Balsamic Vinegar
- a few sprigs of fresh baby rivermint leaves, fresh, to garnish
- vegetable oil (for oiling the grill)

SUBSTITUTIONS

Creative Native Bush Tomato Balsamic: other caramelized balsamic vinegar

ground pepperberry: ground black pepper

rivermint: mint.

METHOD

1. First, pre-heat your very clean char-grill (see instructions for cleaning on p. 23).
2. Cut the haloumi into thick 1-1.5 cm (about ½ in.) slices.
3. If you like, cut the larger cherry tomatoes in half while keeping the smaller ones whole.
4. Trim off the lowest third of the asparagus with a neat diagonal cut of each stalk.
5. Place the haloumi, cherry tomatoes, and asparagus on a tray and brush with some olive oil. Grind black pepper or pepperberry over the top.
6. As it's quite a lot to grill at once, start with the asparagus and tomatoes. Grill for two minutes or so, to give them lovely char-grill markings, turning once or twice. Once ready, put to the side and cover with foil for a couple of minutes while you prepare to grill the haloumi next.
7. Clean down the grill again with an oiled cloth or paper towel. This is critical to stop the haloumi from sticking.
8. Grill the haloumi on one side. If you want, rotate it by about 45 degrees, just once, after the first 30-40 seconds, to give lovely criss-cross markings. Repeat on the other side (it should only need 1-2 minutes per side).
9. Plate up the asparagus and tomatoes, top with the grilled haloumi and drizzle generously with more extra virgin olive oil and the caramelized balsamic.
10. Finish off with a few rivermint leaves. Adding fresh grapes or rocket (aragula) are also fabulous options.

WARRIGAL SPINACH *and* SALTBUSH GOZLEMES

Light – 4 serves

Gozlemes are a delicacy of Turkey made from layers of dough rolled out until paper-thin, folded, then rolled out again a number of times, to make the delicious pastry. They have flavoursome fillings of (usually green) vegetables, cheeses, herbs and spices, as well as meatier versions made with minced or chopped beef, lamb, or even seafood. They are usually grilled or fried on a hotplate. This Australian vegetarian version uses warrigal spinach along with the fresh flavours of rivermint, lemon myrtle, pepperleaf and saltbush.

INGREDIENTS

dough

- 3 cups unbleached plain flour, plus extra for dusting
- 1 cup wholemeal flour
- 1 tsp salt
- 50g (1⅔ oz) vegetable oil
- 1-1½ cups water, luke warm

filling

- 4 tsp extra virgin olive oil
- ½ small brown onion, peeled and diced
- 2 cups warrigal spinach leaves, chopped coarsely and with large stems removed
- 1 cup fresh picked saltbush leaves

- ½ cup fresh rivermint leaves, chopped
- ½ cup sea parsley, chopped
- ½ cup spring onion, chopped
- 200g (7 oz) grated feta (or a mix of feta, haloumi, and cheddar, according to taste)
- 1 tsp ground pepperleaf
- ½ tsp allspice
- 1 tsp ground lemon myrtle

METHOD

to prepare the dough

1. Ideally, make the dough a day ahead. It needs to sit, covered, for several hours (at least 8-10) before cooking.
2. Using an electric mixer with a dough hook, mix together the flours, salt, vegetable oil and just 1¼ cups of the water. If you prefer, you can knead the mixture by hand for about 5-10 minutes.
3. If the mixture becomes too dry, add a little more water, just a few drops at a time, until you get a very soft, elastic dough that's not too sticky to handle.

to make the filling

4. Heat the olive oil in a large frypan and quickly sauté the onion, spinach, and saltbush for 3-4 minutes to wilt, then remove immediately.
5. Spread out on a tray and place in the refrigerator to quickly cool.
6. Once cooled, stir through all the remaining ingredients.

SUBSTITUTIONS

warrigal spinach:
spinach and / or kale
saltbush:
spinach or kale
rivermint leaves:
mint
sea parsley:
flat-leaf (continental) parsley
ground pepperleaf:
pepper
ground lemon myrtle:
zest of a lemon.

a

b

c

d

e

f

g

h

above: making the gozlemes

a. *flouring the workbench*

b. *rolling out the rested dough into a large square*

c. *the rolled-out square*

d. *brushing the rolled-out square with olive oil*

e. *adding the filling and beginning to fold the pastry*

f. *brushing the filled, partially folded pastry with olive oil*

g. *forming rectangular parcels before cutting into triangles*

h. *the cooked gozleme, served with lemon.*

to assemble the gozleme (see photographs on facing page)

1. Dust a kitchen bench with flour (a), then divide the dough into 6 equal balls.
2. Using a rolling pin, roll each one into a flat, square shape as large and thin as possible (b and c). Make sure you use plenty of extra dusting flour to ensure they don't stick.
3. Brush half the square with oil (d) then fold it in half to form a rectangle, with the oil on the inside.
4. Now brush half the rectangle with oil, fold again (keeping the oiled side on the inside), into a smaller square.
5. Repeat the above steps one or two more times, each time dusting and rolling out the smaller square into a large, thin piece, then folding it back down to a small square (it's a bit like making puff pastry where layers of oil are 'laminated' between the sheets of pastry). Allow it to rest and repeat with the remaining 5 balls of dough.
6. Now roll the smaller squares out once more into one large, thin piece each. You should end up with 6 large, roughly square pieces of pastry, each one as thin as possible.
7. Sprinkle a layer of filling about 1 cm (¼ in.) thick towards the lower centre of each large square (e). There should be plenty of pastry left on the sides to fold over the filling.
8. Brush the exposed pastry with oil (f), then fold over the two sides to cover the filling, then fold up to form tidy parcels or 'envelopes' (g).
9. Using a large, clean barbecue scraper or a pizza paddle, lift each gozleme and place on a pre-heated, moderately hot, barbecue hotplate or in a large non-stick frypan. Watch the temperature carefully so that the gozlemes don't burn. They should take 4–5 minutes on each side to cook, but it's all about good heat control to get that lovely golden brown crust.
10. To serve, slide the gozlemes onto a chopping board and cut into smaller triangle wedges, if desired. Serve with lemon wedges.

BUSH TOMATO BUTTER CHICKEN

Main – 6-8 serves

The best curries are made from freshly ground spices, but that takes time so I like to double the sauce and freeze any excess. Great food can then be ready in a flash: just defrost the sauce, cook the chicken, and add yoghurt last. For a vegetarian option, use potato, pumpkin, and carrot instead of chicken. Be warned, though: this curry won't have the same vivid colour common in restaurants because I use fresh ingredients, no colourings.

INGREDIENTS

spice powder

6 tsp coriander seeds
5 tsp cumin seeds
1 tsp black peppercorns
2½ tsp ground black cardamon
5 cloves
2-3 cinnamon sticks

curry

150 g (5 oz) ghee (or butter)

200 g (7 oz) onions, peeled and diced
45 g (1½ oz) fresh ginger, grated
1 large red chilli, finely chopped
8-10 garlic cloves, peeled and chopped
3 tsp smoked paprika
2 tsp turmeric
5 large red capsicums
2¼ tsp fenugreek leaves, crumbled

400 g (14 oz) whole tomatoes, peeled
4 tsp salt
45 g (1½ oz) sugar, or to taste

30 g (1 oz) dried bush tomatoes, chopped
2 cups cream
45 g (1½ oz) almond or cashew meal.
1.2 kg (2 lb) chicken thigh meat, skin off diced into 2 cm (½ in.) pieces
coriander (cilantro), to garnish (optional)
sliced chilli, to garnish (optional)
½ cup plain yoghurt

SUBSTITUTIONS

dry bush tomato:
semi-dried tomatoes.

METHOD

to prepare the spice powder

1. Line a baking tray with baking paper, then sprinkle over the coriander and cumin seeds, peppercorns, cardamon, cloves, and cinnamon sticks. Dry-roast in a 170°C (340°F) oven for 8 minutes or until lightly toasted. Keep an eye on them and remove from the oven if they start to over-cook.
2. Grind to a fine powder using a grinder or mortar-and-pestle.

to make the curry

3. Heat the ghee in a hot frypan. Add the onions, ginger, chilli, garlic, paprika, turmeric, capsicum (diced), and fenungreek. Gently fry for 8-10 minutes, stirring often and without browning, then mix through the spice powder.
4. Add the tomatoes, salt, and sugar. Simmer for 5-10 minutes. If you like, you can now purée the sauce if you prefer a silky, smooth texture, or you can leave it a little chunky.
5. Add the bush tomato, cream and nut meal and bring the sauce to the boil. Check the seasoning, and adjust to taste At this point, you can freeze some sauce for later use.
6. Add the diced chicken, cover the pan, and keep it on the boil for about 1 minute. Turn off, and leave covered for 8-10 minutes. The latent heat will continue to cook the chicken in the most relaxed fashion, and you will end up with a superbly moist and tender meat, perfectly cooked.
7. Bring back to a simmer to warm, stir through the yoghurt and serve with steamed rice.

BUSH TOMATO *and* WILD BASIL RATATOUILLE BAKE

Side – 4-6 serves

Ratatouille originated in the south of France, although vegetable stews of this type have long been popular throughout the Mediterranean. It makes a superb vegetarian dish and looks spectacular when laid out as a meal to be shared, along with fresh crusty baguettes and salad, or as an accompaniment to a main meal.

INGREDIENTS

½ cup extra virgin olive oil
2 spanish onions, peeled and chopped into 5-10 mm (¼-½ in.) pieces
4 cloves garlic, peeled and crushed

700 ml (1¼ pints) passata
30 ml (1 fl oz) Creative Native Bush Tomato Balsamic
¼ cup bush tomatoes, chopped
½ tsp wild thyme
1½ tsp salt
4 tsp brown sugar

2 small red capsicums
2 small yellow capsicums
3 zucchinis
2 young, shiny eggplants

spray olive oil

2-3 tsp wild basil
½ cup panko breadcrumbs
2-3 tbs good quality Italian parmesan

SUBSTITUTIONS

Creative Native Bush Tomato Balsamic:
other caramelized balsamic vinegar
bush tomatoes:
sun-dried tomatoes
wild thyme:
thyme
wild basil
basil.

METHOD

1. Heat about 2 teaspoons of oil in a large frypan and gently fry the onions and garlic until the onions are translucent.
2. Add the passata, balsamic vinegar, bush tomatoes, thyme, salt and sugar. Simmer for 5-10 minutes.
3. Halve and de-seed the capsicums and cut them into long, chunky strips. Cut the zucchini into quarters length-wise (if they are long you can first cut them in half, width-wise). Slice the eggplant into 2 cm (½ in.) thick rings (young eggplants will not need salting to remove the bitterness).
4. Heat the remaining olive oil then pan-fry the eggplant until golden-brown on both sides. It will soak up lots of oil.
5. Choose an enamelled baking dish that's nice enough to serve at the table. Spray with olive oil, then arrange the vegetables in beautiful coloured rows inside.
6. Crush the basil over the vegetables, then spoon the sauce over the entire dish. Sprinkle over the breadcrumbs and grated parmesan, then spray with olive oil for extra gloss.
7. Bake in a pre-heated 180°C (355°F) oven for 45-50 minutes, then serve immediately. I love to give it one more final drizzle of olive oil just as I bring it to the table.

WARRIGAL SPINACH SPANAKOPITA PIES

Light – 8 serves

This is my unique version of the classic Greek dish, presented as spectacular open, individual pies, and I love the chunky, rustic filling (rather than a smooth, puréed filling). Cooking the filo pastry shells blind (empty) first, before adding the filling, gives a superb, crunchy-textured pie.

INGREDIENTS

filling

30 ml (1 fl oz) olive oil
30 g (1 oz) butter

500 g (1 lb) approx. warrigal (or bower) spinach leaves, rinsed

5 eggs
¼ tsp ground nutmeg
½ tsp ground pepperleaf
150 g (5 oz) feta, crumbled

100 g (3⅓ oz) ricotta
1 cup hard cheese, finely grated (e.g. parmesan, kefalograviera, pecorino)
½ cup panko breadcrumbs
4 spring onions, finely sliced

pie shells

butter (for greasing pie shells)
125 g (¼ lb) warm melted butter
375 g (12½ oz) packet of filo pastry

* *See overleaf for substitutions.*

METHOD

to prepare the filling

1. Begin by preparing the filling. In a very large frypan, heat the olive oil and butter until foaming and just starting to turn a nut-brown in colour.
2. Immediately drop in the spinach and stir-fry it so that it wilts. As soon as it has wilted, transfer it to a large tray and spread it out, to cool it quickly. You can place it in the refrigerator for a few minutes to speed this up.
3. Next, in a large bowl, whip the eggs together with the nutmeg and pepperleaf until smooth, then fold in the cheeses, breadcrumbs, and spring onions.
4. Fold through the cooled spinach and mix through evenly.

to make the pie shells

1. Pre-heat the oven to 160°C (320°F).
2. Lightly butter 6-8 individual ramekins.
3. Fold a long strip of silicone baking paper over to about 2.5 cm (1 in.) in width. Lay this across the bottom and up and over the edges of each ramekin (see below). The strips will form 'handles' that you can use to lift each pie out of the ramekins once they are cooked.

4. Brush half the first sheet of filo pastry with butter and fold it in half. Brush half the surface again, then fold in half again. Repeat this procedure to get down to one eighth of the size. Line the base of the ramekin with this folded filo, to form the pie base (see previous page), then repeat for the remaining ramekins.

5. Next, work on the pie edges. Brush a new sheet of filo with butter and place on top a second sheet. Brush the top again with more butter, then cut roughly into eighths.

6. Working one piece at a time, gently crumple and place each piece, upright, along the circular inside edge of the ramekin, while leaving excess pastry at the top to form a random, crumpled edge, like a petal of a flower. Repeat this and work your way around the inner edge of the ramekin, making sure you overlap each 'petal' over the next, gently pressing the lower edges into the pastry base, to properly complete the pie shell (with no gaps). Don't worry about perfection; it's meant to have a random, abstract look (see previous page).

7. Press firmly in the centre of the pastry base to compact it, while leaving the edges light and airy.

8. Repeat to finish all the remaining ramekins.

9. Bake the filo pie shells blind (empty) in the pre-heated oven for about 40 minutes, until completely dry and a very light golden brown. Remove from the oven.

10. Carefully spoon the filling into the pre-cooked pie shell, then bake for a further 25–30 minutes, still at 160°C (320°F). until the filling is set, but without browning the pastry much more.

11. Remove from the oven and use the baking-paper strips to lift each pie out of its ramekin mould. Serve immediately, ideally with a crisp garden salad dressed with Creative Native Bush Tomato Balsamic Vinegar and a very good extra virgin olive oil.

SUBSTITUTIONS

warrigal spinach:
spinach, kale, or mix of both
ground pepperleaf:
pepper, freshly ground
Creative Native Bush Balsamic Vinegar:
other caramelized balsamic vinegar.

ROAST BUSH TOMATO BALSAMIC SPANISH ONIONS

Side – 4-6 serves

Serve cold on antipasto platters, or hot as a superb accompaniment for grilled or roasted meats. For an indulgent, more substantial, vegetarian dish, sprinkle Persian feta pieces over the top, and/or add charred multi-coloured cherry tomatoes — both work a treat. Be sure to use clean, well-shaped smaller onions for this recipe as the skin is left on for a rustic look.

INGREDIENTS

500g (1 lb) small-to-medium sized spanish onions, with the clean, inner skins left on and the outer, loose skins removed

¼ cup extra virgin olive oil
2 tsp brown sugar
1 heaped tsp salt
½ tsp ground pepperberries
½ tsp dried wild thyme
¼ cup Creative Native Bush Tomato Balsamic Vinegar
½ tsp dried wild thyme

1 tsp ground dried bush tomato (optional)

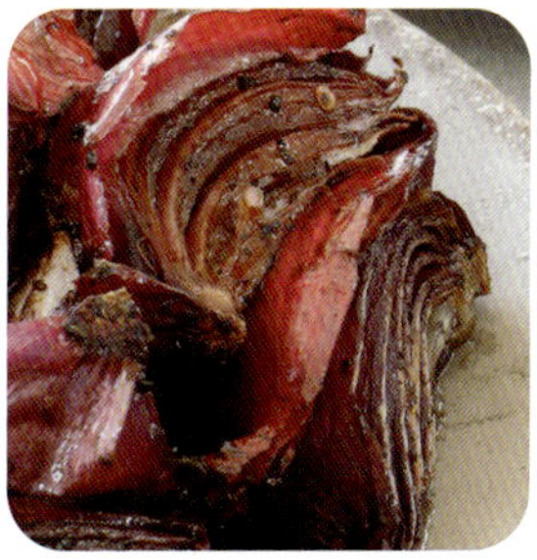

METHOD

1. Carefully trim the onion core of excess roots. Cut each unpeeled onion through the core – base to top – into quarters or sixths, depending on the onion size. Try to keep each piece intact at the base (there should be enough core left to hold the onion together) so they don't break up into smaller pieces.
2. Line a roasting tray with baking paper.
3. Spread the onions out in the tray.
4. Sprinkle the olive oil, sugar, salt, pepperberry, thyme and balsamic vinegar over the top, then gently mix through the onions.
5. Roast in a pre-heated oven at 160-170°C (320-340°F) for 45-60 minutes, until they darken and caramelize. Stir and gently turn them over occasionally.
6. Remove from the oven and sprinkle the ground bush tomato over the top (if using). Stir through, and allow the onions to cool. The juices should become syrupy and coat the onion pieces nicely as they cool.

SUBSTITUTIONS

ground pepperberries: ground pepper
dried wild thyme: thyme.
dried ground bush tomato: sun-dried tomatoes
Creative Native Bush Tomato Balsamic Vinegar: other caramelized balsamic vinegar.

63°C EGGS WITH *with* BROWN BUTTER BEACH SUCCULENTS

Light – 4 serves

This style of 'poaching' an egg has become quite popular in cafes and restaurants in recent years. It produces an extraordinarily textured yolk and white, but takes time to cook (at least an hour) at exactly 63°C (145°F). A sous vide cooker is needed to achieve this critical level of accuracy. There are a few brands perfect for home cooks (I like to use an Anova®). Generally, sous vide cookers 'poach' vacuum-sealed meats, fish, vegetables, and all sorts of ingredients in a water bath, using precisely controlled, slow, gentle heat. They produce outstanding results once the technique is mastered (see notes on p. 21). But, if you don't have one, you can still enjoy this dish by substituting good old 'ordinary' poached eggs.

INGREDIENTS

8 free-range eggs

4 generous handfuls, about 270 g (9 oz) of samphire or other beach succulents such as karkalla or seablite

8 slices of crusty baguette or sourdough bread

2 tsp unsalted butter per person

black pepper, freshly ground.

SUBSTITUTIONS

samphire and other succulents:
spinach, kale, asparagus.

METHOD

1. Place your sous vide cooker in a pot of hot water and set to 63°C (145°F) exactly. Once the temperature is reached, use a slotted spoon to carefully lower in the eggs. They will take an hour to cook, but equally will hold perfectly for another 30 minutes or so at the correct temperature, so you can't really over-cook them.
2. Be sure to trim the samphire (or other beach succulents) of any hard stems and to thoroughly rinse them clean.
3. Shortly before serving, pop the bread in the toaster or on the grill and, while it is crisping up, heat the butter in a frypan until the foaming subsides and the butter starts to go a deep golden colour ('beurre noisette' or 'brown butter'). Quickly toss in the samphire and stir-fry for 30–40 seconds to warm through. Season with pepper.
4. Arrange the buttery succulents on plates in small piles or 'nests' (two per plate). Gently crack an egg (the egg and yolk should stay intact). Serve immediately with the crusty toasted or grilled bread.

GOOLWA PIPPIES *with* GARLIC CREAM *and* BEACH SUCCULENTS

Light - 4 serves

I first had this style dish in France, very memorable. But that memory faded very quickly after eating this dish with friends Rob and Michelle, on Kangaroo Island. We harvested the pippies from the bay and foraged the amazing Kangaroo Island samphire and sea blight from their seafront home, then a glass of local white and views over the bay at sunset . . . bliss.

INGREDIENTS

375 ml (12½ fl oz) or half a bottle of good dry white wine such as riesling or sauvignon blanc
10-12 garlic cloves, peeled and crushed

2½ cups cream

2 additional large garlic cloves, peeled
8 slices of your favourite sourdough baguette

4 tsp extra virgin olive oil
2 tsp butter

1 kg (2 lb) approx. fresh Goolwa pippies (or other clams/molluscs)
1 heaped cup of fresh assorted beach succulents, such as seablite, karkalla and samphire (just the young tips and leaves, no hard wood stems)
½ cup freshly chopped sea parsley

SUBSTITUTIONS

beach succulents:
salt-seasoned asparagus spears
sea parsley:
flat-leaf (continental) parsley.

METHOD

1. Simmer the wine and the garlic in a wide frypan over medium to high heat, until the volume has reduced down to about 50 ml (1⅔ fl oz) of syrupy essence. While doing this, it's very important to make sure the flame does not reach up the side of the pan and burn the syrup at the edges.
2. Once reduced, add the cream. Simmer again for about 8-10 minutes until it has reduced by half (or to about 1¼ cups). The sauce should now be getting a little thick. Meanwhile, pre-heat your clean char-grill on high.
3. Cut the additional garlic cloves in half and rub them generously over the bread slices.
4. Gently warm the olive oil and butter until the butter has just melted. Brush this over the bread.
5. Add the pippies to the sauce and cover with a tight-fitting lid. Bring to a rapid boil over a high heat, to generate the steam to cook them (this will only take 3-4 minutes). Just when the first few shells are starting to open, toss in the succulents to warm them through.
6. Simmer for a few seconds more, then turn off the heat. Leave the lid on, and allow the latent heat to complete the cooking process. This should only take another 2-3 minutes. (Many people cook shellfish for too long I think, forgetting to allow for continued cooking from latent heat.)
7. Grill the bread on the char-grill until golden brown on both sides. If your timing is right, the pippies should be super moist, relaxed and succulent just as the bread is grilled.
8. Use a large spoon to serve up the shellfish and the broth into four wide bowls. Sprinkle with parsley and serve with the crusty garlic bread to mop up all that superb sauce.

Australia's
Wild Nuts *and* Seeds

Macadamia — *Macadamia spp.*

AUSTRALIA'S WILD NUTS *and* SEEDS

Summary

This table is a summary of the notes on some of Australia's native and wild nuts and seeds used in my book and is intended as a brief introduction to their use in home cooking. A list of suppliers and wild food stores is included on page 280. The table includes information about the commonly eaten parts ('edible parts'). It should be noted that some plants might include other edible parts but only those that are used in this book and tested in the recipes are listed here.

Common name	Botanical name	Edible part	Form	Preparation and use	Flavour	Sourcing
BUNYA NUTS						
bunya nuts 	*Araucaria bidwillii*	the white 'nut meat'	dried, fresh, or frozen seed (nut)	*These are the edible seeds of the bunya bunya pine. The 'nut meat' is found inside the hard outer casing, which is removed (along with the thin brown seed coat) before eating. They can also be eaten raw or boiled; they may also be roasted but tend to dry and toughen and also easily burn.*	*Eaten raw, their texture compares to chestnut: dry and chewy and slightly sweet with a potato-chestnut-like flavour. When cooked, they become waxier in texture and more subtly flavoured.*	*The nuts are available from native food stores and on-line suppliers.*
KURRAJONG SEEDS						
kurrajong seeds 	*Brachychiton populneus*	the seed	dried seed and flour	*These seeds are found inside the pods of the kurrajong tree. They are covered in fine hairs that need to be removed before roasting and eating. They are not eaten raw.*	*Once roasted, the hard-shell coating becomes brittle, and the inner seed a lovely rich nutty brown with a floury texture and flavour.*	*The seeds and ground flour are available from native food stores and on-line suppliers.*
MACADAMIA NUTS						
macadamia nuts 	*Macadamia spp.*	the 'nut meat'	dried seed (nut)	*The nuts are found inside an extremely tough outer shell. Both the shell and thin seed coat are removed before eating. The nuts can be eaten raw, but are definitely most delicious when roasted and seasoned.*	*A buttery-crisp texture with a slightly sweet and mild nutty flavour.*	*Widely available in supermarkets and other food stores as well as through on-line suppliers.*
			oil		*Macadamia oil is excellent for frying but is also used in salad dressings.*	

Common name	Botanical name	Edible part	Form	Preparation and use	Flavour	Sourcing
SANDALWOOD NUTS						
sandalwood nuts 	*Santalum spicatum*	the 'nut meat'	dried seed (nut)	*Like all nuts, these need to be released from their hard outer casing. Their fine brown seed coat is left intact and eaten. They may be eaten raw, but light roasting enhances the very subtle flavour.*	*Their texture is creamy with a soft crunch, and once roasted they have a mild nutty flavour with subtle, unique 'medicinal' notes*	*Available through various stores and on-line suppliers.*
WATTLESEED (ACACIA SEEDS)						
wattleseed 	*Acacia spp.*	whole seed	dried seeds	*Wattleseeds are generally quickly roasted before used. Once roasted, they can be used like a grain (after softening in liquid) in risottos, salads, breads, and other dishes, or ground into a flour. Wattleseeds can also be sprouted, to produce sprouts that are similar in appearance to alfalfa sprouts and used in salads, or sprouted then toasted to produce flavoursome malted, wattleseed crisps. See also 'Using wattleseeds: methods and options' on page 28 for detailed notes on the various culinary uses of wattleseeds. Importantly, wattleseeds are gluten-free and they are also a legume, so have a high protein content*	*Wattleseeds can have a wide range of flavours, from 'mild grain nutty' to 'dark-coffee nutty and/or chicory'; it's very much dependent on the tempera-ture and length of roasting.*	*Ground wattleseeds are readily available from several native food stores and on-line suppliers. Whole wattleseeds are also available from native food stores and also on-line, although as at the time of writing there are fewer suppliers (Creative Native Foods in Adelaide has Australia's widest range of wattleseeds as well as other native ingredients available on-line.)*

AUSTRALIA'S WILD NUTS *and* SEEDS

Australia's wild nuts and seeds include the bunya, macadamia, and sandalwood nuts, as well as wattle (acacia) and kurrajong seeds, amongst others. They have always been a traditional source of sustenance and enjoyment for Indigenous Australians, eaten simply as nuts and seeds, but also soaked to form soft gruels or ground into flour and mixed with water to bake a bread or damper in hot ashes. Native Australian grass grains like rice and millet also grow prolifically in the wild and were a traditional Indigenous staple food source, but recipes utilising these grains are not included here because, as at the time of writing, they are not yet available at all for domestic culinary use – although it is hoped this will soon change.

Bunya Nuts

These large nuts come from the majestic Australian bunya bunya pine that is endemic to rainforests in parts of Queensland. It's not a true pine of the genus *Pinus,* but rather is of the genus *Araucaria* and related to South America's monkey puzzle tree. Hence, it is sometimes called the 'false monkey puzzle tree'.

bunya bunya pine — *Araucaria bidwillii*

Bunya nuts are the edible seeds of the bunya bunya pine. Their husks are neither oval nor round, but shaped more like a small, pointy eggplant. They are much larger than most nuts, however, growing to 4-5 cm (1½-2 in.) in length, and are found inside the tree's huge, heavy cone. It grows to about 30 cm (12 in.) or more in length and can hold anything from 30 to 150 nuts. When mature, it drops heavily to the ground, and then the nuts can be collected.

Bunya nuts can be eaten raw or boiled, and some say they are best eaten hot. They can be baked or toasted but these dry cooking methods toughen the flesh in my experience. Raw, they have been compared in texture to a floury chestnut, with a nutty, sweet, almost potato flavour. When cooked, they develop a milder flavour and waxier texture, and they smell like potatoes when boiling.

bunya nut

It is the white meat of the nut that is used in food preparation, so it first needs to be removed from the hard outer casing (the husk). This is easiest done *very carefully* when the nut is still warm and the casing softened by cooking, using a heavy sharp blade or utility knife and a steady hand. The nut's brown seed coat can then be removed, and the white meat extracted.

The nuts can be eaten whole or sliced, puréed, or ground into flour after drying. Puréed, they work well in place of chickpeas in various dips or spreads, in much the same way cannellini beans are sometimes used. Creamy boiled nut meat (whole, sliced, puréed or chopped) is used in various sweet and savoury dishes.

Unlike most other tree nuts, they are low in fat, although they are a good source of protein and carbohydrate. They have long been appreciated by Indigenous Australians, and it is said that at times hostilities between tribes were suspended to enable participation in a bunya nut festival: 'The Aboriginals held a bunya feast every three years, during which a truce was called between warring tribes.'[1]

1. F. Bodkin, *Encyclopaedia botanica*, p. 95

Kurrajong Seeds

The kurrajong tree features intriguing boat-shaped pods (the home of its tasty seeds). It is also a close relative to, and sometimes confused with, the bottle tree (*B. rupestris*), which has a swollen, bottle-like trunk that holds water. While the kurrajong tree may have a thick trunk, it is in its root system that it is able to store water, and this enables its survival under intense dry conditions. The kurrajong tree is endemic to the eastern states of Australia and the Northern Territory.

Kurrajong — *Brachychiton populneus*

This unusual tree is small to large in size and the bearer of the boat-shaped pods. They grow to about 7 cm (about 3 in.) in length and are woody and green when young, before ripening to a brownish black and splitting on one side to release 20 hairy, yellow seeds (at times, the pods look almost like a little hooded chair or sling, cradling the cheeky little seeds within). The fine hairs are an unpleasant irritant and must be removed before the seeds (or 'nuts') can be roasted and eaten (they are not eaten raw). Once roasted, they become brittle on the outside and floury on the inside, while developing a nutty flavour that is enhanced with seasoning. They are high in protein (about 18%) and fat (25%) and belong to a traditional Indigenous diet. It is said the tree was also put to other interesting uses: water was tapped from the trunk, pods were used as a child's rattle and, in colonial times, newly arrived Europeans roasted, pounded, ground, then boiled and strained the nuts to make what sounds like a very much-needed coffee-like beverage.

kurrajong pod and seeds

Macadamia Nuts

These nuts are regarded as the world's finest, and there are two edible types: the smooth-shelled macadamia (*Macadamia integrifolia*) and its rough-shelled cousin (*M. tetraphylla*), which have similar flavours and nutritional profiles and can be used interchangeably. A third (*M. ternifolia*) is inedible.

Macadamia — *Macadamia spp.*

Macadamia nuts have a buttery, slightly sweet flavour and a delightful texture that is crisp and clean on biting but then becomes smooth and creamy in the mouth. The nuts are a pale cream in colour and about 1.2 cm (½ in.) in diameter, sometimes bigger, and seem almost to resemble a button of white chocolate. Although they can be eaten raw, they are generally roasted and sometimes salted, and can also be ground into flour. They are delicious eaten on their own as a snack and also in sweet baked goods, where they add a buttery crunch. They pair very well with chocolate, caramel, and other rich, sweet flavours and can also be added to muesli and various toppings. Although they have an affinity with sweet dishes, I also use them in a satay sauce in place of peanuts, in crumbed coatings, in stuffings, and the like. The ground flour works well in certain baked goods, while macadamia oil is excellent for frying and also imparts a sweet nutty flavour to salad dressings. The macadamia nut is renowned for its extremely hard shell, with rocks and bricks at times being used to forcefully smash them apart to reach the delicate culinary treasure tucked away inside. Thankfully, modern nut crackers can do the job, but they are mostly sold shelled already Once opened, the thin brown seed coat is removed to expose the creamy nut meat within. The nuts can then be eaten raw, but the flavour is enhanced with gentle roasting.

macadamia nut meat

Macadamias are an energy-rich food, however, on account of their high fat content (about 75%), with a single 30g (1oz) serve yielding over 200 calories, or more than 800 kilojoules. They contain about 7% carbohydrate and 3% protein, and are a good source of thiamine and manganese. They are also a part of traditional Indigenous diets and have always been enjoyed immensely. Today, such is their delicious flavour and popularity that they are now one of Australia's largest horticultural enterprises and longest standing native Australian food crop currently servicing a demanding world market.

macadamias

Sandalwood Nuts

These are seeds of the Australian sandalwood tree (*Santalum spicatum*), native to Australia's west and south and related to the bush plum (*S. lanceolatum*), which produces blue berries.

Australian sandalwood — *Santalum spicatum*

Australian sandalwood has a precious, highly valued fragrant wood and oil. The aromatic oil is used in many ways, from aromatherapy through to health care, while it is known that Indigenous Australians boiled sandalwood bark to produce a cough remedy. But, here it is the nuts that are the culinary feature. They can be eaten raw, but develop an intriguing 'stringy-gum texture' on the palate. Roasting enhances their subtle flavour, and they can also be used whole or crushed, sliced or blended then used in various recipes including baked cakes, biscuits, curries and dukkahs. Their texture is a soft brittle rather than crunchy and their unique flavour is very mild. Like that of the quandong, the whole seeds are still used today in craft jewellery. They were also used as marbles in the board game Chinese Checkers. Nutritionally, they contain approximately 40% fat (oils), 20% each of protein and fibre, and only 1% of digestible carbohydrates, along with traces of other nutrients.

sandalwood nuts in their husks

Wattleseeds

Botanically, wattles are plants of the genus *Acacia*. There are thought to be well in excess of 1,200 species in existence globally but, importantly, not all are edible (a question that is still under research). The edible species are flavoursome and highly nutritious. As a legume, they are a good source of plant-based protein, as well as other nutrients. They are also gluten-free.

Wattleseeds (acacia seeds) — *Acacia spp.*

The golden wattle, one of many types found all over Australia, is the nation's floral emblem. It is embedded in the national psyche, along with its green and gold colours, as a symbol of contemporary Australian identity and yet, for millennia, wattles, and most significantly their seeds, have been a major food source for Indigenous Australians. Young green seeds of certain species have long been flash-roasted and eaten like a fresh green pea or bean. Mature, dry seeds were roasted and ground into flour, like a grain, to be mixed with water and baked in hot ashes — the original damper! — while sweet, sticky gum flowed or was tapped from the trunks of some wattles and grazed on as a 'bush lolly' (not all — the gum of many is too astringent for consumption).

Dry wattleseeds are nutritious and abundant most of the time. They have a mild, nutty taste when lightly roasted, but develop a strong coffee, chicory-like flavour with more bitter notes when very dark-roasted. They are a rich source of protein, carbohydrate and various micronutrients. Although their composition will vary a little according to the species and growing conditions, they contain approximately 20–30% protein, 30% each of usable (digestible) carbohydrate and fibre, and 7% fat, along with trace amounts of various vitamins and minerals. They also contain antioxidants. Roasting then cooking is generally necessary to make them digestible and to release all the beneficial compounds that may otherwise be unavailable to the body. Not all wattle species are edible, however, and it's Indigenous Australians who have been the best teachers on this subject. Of the many confirmed edible wattles, I personally favour the Hall's Creek (*A. cowleana*), Desert Oak (*A. coriacea*), Whipstick (*A. adsurgens*) and elegant or 'prickly' (*A. victoriae*) wattleseeds, not least because of their commercial availability. They can be roasted, soaked (activated) and ground to be used in several recipes, while the sprouted seeds can also be toasted to make 'malted wattle', a tasty, nutritious and crunchy garnish.

Although there are subtle differences between the flavours and colours of these wattleseeds, they have similar nutritional profiles and can be used interchangeably. Very importantly, wattles are a legume, plants that hold their seeds in two-seamed pods and which, in both their fresh and dried forms, contain high amounts of plant protein, so have a valuable role in vegetarian and plant-based diets. Recipes for the young green seeds are not included here as they are not as yet easily purchased, but perhaps this will change in the future, and there will be another fresh native ingredient to add to the repertoire of Australian foods.

desert oak wattleseed

mature, dry wattleseed pods

BUNYA NUT HOUMOUS *with* BROWN BUTTER, CUMIN *and* SALTBUSH SEEDS

Light – 10-15 serves

Traditional houmous can be creamy, garlicy, tangy, or sometimes stronger on the sesame or chickpea flavours. They vary tremendously. This great version uses bunya nuts in place of chickpeas and can be used as a dip or sauce. Once slowly simmered, the bunya nuts lose their floury starchy texture and become waxy and pasty. As well as a great entertainer — as a dip on antipasto platters, or in wraps and sandwiches — it's also excellent with grilled fish and a squeeze of lemon.

INGREDIENTS

250 g (½ lb) bunya nuts, nut meat only (cleaned of shell and inner brown seed coat)

½ cup cream
1 cup milk

75 g (2½ oz) tahini paste
70 g (2⅓ fl oz) lemon juice
1½ tsp salt
½ tsp ground white pepper
½ tsp ground cumin
4-5 garlic cloves garlic, peeled and crushed
100 ml (3⅓ fl oz) extra virgin olive oil

2 heaped tsp unsalted butter
3 tsp additional olive oil
1 tsp whole cumin seed
3 tsp saltbush seeds
a few additional leaves of saltbush, shallow-fried in a little vegetable oil till crisp, then drained (optional)
seablite or samphire sprigs to garnish (optional)

SUBSTITUTIONS

bunya nuts:
macadamias, cashews or chickpeas
saltbush seeds:
salted rolled oats
shallow-fried saltbush:
shallow-fried kale chips or sage.

METHOD

to make the houmous

1. Cut the nuts into quarters, then pulse in a food processor to a chunky 5 mm (¼ in.) crumb.
2. Simmer the nuts very gently in the cream and milk for 30 minutes, stirring frequently. This is best done in a non-stick pan. All the starchiness must be cooked out.
3. Allow to cool until luke warm.
4. Whisk in the tahini, lemon juice, salt, pepper, cumin and garlic.
5. Now slowly pour in the oil in a steady stream, while continuing to whisk briskly.
6. Check seasoning, then refrigerate until ready to serve.

to serve

1. Spread out the houmous onto a large serving platter.
2. Add the olive oil and butter to a frypan. Cook over a high heat until the foaming subsides, then immediately add the cumin and saltbush seeds. Shake the pan continuously and stir so the seeds are toasted and the butter almost burns.
3. Drizzle immediately over the houmous then scatter with shallow-fried saltbush and, if available, tiny sprigs of salty beach succulents.

WATTLESEED *and* SEA PARSLEY TABBOULEH

Side – 8-12 serves

This is a marvellous, super-healthy salad based on the classic tabbouleh salad of the Middle East. If you want a gluten-free option, the salad can be made entirely with any of the cooked edible wattle-seeds. Here, I have garnished the salad with some lovely wattleseed sprouts (p.30). Any left-over tabbouleh will keep, covered, for 2–3 days in the fridge.

INGREDIENTS

grains and wattleseed

150 g (5 oz) whole desert oak wattleseed

300 ml (10 fl oz) water

80 g (2⅔ oz) bulgur (or freekeh green wheat or pearl barley)
160 ml (5⅓ fl oz) additional water

dressing

juice (about 100 ml / 3⅓ fl oz) and zest of 2 large lemons
⅓ cup extra virgin olive oil
2-3 garlic cloves, peeled and finely chopped
2 tsp sea salt (or to taste)
1 tsp black pepper, freshly ground

150 g (5 oz) sea parsley
50 g (1⅔ oz) fresh rivermint leaves, coarsely chopped
1 medium tomato or a small handful of cherry tomatoes, diced (optional)

SUBSTITUTIONS

desert oak wattleseed:
other edible whole wattleseed, or freekeh or bulgar wheat
sea parsley:
flat-leaf or continental parsley
rivermint:
mint.

METHOD

to prepare the grains and wattleseed

1. Preheat the oven to 170°C (340°F).
2. Scatter the wattleseeds onto a shallow baking tray then roast for a good 8-10 minutes until they are just starting to smoke and some seeds are starting to pop and crackle. (See also p.28 for more information on ways to prepare wattleseed.)
3. Transfer the seeds to a small saucepan and add 300 ml (30 fl oz) of the water (double the weight of the wattle-seed). Simmer very gently, covered, for 45 minutes, then check for tenderness. If there are still a few hard ones, top the saucepan up with water and simmer for a little longer until they are all tender.
4. Remove from the heat and allow to cool completely while still covered. This will allow the wattleseeds to 'plump up'.
5. Place the bulgur in a bowl. Boil the additional water then immediately pour it over the top. Stir, then allow to cool completely and 'plump up'. If using green wheat freekeh or barley, cook according to the packet instructions.

to dress the salad

1. In a large salad bowl, whisk together the lemon juice, zest, olive oil, garlic, salt and pepper to make the dressing.
2. Stir the dressing through the cooled 'grains'.
3. Finally, mix in the sea parsley, rivermint and tomatoes, if using. Chill until ready to serve.

BLOOD LIME, SESAME *and* SOY SASHIMI POKÉ BOWL

Light – 4-6 serves

This is a simple adaptation of a rice and tuna salad made famous in Hawaii — fresh and summery. My 'native' version uses blood limes in a really nice sesame soy dressing. The base flavour is also far richer if using my Broom Wattleseed and Brown Rice Pilaf, instead of plain steamed white rice.

INGREDIENTS

350 g (12 oz) approx. sushi- or sashimi-grade salmon (or blue fin tuna) diced into 1 cm (⅓ in.) cubes.
1½ cups Soy, Blood Lime and Sesame Dressing (p. 248)

---

4 cups Broom Wattleseed and Brown Rice Pilaf, chilled (p. 225)
2 tsp freshly toasted sesame seeds (p. 260)
4 spring onions, white parts only (reserve the green parts for the garnish)
1 tsp salt, or to taste
½ tsp ground pepper, or to taste

---

1 avocado, peeled and sliced into fan shapes
¼ continental cucumber, thinly sliced
1 cup edamame beans
1 shredded carrot
4-6 radishes thinly, sliced
reserved green parts of spring onion, sliced
finger lime 'caviar' ('pearls' or 'vesicles', optional)

SUBSTITUTIONS

finger lime:
a squeeze of lime or lemon.

METHOD

1. In a bowl, add the diced fish and the Soy, Blood Lime and Sesame Dressing. Toss to coat, then refrigerate for at least 15 minutes, and ideally up to an hour.
2. Thinly slice the white parts of the spring onions (reserve the green parts to use as a garnish later).
3. Using a slotted spoon, remove the marinated fish from the bowl and put to one side. Reserve the left-over dressing.
4. Add the pilaf, half the toasted sesame seeds and the white spring onion to the bowl and mix together with the reserved left-over dressing.
5. Taste to check the seasoning. Season with salt and pepper and add more dressing or extra soy sauce if you wish.
6. To serve, place the pilaf mix in the bottom of four bowls. Arrange the fish over the rice, together with the beautiful array of toppings – the avocado, cucumber, edamame beans, carrots, and radishes.
7. Garnish with the green parts of the spring onions, diagonally sliced, and the remaining sesame seeds before serving.
8. Finger lime makes a wonderful addition, if available, providing a superb citrus crunch.

BUNYA NUT GARLIC BUTTER SCALLOPS

Light – 3-4 scallops per serve

These delicious scallops make use of my Bunya Nut Garlic Butter (p. 247). In this recipe, the egg yolks and breadcrumbs are optional, but they work exceptionally well when the butter is used with scallops and fish, because they provide the lovely crunchy structure and crumb that is left behind as the butter melts away and bastes the seafood during cooking — mouth-wateringly delicious.

INGREDIENTS

3-4 scallops on the shell, per person
1 small roll of Bunya Nut Garlic Butter (p. 247)

METHOD

1. Pre-heat your oven to its highest heat, at least 240°C (465°F), or set an overhead broiler/grill to medium heat.
2. Place all the scallops onto a crumpled foil-lined baking tray.
3. Slice rounds of butter, 5mm (about ¼ in.) thick each, and place one on each scallop (return any unused butter to the fridge or freezer).
4. If using the oven, bake the scallops for 6-8 minutes until cooked and golden brown, then serve immediately (scallops are much nicer if slightly under-cooked; medium-done is perfect).
5. If using an overhead grill or broiler, really watch these carefully so that they don't burn. As soon as they are barely cooked and a lovely golden brown (about 1-2 minutes on each side), they are ready to serve.

above: making the poori, from top left

a. *the dough 'sausage'*
b. *the cut pieces*
c. *preparing the dough for rolling out*
d. *rolling out the dough*
e. *pressing the poori deeper into the oil*
f. *very carefully splashing the poori with oil.*

PUFFED WATTLESEED POORI

Makes 10-12 pieces (depending on size)

Poori, or puri, is an unleavened deep-fried bread (or wafer) often served with Indian curries and, just like some pappadums, has spices like pepper or chilli scattered throughout — I love the nutty wattle crisps in this version. If the poori are rolled out really thin, they can cook up very crisp, but if left slightly thicker, they can have a softer inner dough with a crisp outer, depending on how long they are cooked.

INGREDIENT

1¾ cups atta (a type of whole wheat flour)
1 tsp salt
¼ cup vegetable oil

1½ tbs Malted Wattleseed Crisps (p. 265)
additional flour, for dusting

---

1 litre additional vegetable oil, for deep frying

SUBSTITUTIONS

malted wattleseeds:
roasted ground wattleseeds, chopped nuts or cracked pepper.

METHOD

1. Using a mixer with the dough hook attached, mix together the flour, salt and the quarter-cup of oil until a soft dough forms. Alternatively, knead by hand for about 5 minutes, to develop the gluten (this is what gives the dough its elastic or 'stretchy' quality).
2. Add the malted wattleseed crisps and mix for one minute.
3. Set aside to rest, covered with a clean tea towel or kitchen film, for 15-20 minutes.
4. Meanwhile, heat the deep-frying oil in a deep pot, wok, or deep fryer to about 190°C (375°F).
5. While the oil is heating up, flour the workbench with the additional flour. Place the dough on the floured surface and roll it into a long 'sausage' shape (a).
6. Cut the sausage into smaller pieces of dough (b). Flatten them a little with your fingers (c), then roll them out into thin discs with a rolling pin (d). They should be 12 cm (about 5 in.) in diameter.
7. Fry one poori at a time. Very carefully slide it into the hot oil and, using a flat slotted spoon, press gently on the middle to push it deeper into the oil (e). This will help it to puff up. Use the spoon to carefully splash small amounts of hot oil on top of the poori (f). Take every caution when working with hot oil.
8. Cook the poori for about 20-30 seconds on each side. Remove from the oil with the slotted spoon and drain on a paper towel. The poori should be golden and crisp with a soft, chewy inner dough, with the lovely added crunch of wattleseed. Serve immediately.

BUNYA NUT MALAI KOFTA *and* WATTLESEED POORI

Light – 4–6 serves

A favourite vegetarian Indian dish in my family for many years, this is made from scratch, and has the unique starchy texture of bunya nuts. There's a fair number of ingredients and preparation involved, so I like to make big batches of sauce and freeze down any extra for use on another day. This is one reason I recommend weighing ingredients where possible: it's much easier to double or triple the recipe and still get great results.

INGREDIENTS

sauce

1 tsp garam masala
2-3 black cardamom pods
1-2 green cardamom pods
3 cloves
½ tsp turmeric powder
½ tsp red chili powder
½ cinnamon stick
¼ tsp mace

40 g (1⅓ fl oz) vegetable oil
40 g (1⅓ oz) ginger, peeled
8-10 garlic cloves, crushed
2 small onions, peeled and diced into 5 mm (¼ in.) pieces
400 g (13⅓ oz) diced tinned tomatoes
100 g (3⅓ oz) lightly roasted and fine ground macadamia or cashew nuts
2 tsp dried fenugreek leaves
1 tsp salt
15 g (½ oz) brown sugar
1 tsp dried white kunzea, (optional)
2½ cups vegetable or chicken stock

kofta

210 g (7 oz) bunya nuts, nut meat only

2 medium size potatoes

120 g (4 oz) paneer (cottage cheese)
25 g (approx. 1 oz) rice flour
4 tsp almond meal
¼ tsp red chilli powder
½ tsp garam masala powder
1 tsp salt
1 litre additional vegetable oil (for frying)

METHOD

to make the sauce

1. Pound together the garam masala, cardamon, cloves, turmeric, chilli, cinnamon and mace in a mortar-and-pestle.
2. Heat the oil and gently fry the spices until fragrant and toasted.
3. Add the ginger and garlic and simmer over a low heat for a few minutes until they just start to brown a little on the edge, then add the onions and simmer for a further 2-3 minutes.
4. Add the tomatoes, cashews, fenugreek, salt, sugar, kunzea, and stock. Simmer very gently for 5-10 minutes, then purée with a stick blender until smooth. Leave in the pot.

to make the kofta

1. Cover the bunya nuts in water and simmer for 15-20 minutes until tender and all the starch is cooked out.
2. Separately, boil the potatoes in their skins until tender.
3. Drain the nuts and allow to cool. Also drain the potatoes and allow them to cool a little, so they are still warm.
4. Grate the potatoes into a bowl. Cut the nuts into 5 mm (¼ in.) chunks then add to the bowl. Then grate in the paneer, followed by the rice flour, almond meal, chilli, garam masala, and salt. Mix together well, then, shape the dough into large golf-ball sized pieces (you should get 10-12).
5. Heat the additional oil in a pot or fryer to 180°C (350°F). Lower in the kofta and deep-fry until golden brown (about 5 minutes). Scoop out with a slotted spoon and drain on absorbent paper. Add the kofta to the sauce. Simmer for 5-10 minutes, then serve.

SUBSTITUTIONS

bunya nuts: chestnuts.

ANCIENT AUSTRALIAN SUPERGRAINS SALAD

Side – 12-15 serves

Re-introducing ancient grains and seeds into our diet is a flavoursome and healthy trend. I like to include wattleseeds, which sprout and cook up so easily. In the years ahead, I hope we'll also see native Australian millets and rices on our pantry shelves, as native food cultivation becomes increasingly established. This recipe will serve many at a gathering, but left-overs will keep well, covered, in the fridge for 4–5 days.

INGREDIENTS

1 cup (150 g) whole desert oak or other whole edible wattleseeds: Halls Creek, Broom Wattle, etc.

½ cup freekeh or burgul wheat
½ cup quinoa

---

150 g (5 oz) pumpkin, peeled and diced into 1 cm (¼ in.) chunks
150 g (5 oz) sweet potato, peeled and diced into 1 cm c chunks
180 g (6 oz) red capsicum, diced into 1 cm (⅓ in.) chunks
1 tsp ground cumin
½ cup extra virgin olive oil

---

400 g (13⅓ oz) tinned chickpeas, drained
½ cup currants
1 large bunch coriander (cilantro) chopped
½ bunch (about 50 g / 1⅔ oz) parsley, chopped
1 spanish onion, peeled and diced
⅓ cup pistachios, shelled and ideally peeled (to show their brilliant colour), coarsely chopped

---

1 cup Bush Tomato Balsamic and Pomegranate Dressing (p.245), or to taste
1-2 tbs Wild Savoury Crumble (p.265)
1 tbs pomegranate arils or fresh riberries, for garnish (optional)

SUBSTITUTIONS

wattleseed:
small lentils, or any edible grains of your choice.

METHOD

1. Preheat the oven to 170°C (340°F). Once hot, scatter the wattleseeds onto a shallow baking tray then roast for a good 8-10 minutes until they are just starting to smoke and some seeds are starting to pop and crackle. (See p.28 for more information on ways to prepare wattleseed.)
2. Transfer the seeds to a small saucepan and add 300 ml (10 fl oz) of the water (double the weight of the wattleseed). Simmer very gently, covered, for 45 minutes, then check for tenderness. If there are still a few hard ones, top the saucepan up with water and simmer for a little longer until they are all tender.
3. Cook the freekah (or burgul) and quinoa according to their packet instructions.
4. Allow these cooked grains and seeds to chill in the refrigerator while preparing the other ingredients.
5. Mix the pumpkin, sweet potato, capsicum and cumin together with the olive oil. Spread in a single layer on a tray and roast in a moderate 200°C (390°F) oven for 20 minutes until tender and just starting to brown on the edges. Allow to chill in the fridge completely.
6. Once the seeds, grains, and roasted vegetables have all chilled nicely, place them all in a large salad bowl.
7. Mix through the chickpeas, currants, coriander (cilantro), parsley, onion and pistachios.
8. Toss through the Bush Tomato Balsamic and Pomegranate dressing.
9. Sprinkle with my Wild Savoury Crumble Mix and pomegranate arils if desired, for a superb extra crunchy texture.

PEPPERBERRY BEETS, GOATS CHEESE, *and* BROWN RICE *and* WATTLESEED RISOTTO

Light – 4 serves

These beautiful, vibrant beets are delicious when re-heated as a hot vegetable. This recipe makes a large amount, so it can easily be halved if desired, but the beets will keep for many weeks in the fridge. I like to use baby beetroot, but large beets also work well; just be sure to cut them into halves or quarters, keeping all the pieces at a similar size to ensure even cooking. Also keep in mind that cooking the pepperberry will dissipate its natural heat compounds, so it will lose heat while retaining flavour. As with all native-pepper cooking, to retain the kick of heat, add a little extra right at the end of the cooking, just before serving. This dish is also great with extra roast chopped walnuts or macadamias, for texture.

INGREDIENTS

4 bunches of baby beetroot, or 1-2 bunches large beets

---

4 cups white vinegar
2 cups water
300 g (10 oz) castor sugar
5 tsp salt
1 tsp ground pepperberries

---

1 recipe batch of Wattleseed and Brown Rice Pilaf, chilled (p. 229)
½ cup cream (optional)

---

100 g (3⅓ oz) goats cheese (chèvre)
Sea Parsley Oil (p. 255)

SUBSTITUTIONS

ground pepperberries:
white, black or green peppercorns.

METHOD

1. Cut the tops off the beets, leaving the pointy tails (roots), and saving the beautiful young leaves to use as a garnish later, if desired, then place the trimmed beetroot, vinegar, water, sugar, salt and half of the pepperberry in a saucepan. There should be enough liquid to just cover the beets.
2. Simmer for about 8-10 minutes, or until the beets are barely cooked. To check, pierce the beets with a small knife or fork; they should only offer the slightest of resistance.
3. Allow the beets to cool, until the liquid is luke warm, then drain. Reserve the finely strained liquid for use as a glaze or dressing later.
4. Peel the cooked beets by smearing off the skin with your fingers, while trying to keep the root intact. Reduce the beet liquid over a gentle heat, until it becomes a thin, sticky syrup of about 100 ml (3⅓ fl oz). Return the beets to the strained liquid, as this will allow their vibrant colour to leach out into the liquid further.
5. Add the remaining pepperberry and reheat the beets when ready to plate up
6. Prepare the Wattleseed and Brown Rice Pilaf. Keep the rice a little wetter by adding extra stock or finishing with a little cream, so it has a risotto-like texture.
7. Serve the beets topped with crumbled goats cheese and a drizzle of sea parsley oil and the reserved beetroot glaze.

MACADAMIA *and* LEMON MYRTLE SATAYS

Light – makes 10-12 satays

The marinade used here is popular in Thailand with pork, but it is also great with beef, chicken, prawns, squid, and so on. If you are using an open charcoal barbecue, it is a good idea to soak the bamboo satay sticks in hot water for at least a few hours, or the day before, to stop them from burning over the open flame.

INGREDIENTS

12 pre-soaked bamboo satay sticks

marinade

2 tsp coriander (cilantro), stems and roots, chopped fine
1 tsp chopped garlic
½ tsp white ground pepper
2 tsp light palm sugar, shaved
3 tsp fish sauce
3 tsp vegetable oil

500g (1 lb) approx. pork shoulder, or chicken thigh meat, or tofu for a vegetarian option

2 cups Macadamia and Lemon Myrtle Satay Sauce, warmed (p. 264)
1 cup Cucumber and Rivermint Pickle (p. 260)

METHOD

1. First, make the marinade. In a large bowl, whisk together all the marinade ingredients (everything except the pork, satay sauce and pickle) until all the palm sugar has completely dissolved.
2. Slice the pork meat into small 1 cm (or about ¼ in.) cubes or strips and mix evenly through the marinade.
3. Skewer the meat onto the satay sticks and refrigerate until required. Ideally, allow the satays to marinate for at least an hour or two before cooking.
4. When ready to cook, first prepare and pre-heat your barbecue or (see instructions on p.23).
5. Sear the satays over a high heat, turning regularly to caramelize on all sides. They won't take long at all, only 3-5 minutes, depending on the meat thickness and the heat of the barbecue.
6. Serve with the warm Macadamia and Lemon Myrtle Satay Sauce. Another lovely accompaniment is my Cucumber and Rivermint Pickle.

DESERT OAK WATTLE TREACLE BREAD

Accompaniment – 8-10 serves

This is a superb bread for a cheese platter or as part of a bread basket for any meal. It also freezes really well. I like to serve it with a quality hard cheese, such as a really bitey cheddar, gruyère or French comté — it's also excellent with Sunmuscats in Port and Pepperberry. It is best if left for a day before slicing, and it can be warmed in a gentle oven or microwave.

INGREDIENTS

75 g (2½ oz) whole desert oak wattleseed or other whole wattleseed

400 ml (13⅓ fl oz) water

150 g (5 oz) treacle

600 ml (20 fl oz) buttermilk
15 g (½ oz) bicarbonate soda
2 tsp salt

500 g (1 lb) coarse-ground whole wheat flour or standard wholemeal flour

additional water, if needed

good quality cheeses
Creative Native Sunmuscats in Port and Pepperberry, for serving (optional)

SUBSTITUTIONS

wattleseed:
pearl barley or whole wheat, but omit the roasting step.

METHOD

1. Pre-heat the oven to 175°C (350°F).
2. Spread the wattleseed in a single layer in a shallow baking tray and roast for 8-10 minutes. The seeds need to just to smoke and pop – don't burn them.
3. Remove the wattleseed from the oven and tip into a saucepan. Cover with the water.
4. Simmer very slowly for 45-60 minutes, until the wattleseed has softened completely and absorbed all the water.
5. Separately, place the treacle in a mixing bowl and heat briefly in the microwave for a few seconds.
6. Add the buttermilk, bicarbonate of soda and salt to the treacle and whisk together thoroughly.
7. Add the flour and softened wattleseed and mix briefly, to incorporate all into a smooth dough. If the dough seems too firm, you can add an extra 50-100 ml (1⅔-3⅓ fl oz) of water, just a little at a time as needed.
8. Pour (or scrape) into greased log-shaped cake moulds. Alternatively, portion into loaves and roll each loaf in silicone baking paper and then in foil and twist at the end to form cylinders or 'bon bons' (see p.240 for more notes on how to make the bon bons).
9. Bake at 160°C (320°F) for 1 hour. Serve with cheese and the sunmuscats, if desired.

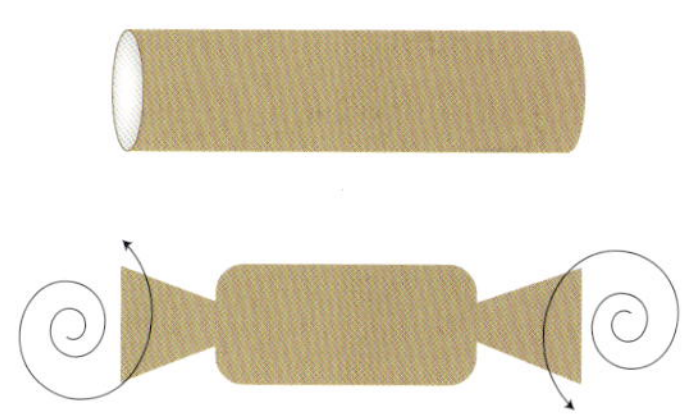

SLOW-BRAISED KANGAROO ZA'ATAR

Main – 4 serves | Light – 6-8 serves

This lovely braised shank is a treat in winter time as a hot meal, served with Date, Cinnamon and Sandalwood Nut Cous Cous (p.230), or shredded in a burger or in Injera Wraps (facing page).

INGREDIENTS

30 ml (1 fl oz) extra virgin olive oil
4 kangaroo shanks

---

30 g (1 oz) Davidson Plum Za'atar (p. 249)
1 tsp salt
2-3 cups chicken or beef stock
(if you are slow-braising)

METHOD

1. In a heavy pan, heat the oil over a medium-high heat until it is hot but not smoking. Add the shanks, turning occasionally, until they are just nicely browned all over.
2. The shanks can be cooked either 'sous vide' (see p. 21) or braised. To cook sous vide, place shanks in a vacuum bag and sprinkle over with the Davidson Plum Za'atar. Seal the bag and cook sous vide for 5 hours at 90°C (195°F).
3. To braise, choose a pot with a tight-fitting lid or a slow cooker. Add the browned shanks, za'atar and stock then simmer, covered, very slowly for 3-4 hours until the meat is just falling from the bone. The stock should reduce to a syrup, but don't let it boil dry (check on the hour and add a little extra stock, if needed).

INJERA WRAPS *with* KANGAROO

To fill the wraps, gather together some strips of the braised kangaroo shanks, thinly sliced spanish onion, roughly diced cherry tomatoes, julienned cucumber, and river or ordinary mint leaves. Lay down the above ingredients in a strip about a half the width of the wrap. Top with some Cucumber and Rivermint Tzatziki, if desired (p. 259). Roll up the wrap, compressing gently as you go, and folding the ends when half-way done.*

Note: wraps are generally more pliable when freshly made or luke warm rather than cold, so you may microwave them for a few seconds just before using.

INJERA WRAPS

Accompaniment – 6 serves

This is my version of the famous fermented Ethiopian flatbread, injera. It has a distinctive sourdough flavour and is great to use as a wrap. It's very easy to make, but the trick is to allow a few days for the natural fermentation process, as that is what allows the lovely, sour, fermented flavours to develop. But, if you are really pressed for time, you can make it all in one day by adding a little instant yeast while still achieving a nice result, albeit without the sour notes. Teff is quite an expensive flour, but you can play around and reduce the amount while increasing that of the other two flours if you wish. Using roast, ground wattleseed instead of kurrajong flour, or a half-half mix of kurrajong and wattleseed, gives further variations, but in that case I recommend using a lightly roasted wattleseed, not dark-roasted (see wattleseed roasting notes on p.270).

INGREDIENTS

1 cup teff flour,
½ cup wholemeal flour
½ cup kurrajong flour, finely sieved
2½ cups luke-warm water.
1 tsp salt
cooking spray, or a small amount olive oil or vegetable oil, for frying

SUBSTITUTIONS

kurrajong flour:
buckwheat flour.

METHOD

1. In a mixing bowl, whisk together the flours and water (leave the salt until later). Lightly cover the bowl with some kitchen film and let the mixture sit undisturbed on a kitchen bench, at room temperature, for 2-3 days.
2. The mixture will start to bubble and froth, but how much time that will take to happen will vary, depending on the weather and humidity. Really, the mixture is ready to be used when it starts to develop that sour, yeasty smell.
3. The fermented dough should have the consistency of a nice batter, somewhere between that of a thin crêpe and a thick pancake batter. Whisk in the salt. Add a little more water if the dough is too thick, or more flour if too thin.
4. Heat a non-stick frypan over medium heat. Lightly spray or brush with some olive or vegetable oil.
5. Pour a ladle of batter into the pan, while carefully swirling it to spread the mixture nicely. Control the heat, and lift the edge of the injera to check it is not burning underneath.
6. Bubbles will soon develop. When this happens, cover with a lid and allow the injera to steam for a couple more minutes until cooked through. There is no need to flip.
7. Remove and repeat steps 4-6 to use all the batter. Serve hot or luke warm as an accompaniment to dips, curries and other dishes, or roll up and use as a wrap.

BRAISED RED CABBAGE *with* MALTED WATTLESEED CRISPS

Side – 4 serves

I learnt this braise while working for three months on just the 'vegetable section' in London's Savoy Grill restaurant several years ago. These days I complement the sweet-sour syrupy cooking liquid with some uniquely Australian nutty texture, from the malted wattleseeds.

INGREDIENTS

¼ large (about 500 g/1 lb) red cabbage

⅓ cup red wine
⅓ cup good quality red wine vinegar
⅓ cup Creative Native Lillipilli Conserve (jam)
1 tsp salt

1-2 tsp brown sugar, or to taste

½ tsp ground pepperberry
4 heaped tsp Malted Wattleseed Crisps (p. 265)

SUBSTITUTIONS

Creative Native Lillipilly Conserve:
red currant jelly
ground pepperberry:
ground pepper.

METHOD

1. Shred the red cabbage into fine 2-3 mm (½ in.) strips.
2. Put the wine, vinegar and jam into a stainless-steel saucepan followed by the cabbage then the salt.
3. Bring to a gentle simmer with the lid on, stir occasionally, and allow to cook for 25-30 minutes. The liquid will reduce to a lovely, sweet, tangy, and brilliant-coloured glaze as the cabbage steams and reduces in volume.
4. Taste the cabbage, now coated with the glaze, and adjust with extra sugar (or more jam) if desired, to balance the acidity.
5. If using immediately, fold in the pepperberry and malted wattleseed and serve. Otherwise, only add the wattleseed and pepperberry just before you serve.
6. This cabbage keeps for 1-2 weeks in the fridge with its acidic glaze. It then reheats easily in the microwave and also freezes surprisingly well.

BROOM WATTLESEED *and* BROWN RICE PILAF

Side – makes 4-6 serves

There are many wonderful, edible wattleseeds and they can all be cooked and served up beautifully, in a similar way to a grain, such as rice. They're also very nutritious. If you want to use another type of wattleseed rather than broom wattle, choose one of the edible smaller to medium seeds, so they take about the same amount of time to cook as the rice. Larger seeds like 'elegant' or 'desert oak' wattleseed will take a lot longer. You can vary the proportions of rice and wattle, as you wish.

INGREDIENTS

½ cup whole broom or other small wattleseeds

30 g (1 oz) butter
30 ml (1 fl oz) extra virgin olive oil
½ small brown onion (about 75g / 2½ oz), peeled and chopped

1½ cups brown rice

600 ml (1 pint) approx. vegetable or chicken stock or 30 g (1 oz) stock powder mixed with 600 ml (1 pint) water
1 tsp salt, or to taste (optional)

METHOD

1. Preheat the oven to 160°C (320°F). Once hot, scatter the wattleseeds onto a shallow baking tray then roast for a good 6–8 minutes until they are just starting to smoke and some seeds are starting to pop and crackle.
2. Heat the butter and oil in a frypan, then add the onion.
3. Fry gently, stirring occasionally, until the onion is just starting to brown at the edges (5–8 minutes).
4. Add the rice and roasted wattleseeds and stir over the heat for another minute, until they are thoroughly coated with the oil and butter.
5. Add the stock and salt (if using), stir, then bring all to a gentle simmer.
6. Cook very slowly for about 40–60 minutes or until the grains are tender, stirring once of twice.
7. Cover and allow to stand for 5–10 minutes before serving.

DATE, CINNAMON and SANDALWOOD COUS COUS

Side – 4 serves

This is such a tasty fragrant side dish it can easily be a meal on its own, or complemented with grilled chicken, lamb cutlets, roast sweet potato, pumpkin pieces, and other vegetables. I also love to spice it up with freshly chopped red or green chillies or finely chopped fresh pepperleaf, to add another layer of flavour. Cooking the cous cous in stock may not be traditional, but it adds amazing depth of flavour, much more so than if using only water.

INGREDIENTS

300 g (10 oz) pearl cous cous
½ tsp salt
½ tsp white pepper
600 ml (1 pint) vegetable or chicken stock, or 30 g (1 oz) stock powder dissolved in 600 ml (1 pint) water
½ tsp ground cinnamon
4 tsp extra virgin olive oil

90 g (3 oz) approx. dates, pitted and diced into 5 mm (¼ in.) pieces

40 g (1⅓ oz) sandalwood nuts, lightly roasted* and coarsely chopped

handful of fresh sea parsley, chopped

* *See page 16 for notes on roasting nuts.*

SUBSTITUTIONS

sandalwood nuts:
almonds, brazil or hazelnuts
sea parsley:
flat-leaf (continental) parsley.

METHOD

1. Place the cous cous, salt and pepper, stock, cinnamon and olive oil into a stainless-steel saucepan. Bring to a simmer, and cook for 5 minutes, stirring once or twice.
2. Turn off the heat, cover, and leave to cool completely, until the cous cous is tender and the liquid has been absorbed.
3. Once the cous cous has cooled, stir through the dates. Place in a microwave dish (or glass bowl covered with kitchen film), then microwave on high for 1-2 minutes, until piping hot.
4. Quickly stir through the nuts, then turn out onto a serving platter.
5. Garnish with the parsley and coriander (if using), and serve. Alternatively, the finished dish can be allowed to cool and served as a salad.

BUNYA NUT and MUNTRIES STUFFING

Accompaniment – 6-8 serves

This classic stuffing recipe is very versatile, and it's a great option for filling a roast duck or chicken (see Chicken in Paperbark with White Kunzea, p. 79), or even a hollowed-out roast pumpkin. There are endless variations, so try using fresh sea parsley, wild thyme, and herbs. Caramelized bacon or prosciutto pieces and chopped desert or sunrise limes also make tasty additions.

INGREDIENTS

1 tbs extra virgin olive oil
2 tsp butter

---

1 small onion, peeled and finely chopped
2 garlic cloves, peeled and finely grated

---

1 cup milk
50g (1⅔ oz) bunya nuts, white 'meat' only, coarsely chopped

15-18 slices (about 150g) stale (1-2 days old) wood-oven or wholemeal bread, cut roughly into 2-3cm chunks.

50g (1⅔ oz) fresh muntries
2 eggs, beaten
2 tsp fresh coastal rosemary, coarsely chopped
2 tsp pepperleaf, chopped coarsely (or 1 tsp dried ground pepperleaf)
1 tsp River Murray salt

SUBSTITUTIONS

bunya nuts:
hazelnuts or brazil nuts
muntries:
try chopped dried apple
coastal rosemary:
sage
pepperleaf:
freshly ground black pepper
River Murray salt:
sea salt or table salt.

METHOD

1. Heat the olive oil and butter in a frypan until foaming and barely beginning to brown.
2. Add the onion and garlic and simmer over a gentle heat for 3-5 minutes until the onion is translucent but not coloured.
3. Add the milk and bunya nuts, cover, and simmer very gently for a further 1-2 minutes.
4. Pour the warm mixture over the chunks of bread. Mix through and cover, then allow 10-15 minutes for the liquids to be absorbed into the bread.
5. Finally, add the muntries, egg, rosemary, pepperleaf and salt. Work everything into the bread (this is easiest if done by hand).
6. Refrigerate until ready to use.

WHIPSTICK WATTLESEED PORRIDGE

Light – 2 serves

You can use any type of the edible malted wattleseeds to make this simple winter warmer. Here I've also added a berry compôte with sprinkled malted wattleseeds over the top for added crunch.

INGREDIENTS

4 tsp Malted Wattleseed Crisps* (p. 265)

1 cup instant or rolled oats
½ tsp cinnamon
½ tsp strawberry gum
1½ cups milk
3 tsp (about 25 g) honey

additional honey, to serve (optional)

* *Whipstick wattle works well for this recipe.*

SUBSTITUTIONS

strawberry gum:
a few drops of strawberry essence.

METHOD

1. Reserve half of the wattleseed to use as a garnish, then place all the remaining ingredients (except the additional honey) into a small saucepan.
2. Gently bring to the boil over a moderate heat, stirring regularly. Simmer for 1–2 minutes, or a little longer if using rolled oats rather than instant, until suitably softened. Or, microwave in short bursts of about 30 second each, stirring between times, until the oats are cooked (this will vary depending on the oven and type of oats).
3. Pour the hot porridge into bowls. Drizzle over additional honey and more milk if desired, to taste. You can also use lemon myrtle, white kunzea or anise myrtle instead of strawberry gum for some interesting flavour variations.

WATTLESEED CREAM

Accompaniment – makes x cups

This is a delicately flavoured cream to accompany desserts. You can also vary the type of wattleseed used and the roasting times to create different flavours. Only use the gelatine if you want the cream to hold a shape over a period of a few hours. This recipe is very light on the sugar, but you can adjust to suit your own taste.

INGREDIENTS

25 g wattleseeds of your choice, roasted for 8–10 minutes until starting to smoke and seeds are starting to pop and crackle (see p. 270 for roasting notes)

2 leaves gelatine (optional)

40 oz (1⅓ oz) castor sugar
75 ml (2⅔ oz) water

600 ml bottle (1⅓ pint) cream

METHOD

1. If using gelatine, soften the leaves in ice-cold water for 20 minutes at least, so it is fully hydrated.
2. Briefly bring the roasted wattleseed, sugar, and water to the boil, to make the 'wattleseed essence'. Add the softened gelatine (if using) and stir well. Cool to luke warm.
3. Separately, whip the cream to medium peaks, then add the luke-warm wattleseed 'essence' to the cream.
4. Continue to whip until stiff peaks form. Chill until ready to serve.

WATTLESEED *and* ESPRESSO CRÈME BRÛLÉE

Sweet – 8-10 serves

Wattleseed once dark-roasted is a great partner to coffee and chocolate. This classic French brûlée is so richly flavoured you might not need that after dinner coffee! The only downside is that it's harder to see easily when the dark toffee topping is perfectly cooked because the cooked custard is also nice and dark. Wattleseed alone makes for a great brûlée too, by the way — adding coffee is just me being a die-hard coffee fan.

INGREDIENTS

200ml (6⅔ fl oz) water
2½ cups cream
180 g (6 oz) sugar
50g (1⅔ oz) coffee beans, freshly ground

---

2 tsp roasted wattleseeds (p.270), ground

---

10 egg yolks
2 tsp pure vanilla extract

8-10 tsp fine castor sugar (2 tsp per serve)

Strawberry Gum and Sandalwood Toasts, to serve (p. 240)

METHOD

1. Whisk together the water, cream, sugar, and ground coffee beans. If you want a smooth brûlée, add the wattleseeds now, too, but if you prefer a lightly textured brûlée, as I do, add them to the egg yolks in step 4 instead.
2. Place these ingredients in a pot over the stove and bring briefly to the boil then turn off.
3. Allow to cool for 10 minutes to infuse the coffee flavour, then use a very fine sieve to remove the coffee grounds, and ground wattleseeds (if already used).
4. Separately, whisk together the egg yolks, and vanilla. Add the ground wattleseeds if you have not already done so.
5. Continue whisking while gradually pouring in the sieved coffee mixture.
6. Pour the mixture into 8-10 (depending on size) individual-serve ramekins or other moulds on a baking tray.
7. Bake in a 100°C (212°F) oven for 30-40 minutes (depending on how warm the mixture is when placed in the oven). Cooking is complete when you can wobble the tray and see the centres of the desserts are just holding a shape, not runny. Allow to cool a little before chilling in the fridge (this can be done a few days ahead; they'll keep for at least a week).
8. Just before serving, sprinkle two teaspoons of castor sugar over each one. Roll it around to spread it evenly in a nice 1 mm (thin - about 1/25th of an inch) layer. This much is needed for caramelizing.
9. Using a kitchen blow torch and applying continuous circle strokes, caramelize the sugar evenly to make a bubbling and even toffee crust. Serve with toasts. Your choice of fresh berries is also a nice option.

MALTED WATTLESEED *and* CHOCOLATE BROWNIES

Sweet – it never makes enough!

Addiction warning! These brownies are so good with the wattle crunch, you might need to make a couple of batches and hide some in different locations around the house. You can vary the type of nuts easily, but I love the combination of hazelnut, macadamia and sandalwood.

INGREDIENTS

chocolate mixture

70 g (2⅓ oz) unsalted butter
40 ml (1⅓ fl oz) vegetable oil
270 g (9 oz) dark couverture chocolate (broken pieces or buttons)
1 tsp strawberry gum

egg mixture

3 eggs
3 cups brown sugar

flour mixture

50 g (1⅔ oz) plain flour
1 heaped tsp baking powder
40 g (1⅓ oz) best quality dark cocoa powder
⅓ tsp salt

finish

100 ml (3⅓ fl oz) sour cream

80 g (2⅔ oz) white couverture chocolate buttons
80 g (2⅔ oz) milk couverture chocolate buttons
210 g (7 oz) mixed nuts: hazelnuts (skin removed), macadamia and sandalwood nuts
4 tsp Malted Wattleseed Crisps* (p.265)

SUBSTITUTIONS

strawberry gum:
peppermint gum,
few drops strawberry essence.
sandalwood nuts:
cashews, almonds or brazil nuts.

METHOD

to make the chocolate mixture

1. Place the butter, vegetable oil, dark chocolate couverture and strawberry gum into a stainless-steel bowl. Bring a partially filled saucepan of water to the boil and place the bowl over the saucepan, keeping the base of the bowl well clear of the boiling water at all times (see 'double boiler' notes, p. 22). Turn off the heat and leave until the chocolate and butter have melted completely. Stir the mixture until smooth and keep it warm, about 50°C (120°F).

to make the egg mixture

2. Using a stand mixer, whisk the eggs and sugar on high speed until light and fluffy (about 5 minutes).

to make the flour mixture

3. Sift the flour, baking powder, cocoa and salt into a bowl.

to finish the mix

4. Using a spatula, gently fold the sour cream and the chocolate mixture into the egg mixture.
5. When almost smooth, fold in the flour mixture, taking care not to over-work the mixture – it should be only just combined.
6. Finally, stir in the remaining chocolate buttons, nuts and wattleseed, then pour the mixture into a shallow, square cake tin, about 15 × 15 cm (6 × 6 in.), lined with baking paper.
7. Bake in a pre-heated oven at 180°C (350°F) for 35–40 minutes. The top forms a lovely crust and should feel firmish but spongy to touch. Allow to cool completely, then cut the brownies into squares or fingers to serve.

WATTLESEED PAVLOVA

Sweet – 6-8 serves

The pavlova, an antipodean classic (although whether first from New Zealand or Australia is a contentious point) was created in the 1920s in honour of the Russian ballerina Anna Pavlova, who visited at that time. It was re-invented by an old friend, Jean Paul Bruneteau, as a Wattleseed Pavlova Roll back in the 1980s at Sydney's Rowntrees restaurant, Australia's first specialist native-food restaurant. This is my version, presented in a spectacular high-domed shape, more similar to the one cooked already in homes all over Australia. Kids (and I) love being 'artistic' with this, but if you don't want the tall, hollow ring pavlova or don't have time to prepare the mould, simply spread the mixture on the baking tray in the traditional, flatter, rounder shape, leaving a depression in the centre to hold the cream later.

INGREDIENTS

7-8 egg whites, room temperature
2 tsp lemon juice
1½ cups castor sugar
15 g (½ oz) cornflour (cornstarch)

10-15 Malted Wattleseed Crisps, (optional, p. 265)

Wattleseed Cream (p. 233)
Rainforest Berry Compôte (p. 169)
neutral (flavourless) cooking spray

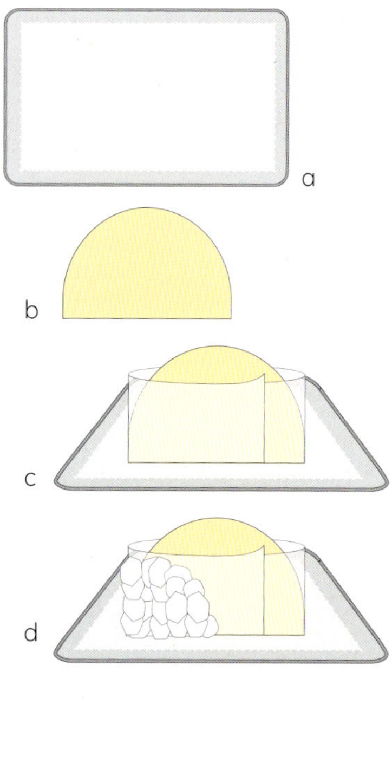

a, b, c, d

METHOD

1. Pre-heat the oven to 140°C (280°F), making sure there's plenty of room for this high dessert by removing the top oven rack.
2. Line a large baking tray with silicone baking paper (a).
3. Choose a small (15 cm / 6 in.), round, oven-proof bowl (b) to use as a 'mould', and place it upside-down on the tray. Wrap a strip of silicone baking paper (lightly sprayed with cooking spray to hold it in place) around the outside (c). You will 'build' the hollow pavlova ring around this.
4. Whip the egg whites with lemon juice and a handful of the sugar, to the 'soft peaks' stage. Then, reduce the mixer speed and slowly add the remaining sugar and cornflour.
5. Return to high speed and whip till stiff peaks form. The sugar grains must be fully dissolved – very important! The mixture must be completely smooth, so taste to check there are no grains left. This is why finely granulated castor sugar is used. Gently stir through the wattleseeds now (if using).
6. Using a rubber spatula, spread scoops of mixture up the outside of the mould in a nice, abstract fashion (d), or use a piping bag, large star nozzle attached, to pipe the mixture up the sides, ensuring each strip touches the next, all the way around.
7. Place in the oven and bake for an hour, then switch off the heat and leave in the oven to cool completely. Once cool, gently lift the pavlova shell off the mould and place on your serving dish.
8. Fill with wattleseed cream and top with Rainforest Berry Compôte or fresh fruits of your choice.

STRAWBERRY GUM *and* SANDALWOOD TOASTS

Accompaniment – makes 30-40 slices

Strawberry gum and our unique sandalwood nuts transform this classic almond toast recipe. This will make lots of lovely light crisps, so store them in an airtight container until ready to serve. The 'cake' is best baked the day before slicing. To get lovely thin and even slices, you really need an electric or hand-operated bread slicer, or otherwise a very good sharp knife, very steady hands and plenty of practice!

INGREDIENTS

1 cup castor sugar
7 large (about 200 g / 7 oz total) egg whites, at room temperature

1½ cups plain flour
3 heaped tsp ground strawberry gum
1 tsp vanilla extract with seeds

150 g (5 oz) sandalwood or macadamia nuts

icing sugar, for dusting (optional)

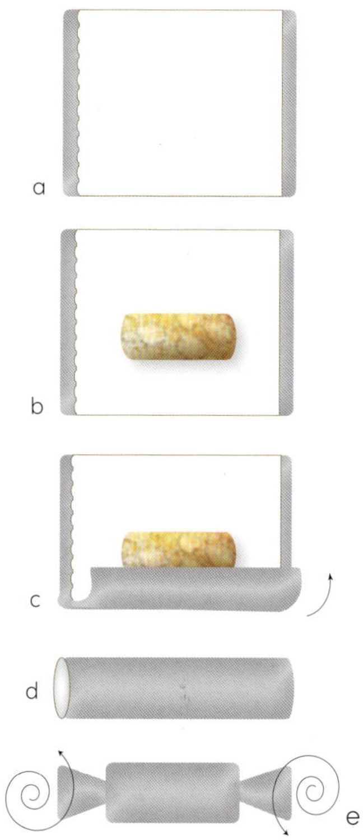

METHOD

1. Preheat your oven to 160°C (320°F).
2. Put 4 teaspoons of the sugar in the egg whites. Use an electric mixer to whisk on full speed until soft peaks form. Reduce the speed a little and slowly pour in the remaining sugar.
3. Return to full speed and whisk to medium-stiff peaks. Sift in the flour, followed by the strawberry gum and vanilla. Using a rubber spatula, gently work through the ingredients to incorporate, scraping down the sides as you go.
4. Fold in the nuts. Do not overwork!
5. You can cook the 'cake' in a small, lined loaf tin, but I love to make a nice log shape: Lay a large sheet of foil on a bench and place silicone baking paper on top (a). Scrape the mixture onto the paper (towards the lower edge). Use a spatula to spread it into a log shape about half the foil's width (b). Now fold over the lower edge and roll into a loose cylinder shape (c, d), with about 3-4 layers of foil around it for strength.
6. Next, twist both ends of the cylinder quite tightly and in opposing directions, to make your 'bon bon' (e).
7. Place the roll on a baking tray, supported with some pieces of crumpled foil around its sides. Bake for 45 minutes, then remove and allow to cool completely (ideally overnight at room temperature, to really firm it up) before slicing into thin 2-3 mm (½ in.) discs. Spread these in a single layer onto baking sheets and bake gently at 150°C (300°F). for 30-40 minutes until light golden grown and crisp. Cool, then store in an airtight container. Dust with icing sugar to serve.

SUBSTITUTIONS

nuts:
almonds, brazil or hazelnuts
strawberry gum:
lemon myrtle.

Condiments *and* Basics

SOY *and* ANISE MYRTLE DRESSING

Condiment – makes ½–1 cup

This simple but rich dressing is used with my braised octopus recipe (p.107) and can be spiced up with a little chilli or fresh pepperleaf. It is also great with green salads and grilled seafood, vegetables, steak or chicken, and it can also be used for interesting pickles when thinned a little with more vinegar.

INGREDIENTS

75 ml (2½ fl oz) sweet soy sauce (ketjap manis)
1 tsp ground anise myrtle
100 ml (3⅓ fl oz) red wine vinegar

½ cup of olive, macadamia or grapeseed oil

SUBSTITUTIONS
ground anise myrtle:
star anise.

METHOD

1. Simmer the sweet soy sauce, anise myrtle, and vinegar in a pan, stirring occasionally, until reduced by half (to about half a cup). It should be a nice, syrupy consistency.
2. Allow to cool and whisk in the oil of your choice.

LEMON ASPEN JUICE

Condiment – makes about ½ cup

In this book I use Lemon Aspen Juice a few times. Having the juice ready at call from the freezer at any time is just the ticket whenever a recipe calls for some lovely tangy, unique acidic flavours — and even for sprinkling over fish and chips. It's perfect if you have no lemons on hand, or you want to make up a fabulous cocktail with coconut cream and vodka after a long day at work, or whip up a simple butter sauce for grilled fish...

INGREDIENTS

100 g (3⅓ oz) lemon aspen
100 ml (3⅓ fl oz) water

* *If you like, even the waste solids still have some flavour. You can infuse these into a tea or a vinegar and strain again.*

METHOD

1. Blend the whole lemon aspen and water together (you can process any amount: just keep the same ratio of water to lemon aspen so the resulting juice strength remains consistent). I find the easiest ways to process the ingredients is in a high speed jug or blender, Thermomix®, or smoothie blender, until it makes a very smooth purée.
2. Pass the purée through a fine sieve, working the solids dry with the back of a soup ladle, to extract all the liquid.*
3. Freeze your Lemon Aspen Juice in ice-cube trays, so you have a permanent supply, ready for use at any time.

ANISE MYRTLE RED CURRY PASTE

Cooking sauce – makes 3-4 cups

Based on the classic Thai paste but with an Australian twist, this recipe makes a generous amount, so freeze any extra into meal-sized snaplock bags for future use. It will also keep in the fridge for about a week or a little longer. I also use the paste as a marinade for barbecued meat or prawn kebabs, just by mixing it with some vegetable oil and seasoning it with palm sugar and fish sauce. For this recipe, for accuracy and balanced flavour the spices should be weighed on metric electronic scales if possible (see my notes on measuring and weighing ingredients, p.18).

INGREDIENTS

120g (4oz) blachan (shrimp paste)

10g (⅓ oz) coriander seeds
12g (⅓ oz) white peppercorns
5g (⅙ oz) star anise
25g (1 oz) cinnamon sticks
6g (⅕ oz) dried red chillies

340g (¾ lb) peeled shallots
260g (9oz) sliced lemongrass, white part only
25g (1oz) coriander (cilantro) roots, coarsely chopped
60g (2 oz) galangal, peeled and thinly sliced
4g (⅛ oz) turmeric
20-24 garlic cloves, peeled
zest and juice of 2 limes
25g (1oz) ground anise myrtle
25g (1oz) sweet paprika

1-2 tbs water or coconut milk (optional)

METHOD

1. Pre-heat the oven to 170°C (340°F).
2. Wrap the blachan in some cooking foil
3. Loosely spread the coriander seeds, peppercorns, star anise, cinnamon sticks and chillies over a lined baking tray in a single layer. Roast until they are aromatic and begin to lightly colour (about 5 minutes, but keep an eye on them and remove them sooner if they are ready, as they can quickly burn).
4. Put the wrapped blachan in the oven to roast at the same time, but allow it more time (about 10 minutes).
5. Using a grinder or mortar-and-pestle, grind the roasted coriander seeds, peppercorns, star anise, cinnamon sticks and chillies to a fine powder.
6. Place the roasted blachan, fine powder, and all the remaining ingredients in a blender. Process on high speed until it forms a smooth thick purée.
7. Add a splash of coconut milk or water, if needed, to assist the blending process.

SUBSTITUTIONS

ground anise myrtle:
star anise.

WILD BASIL LABNEH

Light – 6-8 serves

Make sure you use a really tangy quality Greek yoghurt to make your labneh. Strain it for at least 6-8 hours before using, so it firms up; 2–3 days is even better and left to cure for a week is best of all. This recipe makes more than enough for 4 serves, but you won't regret having to use up the left-overs, which will keep for 3 or 4 weeks in the fridge, marinated in olive oil and herbs if you like.

INGREDIENTS

500g (about 1lb) tangy Greek yoghurt
2 tsp dried wild basil
1 tsp black pepper, freshly ground

SUBSTITUTIONS

dried wild basil:
dried basil.

native basil

METHOD

1. Whisk together the yoghurt, wild basil, and pepper.
2. Line a sieve with cheesecloth, a clean new Chux® cloth, or absorbent paper towel, and place over a medium or deep bowl.
3. Carefully pour the flavoured yoghurt over the top then gather up the edges of the cloth (or paper towel) to completely cover the yoghurt.
4. Place in the refrigerator and let the yoghurt liquid drain into the bowl for 6-8 hours or ideally 2-3 days, or even a week. The sieve, and therefore the draining yoghurt inside it, should be sitting above the liquid that's drained into the bowl, not in it. Discard the liquid periodically. Over a period of days, the yoghurt will become very thick and start to resemble a soft goats cheese texture.
5. You may use the strained yoghurt as a softer labneh, as I do with Hot Roast Wild Basil Tomatoes (p. 67), or cure it for longer to really firm it up.
6. For the longer option, leave a week or more. Using hands oiled with olive oil, roll the labneh into 3-4cm (about 1½ in.) balls and drop them into a preserving jar filled with flavoured oil – garlic, chilli, pepperberry or pepper-leaf – it's your choice. Make sure the labneh is completely covered in oil at all times and the jar sealed when in the fridge.

BUSH TOMATO BALSAMIC *and* POMEGRANATE DRESSING

Condiment – makes almost 1 cup

This is a simple, fruity extension of my Bush Tomato Balsamic Vinegar that lends itself to Middle-Eastern style salads and dishes

INGREDIENTS

75 ml (2½ fl oz) pomegranate molasses
35 ml (1 fl oz) Creative Native Bush Tomato Balsamic
zest, finely grated, and juice of 1 large lemon
¼ cup extra virgin olive oil
1 tsp (6 g) sea salt
1 tsp (2-3 g) ground pepperleaf

METHOD

1. Whisk all the ingredients together thoroughly.
2. Chill until ready to serve. This dressing should keep in a jar or bottle in the refrigerator indefinitely, but will need warming to room temperature before use.

SUBSTITUTIONS

for the recipes on this page

dried wild basil: a few large sprigs of basil
Creative Native Bush Tomato Balsamic: other caramelized balsamic
ground pepperleaf: pepper, freshly ground.

WILD BASIL PIZZA ('NAPOLITANA') SAUCE

Large – makes about 1 litre (2 pints)

This is a simple variation on the classic Italian sauce, wonderful if you can make it in summer — with your own very ripe home-grown tomatoes, of course! It's a brilliant base for pasta and other dishes, too. The addition of sugar is purely to taste — I love a little to balance the natural acidity of tomatoes, but just start with a small amount and taste as you go, adding more if needed.

INGREDIENTS

400 g (13⅓ oz) diced Italian tomatoes
3 cups bottled tomato passata
50 ml (1⅔ fl oz) extra virgin olive oil
1 tsp salt
2 tsp dried oregano
½ tsp wild thyme
1 tsp ground pepperleaf
4 tsp dried wild or native basil, crumbled

4 tsp raw sugar, or to taste

METHOD

1. Simply bring all the ingredients to a gentle simmer, adding the sugar a little at a time (see notes above) and stirring occasionally.
2. Continue to simmer the sauce for 20-30 minutes, allowing it to concentrate.
3. Allow to cool and freeze into meal-size tubs where it will keep for 12 months or more, or pour the sauce while hot into sterilized jars or bottles and keep in the fridge. It should keep, unopened, for several months but once opened should be used within 2-3 days. Either way, the sauce is ready to use on 'easy pizza or pasta nights'.

a.

b

c

d

e.

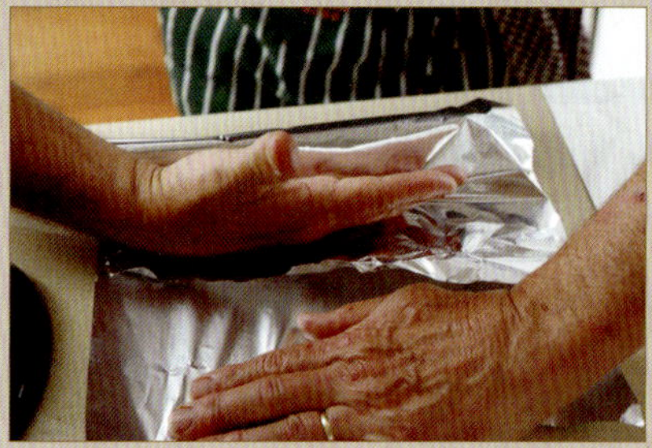

f.

g

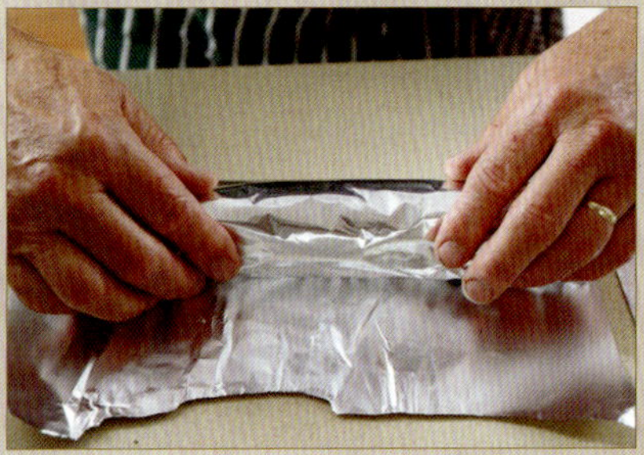

h

i

j

above: making the garlic butter rolls

a. *whipping until light and fluffy*
b. *placing dollops of the butter on to foil*
c. *. . . and shaping into a log*
d. *then perfecting the log shape*
e. *beginning to fold over the foil*
f. *using hands to smooth out air bubbles*
g. *. . . while rolling up into a 'sausage'*
h. *. . . all the way to the end*
i. *then twisting the ends in opposing directions*
j. *. . . to make a lovely, tight 'bon bon'.*

BUNYA NUT GARLIC BUTTER

Condiment – makes 3-4 small rolls

There are endless ways to flavour compound butters and this version of garlic butter is a beauty. As it freezes really well, I always make a large batch at once then wrap it into small aluminium foil 'bon bons' before labelling them and putting them in the freezer. Keep one in the fridge, then slices can easily be dropped onto the simplest of grilled meat, fish or vegetable dishes — another great way to instantly add amazing flavour. This butter is terrific in garlic bread too, of course.

INGREDIENTS

100 g (3⅓ oz) bunya nuts, nut meat only (cleaned of shell and inner brown seed coat)
300 g (10 oz) unsalted butter, at room temperature
30 g (1 oz) dijon mustard
3 egg yolks
15 g (½ oz) chopped sea parsley
15 g (½ oz) chopped chives
5-6 cloves of chopped garlic
3 tsp worcestershire sauce
zest and juice of 1 large lemon
1½ tsp salt
½ tsp ground white pepper
50 g (1⅔ oz) panko breadcrumbs (for a gluten-free option, use gluten-free breadcrumbs)

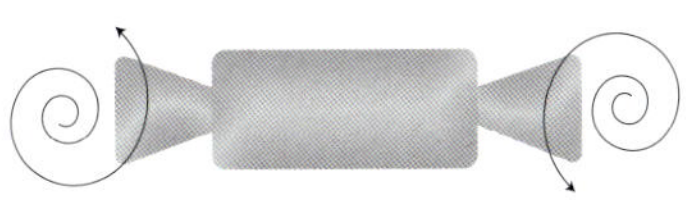

METHOD

1. Steam the bunya nut halves in a Chinese bamboo steamer (or simmer them in a little water) for about 15-20 minutes, to cook out the starch. Drain off any moisture and allow to cool. Chop them to a coarse (about 5 mm / ¼ in.) crumb. If you are doing a large batch, this is certainly easier in a food processor
2. Using a stand mixer with the whisk attachment, whip the soft butter, mustard and egg yolk at high speed until very pale, light and fluffy, for at least 5-8 minutes (see **a**, facing page).
3. Scrape down the sides of the bowl then add all the other ingredients. Mix thoroughly, then check the seasoning. Remember that this wonderful butter needs to be almost over-seasoned, as it will season the food you cook with it.
4. Take a large piece (30 cm/12 in.) square of foil (always use heavy-duty foil, not the thin, light type). Place it on the edge of your bench or chopping board with one third hanging over the edge (**b**). Using the spatula, scoop dollops of butter along this edge, leaving 6-8 cm (2 -3 in.) gaps at the sides (**c**–**d**).
5. Shape roughly into a log and fold over the bottom flap of foil (**e**).
6. Using your hands to smooth down and expel any air bubbles as you go, roll up into a 'sausage' (**f**–**h**).
7. Then, twist the ends of the foil in opposing directions to form a lovely tight bon bon (**i**–**j**). Refrigerate or freeze.

SOY, BLOOD LIME *and* SESAME DRESSING

Accompaniment – makes about 2 cups

This is a brilliant Asian-style dressing that will liven up a host of healthy salads. It will keep in your fridge for many months, but the fruit content settles on the top, so it will need a good shake before use! It's best used after allowing it to warm to room temperature.

INGREDIENTS

75 g (2½ oz) approx. blood limes
75 ml (2½ fl oz) dark soy sauce
100 ml (3⅓ fl oz) rice vinegar
50 ml (1⅔ fl oz) water
90 g (3 oz) sugar
30 ml (1 fl oz) sesame oil
3-4 garlic cloves, peeled
2-3 cm piece peeled ginger, roughly chopped
75 ml (2½ fl oz) vegetable oil
1 red chilli sliced (optional)

METHOD

1. Place all these ingredients into a blender or food processor and blitz on high speed for 20-30 seconds to chop the limes and emulsify.
2. Refrigerate until required.

SUBSTITUTIONS

for the recipes on this page

blood limes: desert limes, tahitian limes, zest and the diced flesh, or grapefruit

davidson plums: plums

ground pepperberry: ground black pepper.

DAVIDSON PLUM CHILLI SAUCE

Condiment – makes about 1 litre (2 pints)

This is quite a large recipe but it's great to make a whole batch and put the excess into sterilized sauce bottles for future use, or halve the quantities if you wish. It will keep for a year or more, and it's amazing in Chinese style stir-fries, or to use as a glaze wherever you would use a plum chilli sauce.

INGREDIENTS

1 kg (2 lb) davidson plums

45 g (1½ oz) ginger, peeled and grated
4-5 large red chillies, chopped, or 4 tsp chilli flakes

½ cup balsamic vinegar
½ cup white vinegar
1½ tsp salt
1½ tsp allspice
900 g (2 lb) brown sugar
1 heaped tsp ground pepperberry

additional chilli, to taste (optional)

50 ml (1⅔ fl oz) water
30 g (1 oz) cornflour (cornstarch)

METHOD

1. Cut the plums in half and remove the two seeds, process them to a fine purée, then add the ginger and chillies.
2. Place the vinegars, salt, allspice, sugar, and ground pepperberry into a large stainless-steel saucepan.
3. Add the purée and simmer slowly for 15-20 minutes, stirring regularly so the sugar does not catch. Now is your chance to boost the chilli if you like the sauce to be really hot.
4. Separately, mix the starch and water together to form a smooth paste. Slowly pour the paste into the simmering sauce, whisking as it thickens. Bring back to the boil once, then you are ready to bottle the sauce. Bottle and cap the sauce while it is still quite hot.

DAVIDSON PLUM ZA'ATAR

Condiment – makes about ⅓ cup

Traditional za'atar is a seasoning used widely in Middle-Eastern and Mediterranean cooking. It's made from a combination of herbs, sesame seeds, sumac (a Mediterranean fruit), and salt. My Australian adaptation uses davidson plum in place of the sumac, to provide a sour and tangy flavour.

INGREDIENTS

30 g (1 oz) sesame seeds

½ tsp wild thyme
1 tsp Greek oregano
2-3 tsp Creative Native Davidson Plum powder (see p. 272 for stockists)

METHOD

1. Pre-heat the oven to 170°C (340°F).
2. Scatter the sesame seeds in a lined baking tray. Dry-roast for 5-6 minutes until the seeds are a very light golden colour. Watch them carefully – they can quickly burn.
3. Using a mortar-and-pestle, pound the roasted sesame seeds together with the thyme, oregano and plum powder, to blend.
4. Store in an air-tight container. The za'atar will keep for 3-4 months.

DAVIDSON PLUM HOI SIN JAM *or* BASTE

Condiment – makes 2-3 cups, depending on reduction

INGREDIENTS

250 g (½ lb) approx. davidson plums

2-3 chillies, roughly chopped

210 g (7 oz) sugar

100 ml (3⅓ fl oz) hoi sin sauce

SUBSTITUTIONS

wild thyme:
thymes; maybe sage
davidson plums
red plums.

METHOD

1. Cut the plums in half and remove the two seeds (no need to peel).
2. Blitz the chillies and plums in a blender to a coarse purée.
3. Place the purée with the sugar in a pot. Simmer gently over a low heat for about 15 minutes.
4. Whisk in the hoi sin sauce and then simmer again. Now you have a choice: you can keep the sauce thin, and use it as a basting glaze, or reduce it to a jam-like consistency. The best way to judge the consistency is to do a 'cold saucer test': put a tablespoon or so on a cold saucer in the fridge and see if it is runny or becomes more jammy. If you want it to be more 'jammy', reduce it further. It will keep in the fridge indefinitely.

VERJUICE *and* DESERT LIME 'BEURRE BLANC'

Condiment – 4 serves or ¾ cup

Beurre Blanc, or 'White Butter Sauce', is a French classic, but so many variations are possible using red or white wine, verjuice, or any acidic fruit juice reduction. Adding chopped sea parsley, chives, dill or other herbs will also add another dimension. I love to use this version when serving crispy-skinned fish. Once you master the simple emulsion procedure, you can quite quickly make all sorts of amazing sauces at home.

INGREDIENTS

½ cup verjuice
2 tsp (10–15g) desert limes, finely chopped
1 heaped tsp sugar

120 g (4 oz) cold unsalted butter, diced into small cubes

salt, to taste

SUBSTITUTIONS

for the recipes on this page

desert limes:
lime zest and juice
lemon myrtle leaves:
thai lime leaves or lemongrass.

METHOD

1. In a small stainless-steel saucepan, bring the verjuice, limes and sugar to a rapid boil, then reduce down to one quarter of the original volume, about 50 ml (1⅔ fl oz). Take care that the flame does not go up the sides of the pan and burn the edges – this can quickly ruin the flavour.
2. Reduce heat to its lowest possible setting and swirl in the butter, 3–4 cubes at a time, allowing it to melt and emulsify. Constant shaking of the pan, or whisking, is essential. I like to move it on and off the heat, to keep it warm, without boiling.
3. Once all the butter is added, you should be left with a gorgeous, shiny yellow, butter sauce. Season to taste and adjust the acidic balance with a little more sugar if you like.
4. Cover and keep in a warm spot until ready to use. Don't let it cool; it will set. If it does need re-warming, do so carefully while stirring. Don't let it boil, as that will break the emulsion.

ORANGE *and* LEMON MYRTLE 'BEURRE BLANC'

Condiment – 4 serves or ¾ cup

INGREDIENTS

½ cup orange juice
6–8 lemon myrtle leaves
2 tsp ginger or galangal, peeled and grated or finely diced

120 g (4 oz) cold, unsalted butter, diced into small cubes

METHOD

1. Simmer the juice, lemon myrtle leaves, and ginger until reduced to about quarter the original volume. Here again, make sure the flame does not go up the sides of the pan and burn the edges, or it can ruin the flavour.
2. Remove the spent leaves. Follow steps 2–4 of the recipe for Verjuice and Desert Lime Beurre Blanc, above.

GERALDTON WAX *and* SPRING ONION SALSA

Condiment – makes 1-2 cups

. . . perfect with my Wild Lemon Herb-Steeped Chicken (p.94), and with grilled fish, tofu or scallops.

INGREDIENTS

10 g (⅓ oz) Geraldton wax leaves, stripped from the stalk, finely chopped
30 g (1 oz) ginger, grated
100 ml (3 ⅓ fl oz) peanut oil

---

150 g (5 oz) spring onions (white part only) finely sliced
50 ml (1⅔ fl oz) shaoxing wine
1 tsp salt
1½ tsp sugar
2 tsp rice vinegar

METHOD

1. Blend the Geraldton wax leaves, ginger and peanut oil together in a food processor or with a mortar-and-pestle.
2. Mix in the spring onions, shaoxing wine, salt, sugar and vinegar, until the sugar has dissolved.
3. Taste for balance; more vinegar or sugar can be added, if desired. The salsa can be stored in the fridge for a day or so, but is much nicer freshly made on the day.

CARROT *and* GERALDTON WAX OIL

Condiment – makes 1 cup

With a brilliant colour and flavour, this oil is great for dressing salads and brushing on grilled fish, vegetables and chicken.

INGREDIENTS

250 g (½ lb) carrots, grated
1 cup peanut oil
30 g (1 oz) Geraldton wax leaves, chopped
2 large red chillies, chopped
20 g (⅔ oz) ginger, grated

SUBSTITUTIONS

Geraldton wax leaves: thai lime leaves and/or lemon grass.

METHOD

1. Place all the ingredients into a wide pan and simmer slowly over a gentle heat for 30 minutes, stirring often, until all the liquid has evaporated. The remaining oil will take on a brilliant orange hue and a lovely flavour. Allow to cool to room temperature.
2. Line a sieve with a clean Chux® cloth, muslin cloth or paper towel. Pour the mixture through the sieve, allowing it to strain completely. Store the strained oil in a jar in the fridge until required. It will keep indefinitely.

PRESERVED DESERT LIME OIL

Accompaniment – makes a little over half a cup

This is a simple way to have a dressing made from preserved desert limes ready to go, for adorning a Moroccan tagine (see Tagine of Rabbit, p.137) or spicing up a roast chicken with dukkah (Saltbush Dukkah-Crusted Chicken, p.104), or even drizzling on grilled fish or a roast pumpkin salad with yoghurt.

INGREDIENTS

⅓ cup preserved desert limes (see below)
¼ cup extra virgin olive oil
½ tsp turmeric

METHOD

1. Gently fry the desert limes and turmeric in the oil for about a minute, to infuse the flavours.
2. Cool then place in a sterile preserving (or Mason) jar and seal and store in your pantry.

PRESERVED DESERT LIMES

Accompaniment – makes 2 cups

Preserved desert limes are a wonderful condiment to add to salads, dressings, dips, tagines and other sauces. Like the preserved lemons used widely in North African cooking, they add strong, distinctive, salty citrus notes to any dish but, unlike preserved lemons, the whole desert lime is used; there is no need to discard any flesh or pith. As always, when preserving, it is most important that you use sterile implements, including preserving jars that can be tightly sealed.

INGREDIENTS

200 g (7 oz) approx. desert limes
150 g (5 oz)
1 cinnamon stick
½ tsp ground turmeric
1-2 tbs extra virgin olive oil
100 ml (3⅓ fl oz) lime or lemon juice

METHOD

1. Mix all the ingredients together.
2. Place in a sterile preserving (or Mason) jar and seal.
3. Turn gently every week or so, for at least a month. The limes will keep indefinitely in your pantry.
4. To use, simply drain then serve.

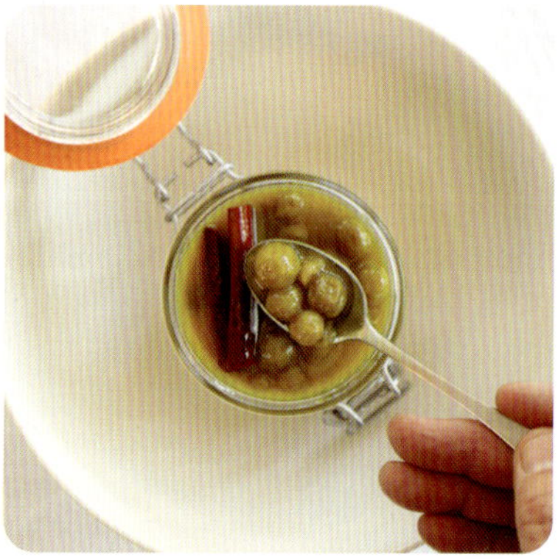

GERALDTON WAX COCONUT CREAM

Condiment – makes 1 cup

This light and fragrant cooling cream makes a beautiful accompaniment to spiced soups (see p.53), curries, and similar dishes, or even with sticky lemon myrtle rice and fresh mango. It takes only a few minutes to make. If you like, you can use a mix of Geraldton wax and lemon myrtle, instead of one or the other.

INGREDIENTS

1 cup coconut cream
2 tsp Geraldton wax leaves, finely chopped

SUBSTITUTIONS
for the recipes on this page

Illawarra plums:
cherries or small plums
ground pepperberry:
ground pepper.
Geraldton wax leaves and lemon myrtle leaves:
lemon verbena leaves, lemon grass, thai lime leaves.

METHOD

1. Mix the aromatic Geraldton wax leaves into half of the coconut cream. Briefly bring to the boil (either on the stove or in the microwave).
2. Allow to cool, then mix in the remaining cream.
3. For a smooth consistency, strain the cream through a sieve to remove the plant fibres, or simply leave as is for additional texture. Refrigerate until ready to serve.
4. To serve, spoon dollops onto your dish. It will keep for 4-5 days in the refrigerator

PICKLED ILLAWARRA PLUMS

Condiment – makes about 1 litre (2 pints)

I developed this recipe many years ago, in the Red Ochre restaurant, based on a traditional pickled cherry recipe. The plums, in a reduction of their pickling juice, make an excellent addition to glazes for game dishes, steak, duck or lamb. They can even be sweetened further, to accompany desserts.

INGREDIENTS

300 g (10 oz) whole Illawarra plums
½ tsp (2 g) ground pepperberry

---

210 ml (7 fl oz) red wine
300 ml (10 fl oz) red wine vinegar
15 g (½ oz) ginger, grated
370 g (13 oz) white sugar
2 cinnamon sticks, crumbled
1 tsp white peppercorns, crushed

METHOD

1. Cut all the plums in half and place in a suitably sized sterile glass jar, together with the pepperberry.
2. Simmer all the remaining ingredients for 5 minutes. Cool to room temperature then strain.
3. Pour the strained liquid over the plums so that they are fully covered. Place in a sterile preserving (or Mason) jar and seal. Allow to steep for 1-2 weeks before use. They will keep indefinitely in your pantry.

SAGE *and* SALTBUSH 'BEURRE NOISETTE'

Condiment – makes about 1 cup

This superb sage-and-saltbush 'beurre noisette', or nut-brown butter, is a variation on the classic brown butter-and-sage combination, and can be used as a quick and easy pasta sauce and is great as a hot dressing over vegetables such as potato, beans, and broccoli. It also works beautifully used in combination with Garlic Cream Sauce (see below), for a double indulgence, and fabulous when chopped nuts such a macadamia, sandalwood, almond or hazelnut are added into the mix.

INGREDIENTS

100 g (3⅓ oz) unsalted butter

4-5 large sage leaves per serve
1 cup saltbush leaves
1 generous handful of sea parsley, coarsely chopped

SUBSTITUTIONS
for the recipes on this page

saltbush leaves:
baby spinach or kale
sea parsley:
flat-leaf (continental) parsley
River Murray salt:
sea salt.

METHOD

1. In a frypan over high heat, melt the butter until it starts to foam furiously and then brown. This might take a few minutes. Some recipes call for burnt butter, and so you can continue to cook the butter beyond brown towards black if you choose, but it will lean towards some bitter notes then.
2. Add the sage, saltbush and sea parsley and cook until they have just wilted (this will only take a few seconds); stir frequently.
3. Use immediately, poured over your dish.

GARLIC CREAM SAUCE

Condiment – makes about 1 cup

Wonderful with almost any vegetable, white meat, or pasta.

INGREDIENTS

1 cup cream
½ tsp River Murray salt
3-4 garlic cloves, grated
⅓ tsp ground pepperleaf or white ground pepper, or to taste

METHOD

1. Just mix everything together in a plastic container and simply bring to the boil in the microwave when you are ready to serve.

SEA PARSLEY OIL

Accompaniment – makes about 1 cup

This is perfect for drizzling over various hot or cold dishes and is especially great over carpaccio, just before serving, to complete the flavours and presentation. Use freshly made; otherwise, it freezes really well. In my restaurant days we'd make a couple of litres at a time and freeze in small tubs ready for service in later weeks.

INGREDIENTS

1 cup best quality extra virgin olive oil
30g (1oz) sea parsley
a few leaves of wild basil (optional)

Murray River salt flakes (optional)

METHOD

1. Process the sea parsley and half the olive oil into a fine purée then microwave on high for 30–60 seconds until it comes to a rapid boil. Immediately add the remaining oil and stir. Place in the fridge to cool quickly. (this helps retain the vibrant colour).
2. When back at room temperature, strain the oil through a fine sieve or muslin cloth to remove the solids, leaving a bright green, clear oil. Stir through the salt just before serving, if using, for a crunchy seasoning.

SUBSTITUTIONS

for the recipes on this page

desert limes:
tiny pieces of lime or lemon
sea parsley:
flat-leaf (continental) parsley
rivermint:
mint
River Murray salt flakes
sea salt flakes.

SEA PARSLEY SALSA VERDE

Accompaniment – makes about 2 cups

This is great with grilled fish, chicken, prawns, cutlets, and vegetables (sweet potato, asparagus, capsicum, etc.). I often double the base and keep extra in the fridge (it lasts for months). Then, when I need a fresh salsa, I just bring it to room temperature then stir through fresh garden herbs, to have maximum flavour in moments.

INGREDIENTS

1 cup extra virgin olive oil
2-3 garlic cloves, roughly chopped
2 tsp desert limes, chopped
15g (½ oz) anchovy fillets
6 tsp capers, chopped

juice (about 3 tbs) and zest of 1 lemon

1 cup sea parsley, chopped
¼ cup rivermint leaves, chopped

METHOD

1. Blend the olive oil, garlic, desert limes, anchovies and capers together in a food processor or with a mortar-and-pestle.
2. Mix in the juice and zest. At this point, the base can be stored in an air-tight jar in the fridge for several months.
3. Mix in the parsley and rivermint just before serving, to retain maximum colour and flavour.

SPICY PEPPERLEAF OIL

Condiment – makes 1 generous cup

I encourage anyone who loves using native foods to buy a native peppertree or shrub and have it growing in a cool, shady spot in their garden or on the patio, so the fresh leaves are available at any time they are needed. Remember there are male and female plants, so if you want the fruit — pepperberry — as well as the leaf, you'll need one of each, for the cross-pollination. Native ('mountain' or 'Tasmanian' pepper) is a cool-climate plant and grows best in a cool, moist environment.

Pepperleaf oil itself is a simple, flavoured oil that will add spice and heat to any sauce, grilled meat, fish or vegetable, or can be used to drizzle over curries, salads and other dishes. It's perfect for adding a burst of unique peppery flavour, in much the same way chilli oils, pastes and sambals are offered with many Asian dishes. The heat in Australian native pepper comes from the compound 'polygodial', but cooking causes it to lose its characteristic heat. As this oil is cold-processed, the heat is preserved. Keep the oil refrigerated, and allow it to come to room temperature an hour or so before use (because the olive oil coagulates and becomes cloudy when cold). I use it as a seasoning on meals.

INGREDIENTS

1 cup extra virgin olive oil
½ cup of Tasmanian pepperleaves, stripped from the stalk
1 tsp salt, or to taste

SUBSTITUTIONS

Tasmanian pepperleaves:
fresh chilli, Dorrigo pepperleaves (see notes on p. 40).

METHOD

1. Simply process all the ingredients to a fine purée in a food blender (like a thin, runny pesto). For a thicker oil or paste, just add more leaves.
2. Store the oil in a jar in the fridge until required. It will keep for a month or two.

SUNRISE LIME *and* CHILLI BLACK VINEGAR

Condiment – makes about half a cup

A simple fruity version of a Chinese table condiment, to cut richness and fattiness in many dishes.

INGREDIENTS

40 ml (1⅓ fl oz) sweet soy sauce (ketjap manis)
40 ml (1⅓ fl oz) Chinese black vinegar
40 ml (1⅓ fl oz) water
1 chilli, sliced
1 sunrise lime, quartered and sliced fine

METHOD

1. Mix all these together and allow to macerate for an hour or so before use. Leftovers with keep for a few weeks in the fridge. (This is very easy recipe; conveniently, sunrise limes – as well as blood and desert limes – have such fine skin that the whole fruit, skin and seeds can be eaten, although the seeds can be removed, if preferred).

TOMATO *and* LEMON MYRTLE CHILLI JAM

Condiment – makes about 4 cups

Chilli jams are an addictive condiment to have handy in the fridge, and of course can be mild or seriously hot, depending on the type and quantity of chillies. They are excellent to use in wraps, sandwiches, on burgers, or to spice up dips and stir-fries — go wild!

INGREDIENTS

20 g (⅔ oz) blachan (shrimp paste)

100 ml (3⅓ fl oz) vegetable oil
75 g (2½ oz) red shallots or spanish onions, peeled and chopped

150 g (5 oz) long red chillies, chopped
4 cloves garlic, peeled and crushed

2 large red capsicums
25-30 g (1 oz) lemon myrtle leaves
400 g (14 oz) tomato paste or very thick passata (tomato purée)
150 g (5 oz) palm sugar
50 ml (1⅔ fl oz) fish sauce
50 g (1⅔ oz) wild native tamarind pulp

METHOD

1. Wrap the blachan in a piece of foil and roast in a 180°C (356°F) oven for 8-10 minutes.
2. Meanwhile, heat the oil in a heavy-based pan over moderate heat then fry the onions for 3-4 minutes.
3. Add the chillies and garlic and continue frying until they are very lightly caramelized.
4. Using a blender, process the roasted blachan, onions, chillies, and garlic to a smooth purée.
5. Place the purée, tomato paste, palm sugar, fish sauce and tamarind pulp in a pot. Simmer very gently for 30-40 minutes, stirring frequently (caution: it can burn) until it's a jammy consistency.

SUBSTITUTIONS
for the recipes on this page

sunrise lime:
orange zest
lemon verbena leaves,
thai lime leaves
wild tamarind:
Asian tamarind purée.

TOMATO, LEMON MYRTLE *and* GINGER SAUCE

Sauce – makes a generous litre (2 pints), depending on the amount of reduction

I love this recipe, which I first developed during my Red Ochre Restaurant years for the mud-crab season. It's based on the classic Singapore Chilli Mud Crab I enjoyed so much during my first international gig as a guest chef, at the Singapore Hilton back in 1996. For the real chilli fans, choose super-hot scud chillies if you're game! The lemon myrtle flavour is deliciously addictive when combined with the tomato and Asian flavours, and the sauce works superbly with chilli crab, mussels, fish, squid and other seafood. It's great on pizza, too.

INGREDIENTS

1½ tsp sesame oil
30 ml (1 fl oz) extra virgin olive oil

30 g (1 oz) ginger, peeled and grated
6-8 garlic cloves, peeled and slivered
1-2 tsp red chilli flakes,
or 4-8 red chillies, chopped

120 g (4 oz) onions, peeled and coarsely chopped

3 cups tomato passata or crushed tinned tomatoes, or a mix of both
110 g (4 oz) sugar or light palm sugar
3-5 whole star anise
150 ml (5 fl oz) rice or white vinegar
10-15 whole lemon myrtle leaves, or 2-3 tsp ground lemon myrtle leaves
25 ml (1 fl oz) fish sauce, or to taste

50 ml (1⅔ fl oz) water (optional)
20 g (⅔ oz) cornflour (cornstarch) or arrowroot

SUBSTITUTIONS

lemon myrtle leaves:
lemon verbena leaves,
thai lime leaves.

METHOD

1. Heat the oils together in a large saucepan.
2. Add the ginger, garlic and chilli. Fry while stirring constantly until they are very fragrant and just starting to caramelize.
3. Immediately add the onion and fry gently for another 3-5 minutes to soften.
4. Add the passata (and/or tomatoes, if using), sugar, star anise, vinegar, lemon myrtle and fish sauce. Bring to a very gentle simmer, stirring occasionally and cook for 20-30 minutes. If you wish, you can now adjust the sweet and salty flavour by adding a little more sugar and/or fish sauce.
5. You can also decide whether you want to thicken the sauce with a little extra water and starch. If so, mix the water and cornflour (or arrowroot, if using) together to form a paste and mix some or all through the simmering sauce. Alternatively, simmer the sauce for a little longer so that it reduces in volume, but be aware that the extra reduction will also concentrate the flavours.
6. Allow the sauce to cool, pour into sterilized jars or bottles and store in the fridge until ready to use. It should keep for up to 2 months, but I freeze it down at home into meal-sized tubs or vacuum bags.

CUCUMBER *and* RIVERMINT TZATZIKI

Condiment – makes 2-3 cups

Refreshing sauces made from yoghurt mixed with ingredients such as cucumber, lemon, garlic, dill, and mint are widespread and go by various names (tzatziki, raita, etc.). They can be used as a cooling accompaniment alongside hot dishes, or as a wonderful healthy sauce or dressing in wraps and salads.

INGREDIENTS

15 g (½ oz) rivermint leaves
5-6 desert limes
4-5 garlic cloves, peeled
1 tsp salt
20 g (⅔ oz) sugar

½ continental cucumber or 2-3 small lebanese cucumbers, grated
500 g (about 1 lb) Greek yoghurt
additional rivermint, for garnish

SUBSTITUTIONS

rivermint:
mint.
desert limes:
flesh and zest of 1 small lime or lemon, peeled and finely diced.

METHOD

1. Finely chop the rivermint, desert limes and garlic on a chopping board with the salt and sugar (adding these granules helps absorb the moisture and oils from the ingredients, instead of them being left on the board surface), or just blitz them very quickly in a food processor.
2. Mix this 'paste' and the grated cucumber into the yoghurt.
3. Cucumber has a lot of water so, as an optional step, line a sieve with a clean Chux® or paper towel. Pour the mixture into the sieve, cover, and place a bowl underneath to catch the drips. The sieve should be sitting above the drained liquid, not in contact with it (see p. 244 for more information about draining the yoghurt and also how to thicken the yoghurt to make labneh). Allow to drain in the fridge until it's thickened nicely, then discard the water and serve, garnished with rivermint if desired.

RIVERMINT YOGHURT SAUCE

Condiment - makes about 1½ cups

INGREDIENTS

1 cup plain yoghurt

---

15 g (½ oz) rivermint leaves
20 g (⅔ oz) green chillies, sliced
1-2 garlic cloves, peeled
zest and juice of 1 lime
20 g (⅔ oz) coriander (cilantro)
20 g (⅔ oz) light (pale) palm sugar
1 cup plain yoghurt

METHOD

1. Put the yoghurt to one side, then process all the remaining ingredients into a fine paste, or pound them together using a mortar-and-pestle.
2. Now stir through the yoghurt (it's important not to process yoghurt in the machine as that destroys the thick texture, and it will be quite runny). Chill before serving.

CUCUMBER *and* RIVERMINT PICKLE

Condiment – makes about 2 cups

This beautiful refreshing pickle will keep for months in the refrigerator. It's amazing in wraps and sandwiches, and on antipasto platters, too — a fantastic alternative to the old-fashioned pickled onions and gherkins!

INGREDIENTS

liquid

- 150 ml (5 fl oz) coconut vinegar
- 100 ml (3⅓ fl oz) water
- 150 g (5 oz) sugar
- 1 tsp salt
- 3-4 garlic cloves, peeled and crushed
- 1 bunch (about 50 g or 1⅔ oz) coriander (cilantro), roots and/or stems, chopped
- 1 handful (about 10 g / ⅓ oz) rivermint

pickles

- 1 large (about 500 g or 1 lb) continental cucumber or small cocktail cucumbers
- 25 g (1 oz) red shallots (or spanish onions), peeled and sliced
- 3-4 large red chillies, finely sliced
- 10-15 g (⅓-½ oz) ginger, finely grated
- 1 handful (about 10 g / ⅓ oz) additional rivermint leaves, coarsely chopped

METHOD

to make the pickling liquid

1. Weigh the vinegar, water, sugar, salt, garlic and coriander and rivermint straight into a stainless-steel saucepan, taring off one after the other as you go (this makes it really easy to get exactly the right quantities and acid sweet balance).
2. Bring to the boil. Simmer gently for 5 minutes, then allow to cool completely.
3. Strain the cooled mixture through a fine sieve.

to prepare the pickles

1. Slice the cucumbers into half or quarter rounds (about 5 mm / ¼ in. thick) and mix with the shallots, chillies, ginger and extra rivermint leaves. Place in a sterile preserving jar.
2. Pour over the strained pickling liquid and refrigerate.
3. Allow to marinate for 3–4 days (preferably a week or more) before using.

SUBSTITUTIONS

rivermint:
mint.

RIVERMINT *and* CHILLI PESTO

Condiment – makes about 2 cups

I love this pesto, very much a 'cross-cultural' recipe, which I only recently refined for commercial production as a food service product. It also freezes really well, in case you want to keep any excess for long periods. The coriander, fish sauce and chilli provide lovely Asian notes, but a vegetarian option, replacing the fish sauce with salt, works just as well. I like to toss it through pasta and green vegetables such as beans and broccolini, to make a complete vegetarian meal. Replacing some of the chilli with fresh native pepperleaf is another flavoursome variation, and adding some grated ginger is also wonderful — as is using our wild basil!

INGREDIENTS

160g (5⅓ oz) cashew or almond nuts

30g (1oz) basil leaves
50g (1⅔ oz) rivermint leaves
60g (2oz) coriander (cilantro), leaves and stalks
5-6 garlic cloves, peeled
30g (1oz) green chillies, chopped
70g (2⅓ oz) Italian parmesan, grated
30g (1oz) brown or light palm sugar
1½ tsp sea salt or 1½ tsp fish sauce, or to taste

200ml (7fl oz) grapeseed or peanut oil

SUBSTITUTIONS

rivermint:
mint.

METHOD

1. Pre-heat the oven to 160°C (320°F). Scatter the nuts on a baking tray and roast gently for about 8-10 minutes, until a very light golden colour. Allow to cool.
2. Place all the ingredients (except the oil) into a food processor bowl. (For this and many recipes, I like to weigh the ingredients directly into the bowl while it is on the scales – see notes on measuring and weighing ingredients on page 18.)
3. Process the ingredients into a chunky paste while slowly drizzling in the oil.
4. Check the seasoning and adjust to your taste. More oil can also be added to make a thinner pesto.
5. If you like it hot, by all means add more chilli.

RIVERMINT *and* ONION CHILLI JAM

Condiment – makes 4-5 cups, depending on consistency

Onion jams are great with roast vegetables, grilled steak, lamb and chicken, or in a sauce with roast meats. This has a mint-and-chilli spice kick and is also lovely on burgers or in toasted ham-and-cheese sandwiches.

INGREDIENTS

80 ml (2⅔ fl oz) extra virgin olive oil
1 kg (2 lb) onions, peeled and diced into 1 cm (½ in.) chunks or finely sliced

---

3⅓ cups dark brown sugar
1½ tsp salt
10-12 garlic cloves, peeled and finely chopped
20-30g (⅔-1 oz) large red chillies (adjust quantity depending on the heat level desired), finely chopped
1 cup good quality red wine or balsamic vinegar
50 g (1⅔ oz) rivermint leaves, chopped

METHOD

1. Heat the oil in a wide heavy-based pan then add the onion. Cook over a low to medium heat, stirring regularly until they are a nice golden brown (about 30 minutes).
2. Add the remaining ingredients and gently simmer to evaporate excess moisture and reduce the mixture to a 'jammy' consistency. To test this, place a small spoonful on a cold saucer in the refrigerator and see how well it sets. It won't set hard, but it shouldn't be too runny, either.
3. Once the jam is the right consistency, add the rivermint. Bring to the simmer again to pasteurise and then decant into sterilised jars and cover immediately with a lid. Store in the refrigerator, where it will keep almost indefinitely.

CARAMELIZED ONION *and* MUNTRIES JAM

Condiment – makes 4-5 cups, depending on consistency

This is similar to the jam above but not as sweet or reduced. It could be made more 'jammy' by adding more sugar and vinegar but is marvellous 'as is' with grilled meats and mashed potato in winter, or on a pizza. It's also excellent with the addition of a little wild thyme.

INGREDIENTS

80 ml (2⅔ fl oz) extra virgin olive oil
1 kg (2 lb) spanish onions peeled and sliced into thin slivers

---

1 tsp salt
½ cup cider vinegar
4 tsp dark brown sugar
1 generous cup muntries
1 tsp ground pepperleaf
2 tsp sage, chopped
1-2 green chillies, chopped (optional)

METHOD

1. In a wide, heavy-based pan, heat the olive oil and add the onion. Cook over low heat, stirring regularly, until the onions are a nice golden brown. This should take about 30 minutes. Don't rush it!
2. Add the other ingredients and gently simmer to a stew while reducing a little. You can adjust the sweet/sour balance by adding more vinegar and/or sugar, and, if you like a hot kick, extra chilli.

SUBSTITUTIONS

rivermint: mint
muntries: diced dried apple
ground pepperleaf: ground pepper.

YELLOW RIVERMINT CURRY SAUCE

Sauce – makes 1½–2 litres (3–4 pints) of sauce (enough for a couple of meals)

This lovely version of the classic Thai yellow curry sauce can be quite tart and sour, but simply adjust to suit your taste. Our amazing native tamarind (also known as the rainforest lychee) fruit, like the Asian tamarind, makes a great acidulant for curries. The sauce is great with any firm white-fleshed fish or chicken, and even vegetables such as eggplant, zucchini, carrot and sweet potato.

INGREDIENTS

20 g (⅔ oz) blachan (shrimp paste)

1 yellow capsicum, diced
75 g (2½ oz) shallots, peeled and chopped
45 g (1½ oz) lemongrass, white part only, sliced
10–12 garlic cloves, peeled and sliced
30 g (1 oz) orange/yellow chillies
15 g (½ oz) turmeric powder or 45 g (1½ oz) grated
30g (1 oz) chopped galangal (or ginger)
15 g (½ oz) rivermint leaves
50 ml (1⅔ fl oz) peanut or vegetable oil
10–12 lemon myrtle or thai lime leaves
zest of 2 limes

2 cups coconut cream

45 g (1½ oz) native tamarind purée
3 cups chicken or fish stock
100 g (3½ oz) palm sugar, grated
80 ml (2⅔ fl oz) thai fish sauce

SUBSTITUTIONS

orange/yellow chillies:
red chillies
rivermint:
mint
native tamarind purée:
Asian tamarind purée.

METHOD

1. Heat the oven to 180°C (355°F).
2. Lightly wrap the blachan in an envelope of foil and roast for 10 minutes.
3. Purée all the paste ingredients – blachan, capsicum, shallots, lemongrass, garlic, chillies, turmeric, galangal, rivermint, oil, lime leaves and zest – to a fine paste in a food processor.
4. Separately, reduce the coconut cream in a heavy-based pan over a slow-medium heat until the cream just starts to split and is very lightly 'toasted'. Do not colour.
5. Add the paste. Gently fry for 5–10 minutes without colouring.
6. Add the tamarind purée, stock, sugar and fish sauce. Mix well, then simmer for 5-10 minutes, stirring occasionally. You can now adjust the sweet/salty/sour/hot balance to your taste, or later, when you finish preparing the dish, if you prefer.
7. The sauce can be used immediately, or will keep, covered, in the fridge for 2–3 days. It also freezes quite well.

MACADAMIA *and* LEMON MYRTLE SATAY SAUCE

Accompaniment – makes about 2 cups

This is certainly a real Aussie version of Indonesia's famous peanut satay sauce, and it keeps very well frozen in small meal-sized tubs or plastic bags. The lemon myrtle adds a unique flavour that lemon grass or thai lime (formerly known as kaffir lime) can't match (although they can be used as substitutes in a pinch).

INGREDIENTS

20 g (⅔ oz) blachan (shrimp paste), crumbled

¼ cup macadamia or vegetable oil
30 g (1 oz) red chillies, sliced
30 g (1 oz) garlic
20 g (⅔ oz) peeled galangal, roughly chopped
2 tsp ground lemon myrtle
2-3 lime leaves

---

250 g (½ lb) plain macadamias, white meat only

---

400 g (13⅓ fl oz) coconut cream
25 g (1 oz) palm sugar
½ cup sweet soy sauce (ketjap manis)
8-10 large fresh lemon myrtle leaves

---

25 g (1 oz) wild tamarind purée

SUBSTITUTIONS

macadamias:
cashews, peanuts
lemon myrtle leaves:
thai lime leaf or lemongrass
wild tamarind purée):
Asian tamarind purée.

METHOD

1. Wrap the crumbled blachan in an envelope of aluminium foil and roast in a moderately hot 200°C (390°F) oven for 5 minutes.
2. Using a food processor, pureé the roasted blachan together with the vegetable oil, chillies, garlic, galangal, ground lemon myrtle and lime leaves to a fine consistency.
3. Reduce the oven heat to about 160°C (320°F). Scatter the macadamia nuts in a lined baking tray and gently roast for about 10 minutes, until they are a light golden-brown in colour. Check frequently, as they can burn easily.
4. Add the roasted macadamias to the puréed ingredients. Using the food processor, pulse through the macadamia nuts to mix in with the purée and create a roughly 5 mm (¼ in.) 'crumb'.
5. Place the coconut cream, palm sugar, sweet soy sauce, lemon myrtle leaves and the nut purée in a heavy-based saucepan. Simmer gently, stirring frequently, for 10-15 minutes. Add the tamarind pulp now to balance the sauce to taste, simmer once more. If it's too thick, add a little water or coconut milk or cream to adjust. If too thin, reduce more.
6. Discard the spent leaves and store the satay sauce in an air-tight container in the refrigerator until ready to use. It should keep for 1-2 weeks.

WILD SAVOURY CRUMBLE

Accompaniment – makes a generous cup

This crunchy, crumbly mix is delicious scattered over roast vegetables, salads, or even used as a crumb or crust on fish and meats — whenever a nutritious, tasty texture is needed to finish a dish. It can also be used as a crumble topping over gently baked or stewed fruits: just omit the savoury dukkah and sweeten it slightly.

INGREDIENTS

30 g (1 oz) pepita seeds
30 g (1 oz) pumpkin seeds
30 g (1 oz) macadamia nuts, chopped coarsely into 3 mm (about ⅛ in.) chunks
30 g (1 oz) sandalwood nuts, chopped coarsely into 3 mm (about ⅛ in.) chunks
30 g (1 oz) Creative Native Saltbush Dukkah or other favourite dukkah
30 g (1 oz) Malted Wattleseed Crisps (see below)

METHOD

1. Pre-heat the oven to 160°C (320°F).
2. Mix all the ingredients together then scatter them over a large, lined baking tray.
3. Gently toast for about 10-15 minutes until just becoming a light golden colour. Keep an eye on them as they can burn easily.
4. Cool and store in an airtight container. They should keep for at least 3-6 months. You can leave the mix coarse, or crush it smaller if you like.

MALTED WATTLESEED CRISPS

Accompaniment – makes about 1 cup

These delicious, healthy little crisps are easy and fun to make — and it's also a very educational process, great for kids! Once made, they will keep in an air-tight jar in the pantry for about 2–3 months. If you don't already know how to activate and sprout wattleseeds, refer to the easy instructions on p.29 (and don't forget, you will need to allow a few days for the sprouting to take place).

INGREDIENTS

1 cup wattleseed
3 cups boiling water

METHOD

1. Activate the wattleseeds (soak them for 12-24 hours, depending on the type, using the method on p.29).
2. Now allow them time to sprout (refer to p.30).
3. Drain the sprouted seeds then roast slowly in a slow-moderate oven (150-170°C / 300-340°F), to caramelize. Depending on whether you want a light or dark roast, this can take 30-60 minutes or more. (See pp.29-30 for more details.)

BASIC PIZZA DOUGH

Large – makes enough for 4 large pizzas

I absolutely love to have a pizza night at home and to fire up my wood oven (an old beauty I built years ago with my dad). It's quite an effort to get everything underway, but it's such a wonderful reward when everyone comes together to enjoy, not just the eating of the meal, but also the 4 or 5 hours of preparation. It's a family tradition for us. The dough can be made the day before to really ferment; once made, just wrap the balls in some kitchen film and refrigerate overnight. The sauces and garnishes can also be prepared in advance.

My wood oven takes at least 3 hours of raging fire to gain a full 'soak of heat' into the bricks. I build the fire in the middle first, then 15–20 minutes before making my first pizza I split the coals and push them to the back and sides and allow the heat on the hearth to equalise. The oven needs to be extremely hot to achieve fast, crispy-based pizzas but, to check it's not too hot, throw a small piece of plain dough into it to see if the base burns instantly. If so, wait a little while for the heat of the hearth to settle, or run a clean, damp old mop (kept just for this purpose) over it to help cool it slightly. As your pizza night progresses, throw in some extra wood or small logs onto the coals as needed. They should quickly burst into flame and provide another surge of heat. Keep an eye on the temperature; you will quickly see if the pizzas are slowing down in cooking time and browning. If your oven is cooling off, it will need that extra heat burst from the additional wood.

When cutting a pizza slice of a properly cooked pizza, you should be able to hold it from the edge, and it should still hold up straight and not bend or sag. Sadly, so many highly regarded pizza restaurants never achieve a crispy base and really miss the point. Another bad practice seen way too much in Australia is over-loaded toppings — so unnecessary. If you invest in the best quality ingredients, less is definitely more. If you don't have a wood oven, cook the pizza in your conventional home oven on a pizza stone: just pre-heat to the highest possible setting for at least a half hour, but you won't achieve quite the same extreme heat that's possible in a wood oven.

INGREDIENTS

500g (1lb) strong bread or pizza flour
7 g sachet (about ¼ oz) dry yeast
4 tsp olive oil or spray oil
1 tsp salt
2 tsp raw sugar
300 ml (10 fl oz) water

To make 'Potato and Garlic Bunya Nut Pizza' (left): Boil 2 medium, unpeeled potatoes until just tender. Cool, peel and slice thinly. Roll out a half-quantity of dough (see instructions on p. 146) then spread 1 cup (total) of softened Bunya Nut Garlic Butter over the bases. Sprinkle the potato and rosemary sprigs over the top, followed by a generous amount of cheese (bitey cheddar or gruyere). Cook in a very hot, pre-heated oven (see p. 146), season then serve.

METHOD

1. Work the ingredients into a smooth dough, by hand or using the dough hook on an electric mixer, then knead for about 5-8 minutes, until the dough is smooth and elastic. Cover with kitchen film and place in a warm spot. Allow to prove for at least 20 minutes, until doubled in size.
2. Knead again to 'knock down' the dough, then shape it into fist-sized balls. Smear over with olive oil (or spray oil).
3. Place on a large tray and cover with a clean, damp tea towel. Prove once more until doubled in size again before using.

STEAMED BAO BUNS

Accompaniment – makes approximately 20 buns, depending on size

For those who love working with bread and pastries, this may take a couple of goes to perfect the technique — but, if pressed for time, you will still get great results using frozen buns from an Asian supermarket.

INGREDIENTS

210 ml (7 fl oz) milk
50 ml (1⅔ fl oz) vegetable oil, plus a little extra for oiling the buns

2 cups plain flour
1 cup cornflour (cornstarch)
4 heaped tsp castor sugar
7 g sachet (¼ oz) dry yeast
½ tsp baking powder

neutral cooking spray

Native Aniseed Five-Spice Pork with Davidsons Plum Hoi Sin (p. 81), served with boa buns.

METHOD

1. Measure the milk and oil into a microwave-proof container and microwave briefly (about 10-15 seconds) to warm a little.
2. Place all the remaining ingredients together (excluding the cooking spray) with the warmed milk and oil in a mixing bowl. Using an electric mixer with the dough hook attached, knead at a slow speed. It should begin to form a sticky dough; if not, you may need to add a little extra milk (this will depend on the flour you are using).
3. Continue kneading the dough until it becomes soft, elastic and smooth to touch. This should take about 5-8 minutes.
4. Cover with kitchen film and place somewhere warm to prove for 30-40 minutes. It needs to rise and double in size.
5. Once the dough is ready, punch it back and knead briefly by hand. Fashion it into a long sausage, about 3-4 cm (about 1-1½ in.) in diameter, then cut into smaller pieces, about 3-4 cm (about 1-1½ in.) in length
6. Use your hands to rub some oil onto the surface of the dough and squeeze it flat.
7. Using an oiled rolling pin, roll out each piece into elongated round discs. Lightly fold each one over in half and place on a large oiled tray. Cover with kitchen film and place in a warm place for about 30 minutes for the buns to rise again.
8. Place a bamboo steamer over a pan of simmering water. Line the steamer tray with baking paper and pierce a few holes here and there, to allow the steam to come through. Spray with spray oil then carefully lay out as many steam buns as will fit comfortably. Place over the simmering water.
9. Steam the buns in batches for 10-12 minutes, or until puffy and soft and cooked all the way through. Serve immediately.

SEA PARSLEY PASTA

Basics – 4-5 large serves | 8 small serves

This is an easy, classic pasta dough. I allow 100g (a little over 3oz) of flour and an egg per person, but that quantity can be tweaked according to appetite. If the dough becomes a little 'tight' or dry (this can happen because the moisture content in flour can vary from batch to batch), add a dash of water to make a thinner, more pliable dough. Various herbs can be added for colour and flavour.

INGREDIENTS

500g (1 lb) bread ('strong') flour
5 eggs
1½ tsp salt
5 tsp extra virgin olive oil
30g (1 oz) sea parsley, chopped very finely
a little extra water, if required

SUBSTITUTIONS

sea parsley:
flat-leaf (contintental) parsley or other fresh herbs of your choice.

METHOD

1. Sieve the flour into a food processor and add all the other ingredients. Pulse until the mixture just starts to come together. (The parsley must be very finely chopped so it doesn't get caught in the pasta-machine rollers later, if using).
2. Pour onto a floured workbench and knead for 5-10 minutes by hand to a smooth, elastic dough.
3. Alternatively, if using a stand mixer with a dough hook, knead for 5-10 minutes. Kneading develops the gluten, which makes the dough elastic and strong. To check, pinch the dough and pull at it slightly. It should stretch nicely. Don't over-work. Cover with kitchen film and allow it to rest for 20 minutes.
4. If you have a pasta machine, start rolling out the dough. To build up layers (or 'laminations'), which improves texture, first feed the dough through the machine (on the widest setting) in a flat sheet, then fold over and feed through again once or twice more if you like, but its not essential. Keep it well dusted with flour to avoid sticking. Now you can run it through the spaghetti or fettucini cutters.
5. Alternatively, if you don't have a pasta machine, do it the original way: roll out with a rolling pin, cut the dough into quarters and wrap in kitchen film until ready to use. Roll the first ball into a large rectangle, dusting lightly with flour as you go, until the pasta is very thin (1-2mm thick, or 1⁄16 in.) then roll up into a sausage and cut with a sharp knife into spaghetti or the wider fettucini strips. Repeat with the remaining dough.
6. Cook pasta in generous amounts of rapidly boiling salted water until 'al dente'.

STEAMED LEMON MYRTLE RICE

Accompaniment - 4 serves

A quick and easy rice dish that works perfectly with plain or spiced dishes.

INGREDIENTS

250 g (½ lb) jasmine rice, washed
400 ml (13⅓ fl oz) water
5-8 lemon myrtle leaves
1 cm (⅓ in.) approx. piece of ginger, cut into 3 thick slices.

METHOD

1. Bring all the ingredients to the boil in a deep, lidded saucepan. Stir once, then cover tightly with the lid.
2. Reduce heat to the lowest setting. Leave rice to slowly cook for 20 minutes.
3. Turn off the heat, remove the lid, and break up the rice by stirring with a fork. Cover again, and leave to stand for a further 5-10 minutes, then serve.

COCONUT LEMON MYRTLE RICE

INGREDIENTS

250 g (½ lb) jasmine rice, washed
400 ml (13⅓ fl oz) coconut milk
5-8 lemon myrtle leaves
1 cm (⅓ in.) approx. piece of ginger, cut into 3 thick slices (optional)

METHOD

1. This is just a variation of the recipe above. Follow the same steps. The recipes are interchangeable.

SUBSTITUTIONS

lemon myrtle leaves:
thai lime leaves,
lemon zest.

ROASTED WATTLESEEDS

Various uses – makes about ½ cup

I use roasted wattleseeds (acacia seeds) in a lot of my recipes, and this is my tried-and-true technique. Then, once the wattleseeds have been roasted, they can be stored in an air-tight jar, in the pantry, for several months. If a recipe calls for ground wattleseeds, freshly ground is best, just before using. I like to use a mortar-and-pestle for this purpose, as it seems to produce the best flavour, but spice grinders or even a powerful blender will also do the job. Always keep in mind that while many wattleseeds are edible, this is not true for all them, so keep with the known edible varieties. See also p. 28–29 for more information on other ways to use wattleseeds, including sprouting, malting, and fermenting.

INGREDIENTS

½ cup of whipstick or Halls Creek wattleseed, or other edible wattleseed

METHOD

1. Pre-heat the oven to 160°-170°C (320°-340°F).
2. Spread the seeds out thinly (a single layer is best) on a roasting tray
3. For a light roast, bake for 5-6 minutes until they are just starting to smoke, as this is what develops their lovely nutty character. For a darker roast, keep baking for an extra 3-5 minutes. They will start to smoke very heavily, so make sure your extraction exhaust fan is on high. They will also start to pop and jump profusely, so I often cover the tray with foil to prevent a lot of the seed ending up on the oven floor! Keep a close eye on them, though, as they can burn easily.
4. Allow to cool before using or storing in an air-tight jar. They will keep for 4-6 months.

ROASTED SALTBUSH SEEDS *or* SESAME SEEDS

For saltbush seeds, follow the same steps as above, but replace the wattleseeds with saltbush seeds and set oven to 160°C (320°F) only. Roast for 6-8 minutes.

For sesame seeds, follow the same steps as above, but replace the wattleseeds or saltbush seeds with sesame seeds and set oven to 160°C (320°F) only. Roast for 5-6 minutes. Watch carefully – they can easily burn.

PEPPERBERRY BRIOCHE

Accompaniment – makes 4 very large hamburger buns or 10-12 traditional, smaller brioche buns

I marvelled at the superb French pastries in Europe when working there as a young chef, and brioche was a favourite. Unlike most other breads, it includes butter and eggs and so it sits somewhere between a bread and a pastry, very rich and buttery. The amazing purple-black pigments and flavour of the Tasmanian pepperberry leach out into the dough during baking, to give it a unique dark hue and mild spice notes. I developed this recipe as an entrée dish in the early '90s with caramelized shallots, warrigal spinach and mushrooms together with a pepperberry and red wine butter sauce — but it also makes a special burger bun, too!

INGREDIENTS

2 x 7 g sachet (about ½ oz, total) dry yeast
150 ml (5 fl oz) milk, luke-warm
30g (1 oz) sugar

---

375 g (13 oz) plain flour
pinch of salt
4 egg yolks
90 g (3 oz) unsalted butter, softened
1 tsp ground pepperberry

---

2 tsp extra milk
1 extra egg yolk (optional)

* *Spare egg whites freeze remarkably well in small 'recipe'-sized tubs — great for the pavlova on page 238.*

SUBSTITUTIONS

ground pepperberries:
ground black pepper.

METHOD

1. Mix together the yeast, milk, and sugar and allow the mixture to sit in a warm place for an hour or so, to prove.
2. Separately, sieve the flour into a large mixing bowl.
3. Add the yeast mixture to the bowl, together with the salt, egg yolks, butter, and pepperberry.
4. Using the dough hook on an electric mixer, mix on a low speed for 5-8 minutes, to form a smooth, elastic dough.
5. Cover with kitchen film and place in a warm spot. Allow to prove for a further 20 minutes or so, and double in size.
6. Knock down the dough and form into 10-12 brioche buns or about 4 large burger buns. Place on a lined baking tray and spray liberally with water.
7. Cover the buns with a second large, deep pan, or tray, or other deep container (like a cardboard box) if you can, to achieve a warm humid environment, important for proving.
8. Leave the buns to prove until they have doubled in size (maybe another 15-20 minutes). It's a good idea to spray the buns with water a couple of times while they prove, to prevent a dry skin from forming.
9. Using egg yolk for a glaze will give a wonderful shine to the finished brioche, briefly beat the remaining egg yolk and milk together to combine, then brush a thin layer over the top of the buns to glaze (or plain milk works well, too.)
10. Bake at 180°C (355°F) for 20-30 minutes, using up to 30 minutes for the larger buns less for the smaller buns.

INDEX

RECIPES, Alphabetically

RECIPES, by native or wild ingredient

Where to get Australian native and wild ingredients

Many of these are now available from bulk and wholefood stores, produce and farmers markets, nurseries, some supermarkets and greengrocers, and on-line. Several can be grown at home. Availability will vary according to season and location, and this book provides substitutions for when they are needed. I also hope it will increase awarenesss, so that when home cooks come across these foods by chance they will want to take them home and try them out. Here are a few places from where to get your native and wild Australian foods:

Creative Native Foods

Australian Native Plants Society of Australia

- ON-LINE – Creative Native Foods (www.creativenativefoods.com.au) has one of the most comprehensive ranges, including dried and frozen herbs, spices, fruit, vegetables, nuts and seeds, including wattleseed. It is also where to buy Creative Native Bush Tomato Balsamic, Satlbush Dukkah and other Creative Native products, as well as in-season fresh produce when available. There are many other online suppliers of native foods, easily located with an internet search, but always choose reputable suppliers to ensure the quality.
- NATIVE PLANT NURSERIES – For a regularly updated state-by-state list of native plant nurseries and some international locations, visit the Australian Native Plants Society of Australia, www.anpsa.org.au/nursery.html
- GENERAL NURSERIES – Most nurseries now stock native food plants, including major chains such as Bunnings, although the range may be limited according to the location.
- HOME GARDENS – I encourage people to visit nurseries, then grow their own native and wild Australian foods. This is a rewarding and sustainable practice and very educational. Growing, harvesting, and eating your own food is also an empowering and highly enjoyable experience. Most of Australia's native 'herbs' and spices (including those that are not true herbs but are used as herbs, such as pepperleaves and gum leaves) wattles, and leafy vegetables are quite resilient and can be grown in most parts of Australia. The fruits, especially tropical fruits, and nuts may need a more specific environment, but your local native nursery will be able to advise you on what native plants would be suitable for your home garden.
- FOOD SHOPS – An increasing number carry Australian native and wild foods. Some you might like to visit are:
  1. The Source: Australia-wide, approximately 50 stores that carry a good range of Australian native foods in the 'bush tucker' category. To find the store closest to you, visit www.thesourcebulkfoods.com.au
  2. The Essential Ingredient: Currently seven stores in New South Wales, Victoria, and ACT with a 'Australian native ingredients' category. To find the store closest to you, visit www.essentialingredient.com.au
  3. Creative Native Foods: of course drop in to say hello to me or my staff at Creative Native Foods, 75a Orsmond St. Hindmarsh SA 5007 (not far from the entertainment centre.) or on market days (see below)
  4. Spice World: Shop 10 Bank Arcade, Hobart, Tas. 7000
- MARKET STALLS: Most produce markets and some farmers markets have stalls that sell Australian native ingredients. It is great fun 'foraging' in those markets to see what fresh Australian produce you can find. A few examples include:
  1. Queen Victoria Market: Melbourne Bush Food Co. (I Shed, Stall 88)
  2. Something Wild, Adelaide Central Market (Stall 55).
- Other retail and market stores (excluding on-line stores) are welcome to contact the Publisher (emma@brollybooks.com) to request inclusion in this list in future editions of this book.

The Source (store locator)

The Essential Ingre (store locator)

NOTE ON AVAILABILITY AND COST: In a commercial sense, the industry is still in its infancy, although supplies and stockists are increasing. The supply of some species is still very reliant on wild harvest or smaller farms. For example, in early 2020, the most well-known wattleseed, *Acacia victoriae* ('elegant wattle') became quite scarce and in turn expensive due to drought, but I can happily report that significant plantings have been going in the ground steadily over the last few years, and these sources are now starting to 'bear fruit'. Additionally, most native ingredients have quite intense flavours so a little goes a long way. Their cost per serve compares very favourably against that of other ingredients, for example, saffron, black peppercorns, and ground cinnamon, which may be many hundreds of dollars per kilo in small packets on supermarket shelves.